The NVA Were Everywhere . . .

I fired back at the machine-gun bunker in front of us and at another sniper, also to our right, until the barrel was too hot to touch and the ground around us was littered with spent shells. My firing had little effect on the bunker, but it kept the sniper off balance so that his fire was not accurate. O'Bryan had discarded his pistol and began using my old rifle, which would shoot only part of the time, but which was still better than a pistol.

I felt like a deer surrounded by wolves, or like a rabbit when a fox sinks its teeth into its back. I just knew the game was over, that I was a dead man, that this was the Big Casino.

But I wouldn't go down without a fight. After a particularly savage burst of machine-gun fire riddled the area around us, making O'Bryan and me hug the ground even closer, I made a decision. "If I'm gonna die," I thought, "I'll be damned if I'm gonna lay here and be picked off like a bird on a limb. I'm goin' down swingin'!"

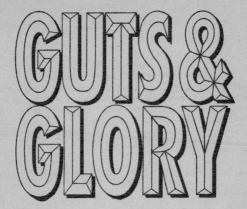

GUTS & GLORY

RANDALL K. McGLONE

POCKET BOOKS

New York London Toronto Sydney Tokyo Singapore

An *Original* publication of POCKET BOOKS

POCKET BOOKS, a division of Simon & Schuster Inc.
1230 Avenue of the Americas, New York, NY 10020

ISBN: 0-671-76062-9

First Pocket Books printing July 1992

10 9 8 7 6 5 4 3 2

POCKET and colophon are registered trademarks of Simon & Schuster Inc.

Cover art by Jeff Wack

Printed in the U.S.A.

Contents

Contents

Author's Note

I have changed the names of most of the people in this book. Every man I wrote about is or was a real person. However, their views of what happened may differ from mine. It has been twenty years, and everyone remembers things differently. Also, the pain of losing a loved one in a war is bad enough without it being brought up again. As I have said, this is my story. Someone else's story might be different.

INTRODUCTION

This is not a history book. It is one man's account of the marines' successful attempt in 1968 to open the vital supply route to Dong Ha and thus to Khe Sanh. This route was in the northernmost part of South Vietnam, in the Quangtri Province. It is granted by everyone, I think, that if we had not opened the route, Khe Sanh would have fallen and the five thousand marines surrounded there by crack NVA troops would have been massacred or marched off to captivity.

This supply route started with the Cua Viet River, which led from the South China Sea to Highway 1, which, in turn, led to Dong Ha. From the air base at Dong Ha, supplies were shipped to Khe Sanh.

To open the supply line, a series of savage, desperate battles was fought in which a battalion of marines, understrength and ill supplied, accomplished the impossible. All the villages along the river were fortified by the NVA's best troops. Our job was to land at the mouth of the Cua Viet River, take these villages one by one, and hold them so that supplies could reach Khe Sanh.

To my knowledge, nothing has been written about these villages. The heroism and acts of valor performed by the marines in these battles were awesome. Rambo really lived, many times over, in the persons of the brave young men who took the river back from the communists, and in doing so, saved the lives of five thousand marines at Khe Sanh.

Every combat action and every scene described in this book actually took place. As for exact times, exact unit sizes, exact number of men involved, and exact locations of battles, I cannot be sure. I was a private when I went to Vietnam, and enlisted men do not know unit sizes, times, and exact battle plans. They, along with a small number of lower-ranking officers, do most of the dirty work and hard fighting, but too often the enlisted men do not know exactly where they are or even what day it is.

This series of battles started with the communist buildup for the Tet Offensive of 1967–68, during which the Battle of Tham Khe (Operation Badger Tooth) took place. At the time I was with the Third Battalion, First Marines, Special Landing Force Bravo. We received two Navy Unit Commendations and one Presidential Unit Citation for these actions. The Navy Unit Commendations describe this series of battles I have written about.

This account is different from any I have read or seen about the Vietnam War. I am tired of reading and seeing how mean, how bad, Americans were over there. And so in this account, Americans are the good guys. That is the way I remember them, and that is the way they were. Americans should know and remember this.

The President of the United States takes pleasure in presenting the
BRONZE STAR MEDAL to

LANCE CORPORAL RANDALL K. MCGLONE

UNITED STATES MARINE CORPS

for service as set forth in the following

CITATION:

"For heroic achievement in connection with operations against
the enemy in the Republic of Vietnam while serving as an Artillery Forward
Observer with Company L, Third Battalion, First Marines, Ninth Marine Amphibious
Brigade. On 27 December 1967, during Operation Badger Tooth, Company L was
conducting a search and destroy operation into Than Tham Khe Village in Quang Tri
Province, a known North Vietnamese Army stronghold. As the Marines approached
the village, they came under intense automatic weapons fire from heavily fortified
positions, sustained several casualties and were temporarily pinned down. Without
hesitation, Lance Corporal MCGLONE moved from his position with the command
group and maneuvered across the fire-swept terrain in an assault against a fortified
bunker. When two of his companions were wounded, he fearlessly exposed himself
to enemy fire in an attempt to assist his fallen comrades. Then, continuing to
advance, he reached the hostile position and, in hand-to-hand combat, assisted in
killing an enemy soldier and overrunning the bunker. After nearly expending all his
ammunition against hostile positions in the village, Lance Corporal MCGLONE
returned safely to friendly lines under cover of supporting fires. His heroic actions
inspired all who observed him and contributed significantly to the accomplishment
of his unit's mission. Lance Corporal MCGLONE's courage, bold initiative and
unwavering devotion to duty at great personal risk were in keeping with the highest
traditions of the Marine Corps and of the United States Naval Service."

Lance Corporal MCGLONE is authorized to wear the Combat "V".

FOR THE PRESIDENT,

H. W. Buse, Jr.

H. W. BUSE, JR.
LIEUTENANT GENERAL, U. S. MARINE CORPS
COMMANDING GENERAL, FLEET MARINE FORCE, PACIFIC

1

Operation Badger Tooth

I ARRIVED IN SOUTH VIETNAM IN JUNE 1967, AND WAS AS-
signed to the First Marine Division, Third Battalion, Special Landing Force Bravo. Spirits were high, drugs were
unheard-of, and we were all young men raised on John
Wayne movies and stories of World War II and Korea. The
recent history of the United States Marine Corps was fresh
in our minds: Belleau Wood, the Inchon Landing, Iwo
Jima, Guadalcanal, Tarawa, and a hundred other battles.
The Marine Corps had never lost a battle, and we were not
about to let it happen now.

In addition to being a rifleman, I was trained as a forward
observer. My military occupational specialty (MOS) was
0846, an artillery scout observer, which, in simpler terms,
meant that I was to crawl up to the enemy's lines, find his
most critical holdings, and call in artillery fire.

During my first few months in country, I went on constant patrols, encountered sniper fire, fought small engagements, ran into isolated ambushes, lived in constant fear,
but somehow managed an occasional beer bust.

It was dangerous. All the time and in the extreme. Marines died every week, as did some of the elusive and tough
enemy. But there wasn't enough fighting to get us really
gassed up or worried. There seemed to be an uneasy lull

1

in the intensive fighting. We didn't know it, but North Vietnam was getting ready for the biggest push of the war, a gamble by North Vietnam's president Ho Chi Minh and General Vo Nguyen Giap to win the war. We were soon to find out what war and being a United States Marine meant.

We were stationed near Marble Mountain, just south of Da Nang, in I Corps, the northernmost section of South Vietnam. Like all young soldiers, we assumed we had the most dangerous and the worst duty there was, so we were elated when orders came down for us to change places with the Battalion Landing Team. It would be a nice break. Not only would we be sleeping aboard ship in real beds, but we would have two weeks of special training in the Philippines. If we had known that the BLT was used for the fiercest fighting, we would not have been so eager.

On returning to Vietnam from the Philippines, we went ashore in landing crafts like those used in the Normandy Invasion. I was attached to L Company, Third Battalion, First Marines. Third Battalion was composed mostly of four marine infantry companies, each containing approximately two hundred men. The battalion also contained an artillery battery, an armor group with tanks and amphibious armored vehicles, a helicopter unit which was usually based aboard ship, a battalion command group and various supply and support personnel. In all, the Battalion Landing Team numbered about twelve hundred marines and Navy Corpsmen. The infantry companies were the backbone of the Battalion Landing Team and we sometimes operated in battalion-sized sweeps and attacks and sometimes in company-sized sweeps depending on the situation. On December 26, we were getting ready for a battalion-sized operation.

L Company landed at the mouth of a river then unknown to me and swept inland toward a large village. Meeting no resistance, we moved through the village without incident. This was the first time any of us had been in an operation so long without making contact with the enemy. Everyone felt relieved, but a nagging feeling told me something was amiss, that not everything was as rosy as it smelled. It wasn't long before my apprehensions proved true.

As we marched along, searching the tree lines and rice

paddy dikes for signs of the enemy, I couldn't help noticing several young men in the village and around the farms. They weren't in uniform, and they seemed out of place. This many young men of draft age in a village was unusual. None of them talked with us, and they avoided contact with us as much as possible. They showed no hostility, showed no weapons, so it seemed we had no reason to attack them. We marched on but kept our eyes and ears open.

That night we slept on a sandy beach and prepared to sweep back through the village the next day and go back aboard ship. Little did we suspect how few of us would board that ship again.

We moved out before daylight after a breakfast of C rations. The sand was deep and loose, and the going was tough. Then we heard it. The unmistakable crack of AK-47s and Chi-Com machine-gun fire. We dropped our packs and scrambled forward as fast as the sand would allow. Word filtered back: First Platoon, our point platoon with almost 50 marines, was caught in a murderous cross fire and believed wiped out.

We looked at one another, not believing. And then the mortars started falling. There was nothing more terrifying than having hell ahead of us, nowhere to go behind us, and mortars coming down on top of us. We dug in. My radioman, with a full-sized pack and a radio on his back, dug a hole like a meerkat, slinging sand like a snowplow.

Hugging the ground like flies on flypaper, we rode out the first mortar volley. Deciding that to stay there meant certain death, another forward observer and I rallied the men and moved toward the rest of the company.

As we drew near, we learned two of our platoons were pinned down in a small creek just as they had entered the village we had swept the day before. Many wounded marines lay scattered around the open terrain between the creek and the enemy bunker complex that had destroyed First Platoon. Enemy machine-gun and rifle fire crisscrossed the creek from a seriers of bunkers located across a one-hundred-yard stretch of open ground to the south of the creek where the marines were trapped. The few survivors of First Platoon were trapped in the open behind some short scrub pine and returned fire with everything they had. It was a scene straight out of Dante's *Inferno:* Marines lay where they fell, blood and guts and brain matter scattered everywhere—a real slaughterhouse.

The 1968 Tet Offensive was on.

Death that day had its horrors: Seeing that death was horrible. Hearing it was horrible. But the worst horror of all was the smell of death. On the battlefield that day, all our senses were tuned to their highest pitch.

Looking around to find the officers and NCOs, I saw my captain and the command group huddled together and making plans. There seemed no doubt about what their decision would be. The NVA had put a hurting on us, and they were going to get some of the same. The captain gave the order, and we charged, like banshees straight out of hell.

Corporal Pope, also a forward observer, our two radiomen, the company clerk, and I were together when the captain ordered the attack.

Pope was one of the finest men I have ever known. He was a little older than the rest of us, maybe twenty-two or twenty-three, and appeared mature for his age. Pope's radioman, Private O'Bryan, was a big, dark Irishman from Chicago. He was new to the bush and didn't say much, but he was a solid man. My radioman, Private Shultz, was a stocky, broad-shouldered man from Ohio. He was a born infantryman. He could walk all day with a radio on his back and never get tired. Corporal Martin, the company clerk, was younger. He was probably smarter than any of the others in Headquarters Platoon. All these were good men and good marines: the best our country had.

When the captain ordered the attack, the NVA were raking the air overhead with death. Bullets from AK-47s whizzed past our heads like hornets from a thousand disturbed nests. We had to do something!

The captain knew his business when he ordered the attack. Sappers—elite North Vietnamese troops who lob grenades and satchel charges into enemy fortifications—were crawling closer. If we didn't do something, satchel charges would soon start hitting in the creek where we were hiding and force us out of the creek and make us open targets.

The NVA were getting a good start in killing us all. We would either have to attack and take a chance on living through it or sit in the creek and die for certain. So we attacked.

I looked at Pope. "Are we goin'?" I asked.

He nodded yes.

I told Shultz to stay put. I didn't want him to go with me. There was a possibility I might not survive, and I wanted to be sure someone would be able to call in the artillery (arty) just in case.

On a nod from Corporal Pope, we went over the top together. We entered another dimension where everything was in slow motion. NVA bullets hit all around us. I fired from the hip as we charged forward, but my fire was not accurate, because I had to manually eject each spent shell as I fired.

NVA sappers and snipers darted like rats back to the line of bunkers ahead. My vision was superaccurate, and all of my other senses were just as sharp. I could almost count the needles on the small scrub pines and could actually see the bullets flying through the air. Out of the corner of my eye I saw the captain fall like a downed grizzly. He fell forward heavily and didn't move. He had been shot through the forehead.

We continued our assault on the enemy bunkers.

Corporal Pope hit the ground beside me as bullets kicked up sand at my feet. I dived for a small clump of scrub pines to my right, about thirty feet from the NVA bunker complex. Machine-gun fire was coming from the bunkers. Snipers and riflemen fired from fighting holes and partly concealed positions around the bunkers.

I looked around to see O'Bryan lying next to me in a small depression surrounded by scrub pine. Corporal Martin lay about ten feet to our left behind a small rice paddy dike that had deteriorated to a mound of sand about ten feet long and two feet high. In front of him, not five feet away, was an NVA sniper in a fighting hole. Corporal Pope, curled into a fetal position, lay motionless in the open between us and Corporal Martin. Dead marines lay all around, and the air was hazy from the smoke of small-arms fire and grenades. It was not a pleasant situation.

We had approached the bunkers under proliferating small-arms and machine-gun fire and had gotten closer to the enemy bunker complex than any of the other marines in the assault. The NVA were determined to kill us for that, as they had killed all the other marines who had made it that far.

A machine-gun bunker lay directly ahead of us, and a sniper tried to plug us from our right. Both of these positions had us in perfect fields of fire, and it seemed we were dead men. NVA gunners raked the area with machine-gun and rifle fire, causing pinecones and needles to rain down upon O'Bryan and me. I got my first lesson in miracles that day, for only a miracle could have kept us from dying. I looked over at Pope.

"Pope!" I screamed. "Git the hell over here before you git killed! What's the hell wrong with you, anyway?"

But Pope didn't answer.

Like a sledgehammer, reality hit me. Everything began to spin. My mind refused to accept the truth. It *couldn't* have happened.

Before I knew it, I was running toward him. Someone screamed behind me.

"Get down!" I heard O'Bryan yell. "Are you crazy?"

NVA machine-gun bullets kicked up dirt around me, but I couldn't stop. I threw myself on top of Pope.

"You'll be okay," I told Pope. "We'll get you out. Don't worry. You'll be okay."

I wouldn't admit it, but I knew what had happened as soon as I landed on top of him. I started crying. I turned Pope over. His head hung grotesquely to one side. His eyes and mouth were full of sand from the way he had landed facedown. A shot in the neck had almost severed his head. I screamed and began jabbering nonsense.

"Don't die!" I pleaded. "You can't die! Get the sand out of your mouth!" I tried to clean his face with my hands. I stuck a finger into his mouth and raked out the sand. His tongue came out, blue and bloated. He stared at me with terrible, sightless eyes.

Fire from the NVA gunners struck all around me, but I wasn't hit. Finally it was as if I lost all feeling. Mechanically I dragged Pope to some bushes and hid him there.

Then, taking his rifle, I ran back to O'Bryan, who was still in the pine thicket.

Martin, in the meantime, had engaged in a gun duel with the sniper still in his fighting hole about five feet in front of him.

"Martin, do you see him?" I yelled.

"It's a bitch!" he returned. "It's a goddamned woman! I can see her."

"I'll throw a grenade at the hole!" I yelled. "When it goes off, you rush her and kill her stinkin' ass!"

It wasn't much of a plan, but it was the best we could come up with at the time. The machine gun to our front continued to shoot through the pines, trying to get us, and we were trapped like ducks on a pond. We had to do something. We didn't have time to make elaborate plans. I pulled the pin on a grenade and threw it at the sniper's hole. It exploded with a loud bang.

As soon as the grenade exploded, Martin, with a fixed bayonet, rushed the sniper. We heard a quick burst of AK-47 fire and saw Martin's head explode. Some of his brains and blood splattered onto O'Bryan and me.

"There goes the bitch!" O'Bryan yelled. "She's running!" He shot at her with his .45. He swore he hit her, and I hoped so, but I never got a shot at her. She kept on running and disappeared over the top of the sand dunes, and we never saw her again.

By that time I had accepted the fact that we were dead. We got down into the sand as low as we could. The scrub pines above our heads were shot to pieces. Most of the branches were blown off, and the ground was littered with cones and needles. We were right under the NVA guns.

We were far ahead of our own lines. Behind us dead marines lay in grotesque positions. Machine-gun fire raked the area, and occasionally a burst tore into the small thicket. We held our breath and dug deeper into the sand as the remaining bits and pieces of pine trees fell on top of us. Miraculously, we weren't hit.

I now had a rifle that worked properly. In the melee, I had picked up Pope's rifle, one of the few M-16s that functioned as it was supposed to. I fired back at the machine-gun bunker in front of us and at another sniper, also to our right, until the barrel was too hot to touch and the ground around us was littered with spent shells. My firing had little effect on the bunker, but it kept the sniper off balance so that his fire was not accurate. O'Bryan had discarded his pistol and began using my old rifle, which would shoot only part of the time, but which was still better than a pistol.

I felt like a deer surrounded by wolves, or like a rabbit when a fox sinks its teeth into its back. I just knew the game was over, that I was a dead man, that this was the Big Casino.

But I wouldn't go down without a fight. After a particularly savage burst of machine-gun fire riddled the small area around us, making O'Bryan and me hug the ground even closer, I made a decision. "If I'm gonna die," I thought, "I'll be damned if I'm gonna lie here and be picked off like a bird on a limb. I'm goin' down swingin'!"

I rolled over, fixed the bayonet on my rifle, and charged out of the thicket in a zigzag run toward the enemy bunkers, screaming and firing my M-16 from the hip. Everything went blank. Then, suddenly and surprisingly, I was crouched at the base of the central bunker. I was still alive. I looked up and saw a communist machine gun sticking out of the bunker's parapet and wondered how its bullets hadn't gotten me.

Quickly checking the situation, I found I was between two bunkers. The one on the right seemed deserted. I hoped its occupants had fled when we attacked. The one on the left was definitely occupied. Smoke rolled out of the machine-gun barrel, and I heard movement inside. About fifteen feet away, to my right and behind a bunker, was the sniper with whom I had been dueling. His spider hole was covered with bamboo shoots and scrub pine branches, but I knew exactly where it was. I could see his hole through the camouflage and saw smoke from his rifle. I was still in a world of shit.

I knew what I had to do. I had watched plenty of John Wayne movies. I had to throw a grenade into that bunker. I reached into my jungle shirt and pulled out a grenade.

As I looked down to pull the pin, something hit me on the top of my head. My steel pot went flying into the sand. I looked up. As in a dream I saw above me an NVA soldier

8

with a small shovel in his hands, the type of small, light shovel that the NVA used for an entrenching tool.

I blocked the next blow with my left wrist and grabbed the soldier by his shirt and pulled him toward me. He screamed and kept hitting me with the shovel. Everything happened in slow motion. I pulled him close enough to lock my hands around his throat and squeeze.

It was as though my hands and arms were not a part of my body. I could not feel them. I willed myself to squeeze as hard as I could. I squeezed harder and harder. The NVA's face turned dark and he struggled less and less. All my willpower was in my hands as I squeezed that man's throat.

Just then I heard something whizz past my head and heard the crack of an AK-47. The sniper had seen everything and was trying to shoot me off his fellow soldier. I relaxed my grip on the man's throat and crouched lower toward the ground to get out of the sniper's line of fire. Reaching with my right hand, I tried to grab my rifle. I planned first to shoot the scumbag who had tried to brain me, then I would, with supreme malice aforethought, go after the sniper, even if it meant a kamikaze charge.

As I reached for the rifle, my assailant broke my grasp, jumped behind me, and leaped onto my back like a mongoose on a cobra. He clawed at my throat and screamed for help. I wedged my wrist between his arm and my throat and kept him from choking me. We struggled like madmen as I tried to shake him off my back.

Suddenly his grip went limp. I shook him free, grabbed my rifle, and shot him in the stomach. When he bent over to grab his stomach, I shot him in the top of his head. Blood spurted all over me. He died instantly.

I looked at the dead man. He was about my age. I felt a little sad at first, but then I thought about Pope and Martin and all the other dead marines lying on that stretch of sand, and felt no remorse. "Well," I thought, "that's one NVA soldier who won't be killing anybody else. If they kill us all, at least we got one of them."

I sat panting, trying to get back my breath and some semblance of reality. After what then seemed like hours, but I now know could not have been more than a few seconds, I looked up and saw O'Bryan lying against the bunker to my left, holding his shoulder. The sniper to our right fired steadily, the rounds striking the bunker against which O'Bryan was leaning, but too high to do any harm. But the sniper let us know he was still there.

"What happened, bub?" I asked O'Bryan.

"You son of a bitch. You shot me!" he swore, and then started laughing. He was still in shock but able to talk. He had seen the NVA hit me with the shovel and had watched us fight. He smiled and said it was the damnedest thing he had ever seen. He had also seen the sniper to our right shooting at me and thought I was a goner, for sure. Then he saw the NVA get away from me and jump on my back. At that time, O'Bryan fixed his bayonet, charged, and bayoneted the soldier I was fighting with. When I shot the NVA through his stomach, the round had passed through him and hit O'Bryan in his shoulder. The wound, though just a crease, was painful.

I grinned back at him and began to laugh, too, from the sheer irony of it all. There we were, just a few hundred yards ahead of our own lines in the middle of a battalion of NVA troops, and I had shot one of our own men! The odds of our surviving that day were small indeed, but right then the situation seemed hilarious.

Shakily I got out a battle dressing and wrapped O'Bryan's arm. His laughing and my shaking made it an ordeal, but somehow we managed to get the dressing in place. The sniper to our right continued with harassment rounds just to keep our heads down.

"Well," O'Bryan asked, "what now?"

"We'd better blow up that bunker," I answered, "before any more of the little bastards get up enough nerve to come out."

The NVA's machine gun was still sticking out of the bunker. Apparently the enemies were still inside. Why they hadn't come out, I don't know. Probably because they didn't want to expose themselves to fire from the marines in the creek. Possibly they might have thought that the sniper had either killed us or would keep us away. As I learned that day and later on in battles, the NVA had a tendency to stay in their bunkers and die rather than come out and fight in the open. Whatever their reasoning, it often proved a fatal mistake.

O'Bryan and I got out grenades and pulled the pins, then together threw the grenades into the bunker parapet. We heard a sudden, excited jabbering, and then the grenades exploded. I watched with pleasure as the heavy Chinese machine gun flew through the air.

The sniper to our right stepped up his firing. He had seen the damage we made and was trying desperately to kill us. I rose up above the bunker on our right and fired a burst from my rifle at him. He and I settled into a personal rifle duel. I would rise up and fire a burst at him, and then he would fire a burst at me. But I had a critical advantage: I never rose up from the same spot twice. I had about ten feet behind the bunker in which to move either left or right. Every time I fired at his spider hole, I fired from a different position. He, in contrast, was limited to firing from one spot. The duel went on for about fifteen minutes, during which time I used up about ten magazines of M-16 ammo.

Finally the sniper didn't return my fire. I hoped he had run out of ammo or that I had killed him. Not knowing drove me crazy.

O'Bryan and I had to make a decision. We were far ahead of our lines. The creek was about one hundred yards behind us across open ground and littered with dead marines. We were right in the middle of a battalion of NVA. Attacking over the dunes into the village was sheer suicide. Two marines, almost out of ammo, and one of them wounded, didn't have much of a chance against fifteen hundred well-entrenched NVA. We were alive only through a miracle, and we didn't want to push our luck too far.

The NVA in the bunkers both to our right and left continued to fire their heavy machine guns at the marines in the creek. Although O'Bryan and I had destroyed the central bunker and the attacking marines had beaten the advancing snipers and sappers, the enemy still had plenty of firepower. Getting back to the relative safe creek appeared totally out of the question, insanity of the first order. But we had to do something.

We fired at the bunkers and threw grenades into the village. Soon we were out of ammo and had one grenade between us. Suddenly we heard two soft thumps and stared in horror at the two Chi-Com grenades that landed between us. We dived for the deck, fully expecting to die. A thousand thoughts ran through my head. I wondered how badly I would be hurt, and thought that if I was hurt really badly, I would play dead and then maybe I would survive the battle.

The explosions and ensuing pain never came. Another miracle! Both grenades were duds. Our amazing luck seemed to be holding out.

Then bullets began hitting the northern side of both bunkers we were hiding between. The bullets got closer and closer. Marines in the creek were firing at us!

O'Bryan and I looked at each other, surprised and scared. It would be a real drag to have gone through all that we had survived only to get killed by our own men. I peeped around the side of the bunker and saw some marines looking out from the creek. They pointed in our direction and seemed undecided about what to do. O'Bryan and I started screaming and waving our arms.

"We're marines, you fuckin' idiots!" I yelled. "We're Americans! Don't shoot, goddammit! Don't motherfuckin' shoot, man! Shit! Fuck! Piss! McDonald's, man! Don't no mothafuckin' gook know nothin' about McDonald's!"

O'Bryan, too, was yelling his head off, screaming everything he could think of to let the marines know we were genuine Americans. He gave a rundown on American culture that would have made a civics or history teacher proud.

The firing stopped and a marine waved at us. Then several marines stuck their heads up and looked at us in amazement, as if we were the feature attraction at a sideshow. I was sure they were wondering how in hell we got where we were. It must have seemed impossible that two men could have made it across that strip of sand, all the way to the bunkers. It seemed impossible to me also.

But the incident snapped us back to reality. To stay there meant certain death. We looked out across that million-mile stretch of barren sand and shook our heads. It would be impossible to cross it, but we had to try. We had no choice.

Since O'Bryan was wounded, we decided I would try it first. I would wait for O'Bryan somewhere in the stretch of sand and put down covering fire for him. If we tried for the creek, we had a chance. A mighty slim one, but a chance.

I sprang from behind the bunker like a runner leaving the starting blocks and entered another dimension as if I had crossed over into the Twilight Zone. I knew I was moving fast, but everything seemed in slow motion.

About halfway across the stretch of sand, I lost my bearings and sense of direction. I dimly remembered that I was supposed to stop and wait for something, but I couldn't remember what for. Bullets whizzed all around me, but I didn't give them a second thought. I didn't care about them.

I was halfway between the enemy bunkers and the creek, staggering around not knowing where to go or what to do, when, as if in a dream, I saw the FAC (Forward Air Control) team behind a small ridge of sand waving for me to get down. I lumbered toward them and fell to the ground behind their ridge of sand.

Suddenly I remembered O'Bryan!

"O'Bryan!" I screamed. "Go ahead and make your break! I'll cover your ass!"

There was no response. Either he had made it back behind me, or he had been killed. All I knew for sure was that the FAC team and I were trapped behind the ridge. Either to advance or to retreat was suicide.

I began to calm down and to look around. There were no signs of movement from the fallen marines except when the NVA fired bursts into their bodies to make sure they were dead. The enemy also kept firing into small pine and bamboo thickets to make sure no marines were hiding in them.

Then in that hell of death I saw something I will always remember. In the middle of that strip of sand and death, a single, unwounded marine refused to leave two wounded comrades. All three were fighting from behind the corpses of marines. The unwounded man cursed the NVA, threw grenades at them, and dared them to come and get him.

I heard the FAC team plotting air strikes and naval gunfire on the bunkers and village. But first they had to get out that marine and his wounded companions. The FAC team finally got the grunt's attention and put down covering fire as he and his wounded companions went for the "safety" of the creek.

The FAC team called in napalm and naval gunfire on the village and bunkers. The salvo had forced the NVA to stop their mortar attack and slow down the machine-gun and rifle fire a little, but the western bunkers continued to keep us trapped in the creek, and eventually pinpointed the FAC team. By the grace of God and the marine cover fire, the Forward Air Control team and I made it back to the creek. We were back in the creek when we heard someone yell.

"Marine coming over! Don't shoot!"

It was O'Bryan! He had somehow worked his way back to the creek. And he was still cussing me.

The survivors of our charge were tired but unbeaten. Looking around, I saw that the charge had taken a terrible toll on our company. The majority of our enlisted men, 128, were killed or wounded; the captain, two platoon commanders and two staff sergeants were also down. Only one staff sergeant and one lieutenant remained. But regardless of the toll, survivors were still fighting the NVA and had no intention of leaving until all our wounded were retrieved and given medical attention.

Our charge had also taken a considerable toll on the NVA. Although it was still certain death to walk around in the 100-yard-long strip of sand, the firing had slacked off considerably. The breaking up of the enemy's front line had erased any danger of our being overrun, and the destruction of the central bunker had weakened their position to the point that they, like us, were just trying to hold their positions.

We did all we could for our wounded, and at the same time kept up a withering exchange of fire with the NVA to keep them at bay and pinned down. The fighting lasted all day. The only supplies we received were crates of ammunition dropped by chopper.

Sometime after dark, we found no one to shoot at, and the firing stopped. The staff sergeant called us together and asked for volunteers to go among the dead marines to check for any who might still be alive. Most of the men joined the search. We found the sniper who had given me so much hell. He was about fifteen feet from his hole, shot through the shoulder, and dead. Evidently I had wounded him and he had bled to death attempting to crawl away in the dark.

Under cover of darkness we carried our wounded back to the beach to be medevacked by choppers. The staff sergeant had been severely wounded during the search for surviving marines. As we put him on the chopper, he swore he would get the little bastards who shot him if he had to slash and burn everything in Vietnam to get the right one.

After I had had time to think it over, I realized what had happened that day. The NVA had already occupied the village that we had swept through so easily. Except for the young men we had seen in the open, apparently scouts, the enemy forces were hidden in family bunkers, in well-placed bunkers in the surrounding area, and in other appropriate spots. We had been duped into thinking the NVA had not yet taken over the village.

When we started coming back through the village, the time and place were perfect for an ambush. They greatly outnumbered us, they had superior firepower, they had the element of surprise, and they had ideal terrain for a surprise attack. The locations of their bunkers gave them perfect fields of fire so that they could command the ground over the one hundred yards of sand and fire down on anyone in the creek or going into the creek.

They hit the First Platoon perfectly. The men were all the way on the sand strip before the NVA opened fire and wiped them out. The captain's decision to attack caught them by surprise and ruined their plans to annihilate our entire company. Our assault destroyed the NVA's front line and their two central bunkers, killed the snipers and sappers, and then inflicted many casualties. Then, when the FAC team was finally able to get napalm and air support in, they knew they were beaten and chose to withdraw under cover of night.

I have no idea what the official interpretation of events were, but one thing I knew for sure: This was the beginning of the end for that NVA battalion. The revenge of the marines would be swift and deadly.

2

After the Battle

IT WAS A SAD AND RAGGED GROUP OF MARINES THAT SWEPT back through the village the next morning. All the villagers had disappeared: how and where to, I never knew.

We had a new commanding officer, new lieutenants, and new staff sergeants. Our new commanding officer looked more like a librarian than a captain in the marines, but he proved to be the best officer I ever had the honor to serve under.

The scene that lay before us at the village fried our brains: Dead combatants lay where they had fallen, in every position imaginable, with some frozen in their last fighting positions.

Our first job was to gather the bodies of our dead buddies and stack them like firewood to be shipped back to the States. The officers and noncoms helped in this grim and sorrowful task.

We searched for abandoned weapons and supplies and then destroyed the entire village. No military discipline was imposed on us for the first time since we had enlisted. To enlisted men, this was a strange and unusual thing. Since marines from other units were protecting our perimeters, we felt safe for the moment and free to roam about the village at will.

As the day wore on, something remarkable happened. While we searched for booby traps and hidden arms, the recent horrors drifted away. Everything seemed unreal, battles seemed remote. Our work became a game and we were little boys playing soldier, only our weapons and explosives were real. We delighted in blowing up everything that looked the least bit suspicious. Grenades exploded constantly and everywhere. A holiday feeling took over!

Noticing chickens roaming about the once prosperous village, I had a brainstorm. I grew up on a forty-acre hillside farm in eastern Kentucky, and after several weeks of sour food aboard a troopship and several more days of C rations, I knew exactly what to do with a chicken. I shot one. Some of us would have a picnic!

Marines gathered around as I cut the unlucky fowl's head off, plucked him, gutted him, built a fire, and put his cleaned carcass on a spit. My radioman collected several bottles of barbecue sauce, which wasn't hard to do since many soldiers carried a supply to flavor C rations.

While we slowly roasted the chicken and basted it with the sauce, my radioman got a whiff of the cooking chicken and decided we needed another. He promptly shot a second chicken! We'd have a double treat!

Many onlookers, especially city dudes, showed disgust as I was cutting the chicken's head off and plucking him, but once they got a whiff of barbecuing chicken, they sprang into action. Not a fowl in that village was safe. It sounded like the battle was on again. Cooking fires sprang up everywhere. Not one chicken survived the onslaught.

Now, back home I had eaten a lot of chicken, but none could compare with the delicious, mouth-watering, delectable barbecued chicken we roasted over an open fire in the ruins of that Vietnamese village.

The respite from fear and horror, the relative freedom, and the youthfulness of the men combined to make us as keenly aware as any five-year-old child. We were really just a bunch of teenagers desperately happy to be alive.

While we were relaxing, officers and noncoms were making plans. We felt a little left out, not being invited to listen in as they held conferences assessing the situation and planning future tactics. Little did I suspect that later on in the

Tet Offensive, although I was only nineteen and a private, I would attend all such conferences. By then I would be the only forward observer in the whole battalion of 500 to 1,000 men and the captain would want me to know what was going on. But on that day Captain Hempel was as far away as God.

By late afternoon we sensed something going on. Headquarters people were building an elaborate bomb shelter and bunker in the middle of the village. Eventually word leaked out. It was astounding! The battalion commander, a lieutenant colonel, God Himself, was coming to the field of battle. I couldn't believe it! In the Marine Corps the men seldom see a lieutenant colonel, much less get close enough to hear one talk or give orders. I wouldn't have been more surprised had I heard "Hail to the Chief" and seen L.B.J. come marching in.

With dusk, the party atmosphere dissipated. A steady, cold rain was falling. Now, Vietnam is hot, but those monsoon rains bring wetness, cold, and misery. Rumors said that the colonel had come to the field because he wanted to be in on an enemy attack expected that night. Since the NVA had left their dead and some equipment behind, he felt they would be back. We would be waiting!

Yesterday's terror returned with the dark. We expected mortars at any minute. The fright was bad, but the cold, wet misery was worse. All the battle survivors camped inside the village perimeter. A camp for field marines in Vietnam consisted of ponchos made into small two- or four-man tents staked with bamboo. The size of a tent varied with how many ponchos men wanted to use. A fighting hole was always dug beside the tent. Right in the middle of the encampment was the colonel's bunker, which, to us, looked like the Taj Mahal.

Most men built tents over cooking fires to get some relief from the cold and wetness. After dark, word came down that all fires were to be put out, for they would be like beacons directing mortar fire on us. My radioman, two members of the FAC team, and I were together in one tent, and we decided we would rather die from a mortar round than from wet and cold misery. We kept our fire. At least death from a mortar round would be quick.

From the colonel came a harsh order for us to put out our fire. Shit! Then a brilliant idea struck us. We had an old iron cooking pot we had found in the village, and we decided to put hot coals in it. We didn't realize that from the outside, our tent looked like the lit end of a huge cigar and could be spotted ten miles away by a half-blind, cross-eyed North Vietnamese.

We had barely accomplished our mission before someone stuck his head and then his whole body into the tent. My companions kind of withdrew into a corner as if they were looking for somewhere to hide or some way to commit hara-kiri.

That left me alone by the fire, so being a true southern gentleman, I invited the guest to warm his hands. Then my heart hit my mouth. In the dim glow of the hot coals I saw a face of pure rage and malevolence. On the shirt collar I saw, shining like a glimmer of doom from the fires of hell, the silver oak leaf of a lieutenant colonel. I had invited God Himself to warm His hands! As my life flashed before me, I envisioned Portsmouth Prison as home for the rest of my life.

After informing the four of us in the tent, and I believe the rest of the encampment was informed, too, of our doubtful parentage and of our immense stupidity, the colonel informed us that if the fire was not put out immediately, what was left of us after he personally destroyed any hopes of us ever fathering a child would be sent on a four-man recon patrol to Hanoi, and if we returned from this, he would really start getting rough. The fire was put out.

That night we four cold, miserable, and scared teenagers slept under a wet poncho. We were more afraid of running into the colonel again than of the whole NVA with General Giap at their head. But my misery had a bright spot. I was important! I had talked to a real live lieutenant colonel!

The expected attack never came. Next morning, after a quick sweep through the area, we boarded helicopters and were flown back to the ship. Our ship, the SS *Navarro,* was used to haul troops to combat and not designed for troop comforts. Ordinarily the enlisted marines had little contact with the crew except for those who served in the mess hall.

Animosity between marines and sailors is legendary. Earlier, while on shore leave in the Philippines, we had many fights with sailors. We called them swabbies, and they called us jarheads, and we knew they were all pussies, and they knew we were all idiots. Even in civilian clothes, there was a big difference. The sailors generally were heavier, cleaner, less nervous, but louder, than the field marines. The marines, in contrast, were razor-thin, never completely clean, nervous, quiet, and seldom smiled. Such differences led to many fights.

As we neared the troopship, I thought back to our former stay on it, of the contemptuous looks and the nasty remarks sailors directed at us. And even today I recall a sailor saying to me as I was getting off a landing craft: "Boy, this place will smell better for a while."

Back aboard, I couldn't believe the change in attitude. Helicopters were still flying dead and wounded marines back to the ship, and navy personnel were handling the remains of the dead and getting the wounded who had not come in the day before off the helicopters. The ship was as quiet as a tomb. Some sailors had tears in their eyes. All were ashen-faced.

Sadness and sorrow was a living, palpable thing. But there was another emotion: rage. Anger grew and grew and finally it broke. As if someone had lit a fuse, the sailors began cursing the Vietnamese.

As they handled the dead, pieces of meat that they had seen so recently as living, breathing young men, helped the wounded, and stared at the ragged, exhausted shells that had returned alive, the sailors' self-control broke. One grabbed a rifle and tried to board a helicopter to go ashore for revenge. He had to be forcibly restrained and taken below. Others tried to volunteer to go back with the marines.

When we were off the helicopters, I noticed sailors milling around, helping when they could, but I think they just wanted to look at us, some twenty survivors from the large numbers who had left the ship so short a time before.

One sailor got fairly close and stared me in the face. He looked as if he had seen a ghost. For a moment it seemed he and I were the only people on earth. He was suntanned, well fed, and looked as if he didn't really know what to say. Finally he spoke. "It couldn't be worth it. You guys actually volunteered for this."

I couldn't think of anything to say. The pain and sorrow in his eyes were just too much. I just stared, and finally he shook his head as tears filled his eyes. He staggered away to help marines trying to get their gear off a helicopter.

I had learned a lesson. Marines and sailors may fight on shore leave, but when the chips are down and our backs are against the wall, we are all Americans. I never again said a bad word about sailors.

I began to feel like a curiosity in a circus. We were filthy, had faces blackened from gunpowder, and we still had blood all over us, some of the blood from the killing we had done and some from trying to help our wounded comrades. We no doubt resembled demons from some dark corner of Hades.

By now we were huddled together in a ragged formation. We seemed addled. The officers and staff sergeants were at a loss about what to do. We stood on display for maybe fifteen minutes, which seemed like fifteen years, while the crew of the ship stared at us. Then our heads started coming up a little higher and our chests started sticking out a little.

"Okay. Here we are. We survived. We're marines. We're not seagoing bellhops in dress blues, nor parade-ground heroes. We eat barbed wire for breakfast and drink blood for lunch. We have tread the valley of death and fear no evil, because nothing worse can happen."

I had been in many formations and parades, dressed to the hilt in Marine Corps regalia, but on that troopship off the coast of Vietnam, bloody, filthy, wet, dressed in ragged jungle fatigues and standing with twenty other survivors in a rough formation before an awestruck navy crew, I felt more pride in myself and fellow marines than I would ever feel again.

I have heard that at some time in every young man's life, he should feel like a Greek god. This was my time. For one small moment we were a shade above mortal men. Today, whenever thoughts of failure loom, or setbacks occur or I think about giving up and maybe ending it all, the memory of that time gives me strength to go on and live another day.

3

The Payback Begins

AFTER THAT FIFTEEN MINUTES OF ETERNITY, WE WERE BACK in the Marine Corps. The staff sergeants came to their senses, barked out orders to fall out and get squared away. We found our living quarters and soon were cleaning weapons, repairing clothing and gear, drying socks and boots, and doing what all soldiers do to get ready for the next venture into hell.

The next day the colonel called a battalion-sized formation on the main deck for a memorial service. As I looked at the battle survivors in the formation, I was struck by their youth and innocent looks. All were clean, and all wore clean jungle utilities. The demons of recent days were gone, and clean, fresh teenagers were back. *Except for their eyes*.

The ceremony was solemn, grave. A few muffled sobs mingled with the words of the chaplain's prayer for the dead.

Then the atmosphere changed. Among the men, a terrible rage built up. You could feel it, touch it, and it became a part of you. Teeth clenched, chins jutted out. We wanted vengeance. We were as one in purpose: North Vietnam would pay dearly for this outrage. There would be many widows and sad mothers in North Vietnam before this year ended.

The colonel gave a short speech. It braced us, encouraged us, gave us a reason to go on. Today I still remember what he said.

"I know there were a lot of heroes out there on 27 December 1967. A lot of men died who will get no recognition for deeds above and beyond the call of duty. Well, they did what was expected and what is called a common virtue for a United States Marine.

"There won't be many medals passed out. What you did is expected of any man who calls himself a U.S. Marine.

"Many of our fellow marines died on that battlefield. Why did they die? They died because the people of the Republic of South Vietnam have a right to choose who governs them. They have a right, just like the people of the United States have a right, to pick their own leaders, not to have their leaders chosen by North Vietnam, China, Russia, or some thugs who call themselves Vietcong."

The colonel paused. His voice broke, but I refused to accept that, for I knew God didn't cry. The colonel had just paused for breath.

He continued. "The totalitarian and communist governments of Russia and China must be stopped here. If South Vietnam falls, so do Laos, Cambodia, and all of Indochina. We will do our best to stop the spread of communism and preserve the right to freedom in South Vietnam."

There was no applause, no cheering, no noise as he finished. Just a cold rage like an evil fog hanging over us all. We were not thinking about politics. We were thinking about killing.

Soon our ship was headed back to Da Nang for resupply and replacements for the dead and wounded. During the trip each survivor was interrogated separately by an officer to try to find out exactly what had happened on that battlefield. Some were questioned by lieutenants, some by other officers, and I by our new commanding officer.

Since there were so few of us and we were given no warning about the interrogations, we had no chance to discuss the battle or make up stories. No doubt the officers were given as truthful and full an account of what happened as could be given by any men.

When summoned to the captain's cabin, I was apprehensive. I felt out of place. As I knocked on the door, I had no idea why I had been summoned, but I was sure it was for screwing up somewhere. But I couldn't think of anything. I had never talked with a captain face-to-face, and I was scared. I would have admitted kidnapping the Lindbergh baby or the assassination of President Lincoln had the captain insisted. When I knocked on the door, only my boot camp training kept me from running. I finally decided, like a man on death row, that I might as well take it like a man. Especially since there was no place to run anyhow.

On entering the cabin, I thought: "This guy must be an admiral or a general or something." He had his own bed, his own desk, his own refrigerator! He lived like a warlord! I stood at rigid attention, didn't eyeball around, and answered his questions. I didn't add or delete anything.

The captain was about 5'11" and about 175 pounds, red-haired, and had a touch of freckles. He would have been right at home as a high school basketball coach. There wasn't an ounce of fat on him, and in a fistfight he would have been hard to whip. But what struck me was something rarely seen in the Marine Corps: This man had compassion! He really cared whether a man lived or died.

Later I got to know the captain better. We were to spend a lot of time together in the field, and we had many good conversations. He liked me. Why, I'll never know. Maybe he smiled at the other officers imitating my hillbilly talk, or the remarks they made, such as "The odds are that crazy hillbilly won't last another month. He takes too many chances." Maybe he just liked someone who volunteered for the bush. Anyway, as time passed I came to realize that Captain Hempel was a born leader, that he was fearless, and that he was the most unselfish man I ever knew.

We reached Da Nang at the beginning of the monsoon season. It was cloudy all the time, but for the time being, it rained only in the afternoon. In the days following we got new replacements, took on food supplies, got our gear squared away, did routine physical exercises, and had several weapons inspections. The officers and noncoms did not harass us, and we actually got to know some of them.

Headquarters Platoon consisted of a lieutenant (new to us), the artillery Forward Observer team, the FAC team, the captain's personal radioman, the interpreter (an infantryman who could speak Vietnamese), the 81-mm mortar Forward Observer team, and usually one or two infantrymen who served as messengers and for security.

The lieutenant was a trained forward observer for artillery. No longer would a nineteen-year-old Kentucky hillbilly call in the artillery fire. At that time my dialect was so pronounced, the Fire Direction Control Center had to keep someone available to interpret what I was saying when I called in a fire mission.

While anchored off Da Nang, we enlisted marines had no shore leave—for several reasons, the most important being that when the BLT (Battalion Landing Team) went back into action, it would not have time to spend two or three days rounding up drunk and disorderly soldiers. And back to action we were going. In a very few days.

4

Before Tet—1968

PRIVATE MEADES AND I KNEW NOTHING ABOUT TROOP plans: the brass hadn't bothered to keep us informed. Meades was an infantryman attached to Headquarters Platoon as an interpreter. He had a bull neck, and even after being in the bush, he looked like a football player. Being from western Virginia, he spoke the same dialect and had the same hillbilly ways as me. We had quickly become friends.

We were nineteen, full of life, sitting on a ship about two hundred yards from shore. Bars, girls, civilization, and unknown delights were at hand, but we were restricted to the ship. Then Meades told me a navy friend would be going ashore and had agreed to let us sneak away with him.

"Let's go!" I exclaimed. I had not yet heard of the word *hesitation*.

We hurried to the landing craft, got aboard, and hunkered down in the boat, scared shitless that somebody would see us. On reaching shore, we tried to act calm, at least until we got away from the dock. I felt sure we would get caught any minute. But luck was with us.

Walking through Da Nang was really something: paved streets, unattached girls in dark bars, and even streetlights! Were we out of place! Civilians were everywhere: some walking, some on bicycles, some on buses, and a few on motorbikes. And there were plenty of military personnel, many of whom stared at us as if we belonged in a Wild West show. They wore T-shirts, new trousers, good boots, were well fed and unarmed, except for the sidearms a few wore. Boy, this was the rear!

In contrast, we were as thin as whips, sunburned, wore ragged jungle fatigues and well-worn boots. Both of us carried hand grenades in our pockets, and I had a K-bar (something like a bowie knife). We carried our rifles in such a way that showed we would use them if the occasion arose.

We stood out like sore thumbs!

The Vietnamese, even the prostitutes, detoured around us. Since we weren't invited into any of the small bars along the way, we headed for a large, well-built, solid building—obviously American.

Seeing no guard on the door, we walked in. We hadn't noticed the sign outside that read:

SPECIAL FORCES
GREEN BERET NCO CLUB
DA NANG, SOUTH VIETNAM

As we walked in, cold air hit us in the face. It couldn't be true! Air-conditioning! As my eyes were adjusting to the dim light, I glanced around. I was in heaven! Here was a real bar with padded seats, a jukebox, cold beer and whiskey, and cool air. My God! They could have kept a division of marines fighting forever on the money the government put into this place.

The men around us had on new fatigues and shined

boots, they sported neat haircuts, and most were older than we were. I thought for sure we were in a generals' club. But then I thought, "No, there couldn't be this many generals. Maybe they're soldiers from a strange country."

Just then someone at a table yelled, "Hey! You boys must have come out of the bush. Come have a beer."

No second invitation was needed. We went to the table and sat down. At first we were a little leery, but cold beer soon loosened us up. When the men found out what outfit we were with, they bombarded us with questions. Evidently word of the battle had leaked out. They seemed anxious to hear all the war stories we had to tell.

We never bought a beer! Our new friends kept us supplied, and we kept talking. Our appearance seemed to fascinate them almost as much as our stories. Apparently most of them had not seen combat other than occasional sniper fire and ambushes. None had that drawn, haggard look that comes from prolonged combat, combat that saps every ounce of strength from the body.

I had the feeling that I had definitely joined the wrong branch of service. These guys had it better in Vietnam than I had ever had it in the States. But the Green Berets were truly nice, and I kept feeling out of place. For one thing, they all outranked us. There were sergeants, gunnery sergeants, staff sergeants, and on and on. In the Marine Corps few people obtained such high ranks, and those who did seldom had time to socialize with privates. Also, they were all spit and polish, and that made me conscious of my own appearance. I felt as if Meades and I were two alley cats at a pedigree cat show.

It was in the rest room that a near altercation developed. Meades was on one side of me, and one of our drinking buddies was on the other. A big man whom I hadn't seen before walked in and stared at Meades and me. He made some remark about the marines; exactly what, I don't know. Well, by this time I had had enough beer that it was unwise for him to say anything. I would probably have had to stand on Meades's shoulders to hit him squarely in the nose, and even then, with his outweighing me by a hundred pounds, I probably couldn't have hurt him. But I thought: "What the hell they gonna do? Send me to Vietnam?"

I swung at him. Lucky for me I was so drunk, I missed by three feet, and our drinking buddy and Meades caught me before I hit the floor. Two other Green Berets grabbed the man and prevented any more trouble. Evidently these two explained to my intended victim who I was, for he came over and shook hands with me, much to my relief, and nothing more was said. Well, we had had a wonderful afternoon, which was over all too soon. It was time to go back to the ship.

Later, while my unit was near Khe Sanh, all marine units in the area were called to the aid of three hundred Green Berets and several thousand Montagnard tribesmen trapped at nearby Lang Vei. It was impossible for any marine units to answer the call. All the trapped men were killed. I have often been saddened while thinking of the dead men and wondering whether some of them were men who had treated Meades and me so well at the Green Beret Club in Da Nang.

But back to that day in Da Nang. Leaving the club, we stepped into sweltering heat. We were zonked! Somehow we made our way to the dock, drunker than boiled owls—and in eastern Kentucky, that is as drunk as a person can get.

At the dock the sailor who had smuggled us to shore waved for us to get aboard. I looked at Meades. Meades looked at me. We didn't speak. We didn't need to. Going aboard in our condition wouldn't be a very good idea. We would put off the inevitable. We waved good-bye to the sailor and staggered off.

I told Meades about Dog Patch. Da Nang was not far from Marble Mountain, where I had been stationed earlier. There is a small village called Dog Patch between our old fire base and Da Nang where soldiers could buy warm beer and a bowl of rice if the proprietors knew them. Meades agreed that Dog Patch was the place to go.

It was getting dark, and the streets of Da Nang were pretty well deserted. Somehow we got through the town and ended up on an old dirt road I recognized from a hundred patrols I had done in the area. Wherever the road led, that was where we were going. We were still drunk enough but were beginning to come to our senses when Private

Meades pulled from his pockets four beers he had smuggled out of the NCO club. We killed one each and decided to drink the other two a little more slowly. That was the end of our coming to our senses.

Here was the situation: Two ragged scarecrows, arms around each other, armed to the hilt, drinking beer, and singing "Blue Moon of Kentucky," were staggering down a dirt road. That might have been a common sight in the hills back home, but not on a dark dirt road right outside Da Nang, Republic of South Vietnam, in January 1968.

We had gone about half a mile when headlights from a jeep hit us squarely in the face. If we had had a cane and straw hat, we could have done an old Al Jolson routine, for we certainly were the center of attention. But just then we heard the safety on an M-16 click from on to off. I said good-bye to Al Jolson, and we sobered up quick. In the light of flares we saw M-16s trained on us and two pairs of steel-hard eyes behind them. This was not the time for lengthy speeches. We put our hands up.

The two marines in the jeep saw we were Americans and assumed we had to be marines. No one else could be that crazy. Our actions and our smell told them we were plastered. They lowered their rifles and helped us into the jeep.

"What the hell are you guys doing out here after dark?" the driver asked.

Meades and I answered at the same time. "I dunno. Uh. We got separated from our unit."

"What *is* your unit?" the driver continued. "Do you know you had the whole damn base on alert? There's suspected enemy movement everywhere, and we almost blew you away with everything we had."

"Aw, what the hell," the other soldier said. "They're just drunk. Let's just take them back to their unit. No harm done."

"Boys, what *is* your unit?" the driver asked again.

"I hope this jeep will float," I giggled.

Finally it dawned on Meades and me that we had screwed up big time. We tried to think of a unit nearby that we could say we belonged to. We could spend the night there and try to get back to the ship next morning.

After we had told our new friends enough phony stories

to keep them driving around for an hour, the driver pulled over and stopped.

"Okay, jarheads. Cut the bullshit. Where the hell are you from?"

Our heads had cleared enough for us to stop giggling and tell the truth. Hell! What were they gonna do? Send us to Vietnam?

We identified our unit and told them we were going on another operation in two or three days and that we did not want to miss it. At that moment the most important thing in the world to me was not to miss the next operation. For the first time in my life I felt duty-bound to be there for my country. I could not let the survivors down. We told the jeep driver that if he could get us back to the ship, we would face the consequences of our actions after the next operation.

The two soldiers were stunned. They, of course, knew about the recent battle. They couldn't believe we wanted to get back into combat. They thought we should prefer jail. Well, it would have been safer in jail, I guess, but spending a week in jail instead of rejoining our unit never crossed our minds.

The jeep patrol decided that the only thing to do was to take us to their duty noncom. So they took us before a grizzled staff sergeant who laughed when he heard our story.

"Well," he said, "I guess we'll have to put these boys in the drunk tank overnight."

He told us not to worry, that we would be back on the ship in the morning and would make the upcoming operation.

Well, we spent the night in jail with seven or eight other men, rear-echelon guys. Both Meades and I felt naked and insecure, for our rifles had been taken from us, the first time we had been without them for many months. The next morning we were awakened early, given our rifles and gear, and rushed back aboard ship.

As young men have probably done since the beginning of time, Meades and I had acted impulsively, stupidly, without giving a thought to what the consequences of our unauthorized vacation might be. What would happen to us? We hillbillies would soon find out.

30

5

Operation Badger Catch

BACK ABOARD SHIP, WE WERE GREETED WITH GLARES AND black looks. Everyone started shouting at the same time.

"Where the hell have you guys been?"

"You're lucky we got a new lieutenant who don't know shit from Shinola, or you guys would hang."

"Better git your gear together, for we're moving out!"

Maybe a tall, lanky grunt said it best: "We knew you'd be back. We couldn't be lucky enough to lose you two idiots."

With sheepish grins we just eased out of sight. They had a right to be pissed off. They had worried about us, wondered what had happened and whether we had drowned or been hurt or killed in a fight. But we always stuck together, and they had covered for us.

It's impossible to keep secrets in the military, and so we weren't surprised that the captain got wind of our adventures. He laughed, but in keeping with good Marine Corps tradition, he chewed the lieutenant out and gave Meades and me unofficial office hours, which amounted to having our asses chewed out.

Our friends told us that the new operation, Badger Catch, would soon get under way. They had no ideas about details but knew we were going after the same North Vietnamese who had hurt us so badly at Badger Tooth.

While the ship moved north during the next two days, we were busy getting gear together, receiving rations, and putting the ship in order. Tension mounted as the significance of what we were going into sank home. War was back on us!

To me this trip to battle was different from the first one. Just looking at the eagerness of some of the youths who had never seen combat made me sad: They just didn't realize that in a very few days, many of them would be stinking meat in body bags. I felt like their big brother. But thinking along those lines can drive a person crazy.

The sergeants were exceptionally tough on inspections: They inspected, reinspected, and then inspected again—everything from flak jackets to rifles and helmets. All men except a few who wanted to keep their old ones were issued new rifles (M-16s). So many of the rifles had malfunctioned at Badger Tooth, we knew something bad was wrong with them. Whatever was wrong cost the lives of many young men on December 27, 1967. I kept mine, the one I had picked up from the side of a dead buddy, Corporal Pope, at Badger Tooth. That rifle worked perfectly.

The ship finally stopped, and before daylight we stood in a loose formation on deck, waiting to go down the rope net to the landing craft. The eyes of many reflected the fear and dread I felt. I wasn't thinking of revenge. I wasn't thinking of glory. I was thinking there was no turning back, that death lay ahead, and it took all the nerve I could muster to keep others from seeing I was close to panic. Because I had been in battle, many of the newcomers looked to me for encouragement. I couldn't let them down.

When we hit the beach, to me everything was again in slow motion. It was like watching a movie as the young marines, all with flak jackets, helmets, and rifles, came ashore. Some of the new men were excited, maybe even thrilled, but the certainty of impending death for so many of us dulled any enthusiasm I might have gotten out of the landing. I just couldn't feel carefree in a situation like that.

As we quickly formed into columns of twos, I saw that at least a few men did not share my feelings. The captain and other officers were excited, enthusiastic. They were like wolves that had gotten the scent of game and were moving in for the kill. For them the hunt was on!

Captain Hempel smiled at me as though I were supposed to be enjoying all this. I hoped my weak smile didn't reflect how I really felt. The new lieutenant in charge of the FO team looked to me for support. It was all I could do to keep my composure. I was thinking, "Don't you and the other new men in our company lean on me. I'm more scared than you are."

Somehow I managed, more or less, to keep my trembling under control as we started the forced march to catch the NVA battalion. I don't know whether I set a good example for anyone looking to me for reassurance. I just did the best I could.

I have been on some killing marches in my life, but none could compare with this one. The captain had not told us where we were going. As the march went on and on, I became numb. I couldn't even feel the ground as I pushed one foot ahead of the other. Finally we came to a small village, but the captain barely paused long enough to question a few villagers before moving out again.

About dark we moved into a larger village. The captain, with the help of Meades, his interpreter, started questioning the people. I sat in on some of the sessions, and later Meades filled me in on details I had missed.

The NVA had left only a few hours before our arrival. The people were angry. The South Vietnamese had never bothered them, but the NVA had impressed them into slave labor. This had been especially insulting to the old people.

The village elders told the captain that the NVA had planned to use villagers to build fortifications and bunkers. But before they could get much done, their leaders had become agitated and nervous. After a quick discussion, they had quickly moved out. Now the villagers knew why.

Boy! Did we welcome the rest and a quick meal of C rations. I saw, just before falling asleep, that the officers and staff sergeants were having a meeting in the middle of our encampment. Before long we would know what hell they had cooked up for us.

It seemed I had just fallen asleep when I was awakened by activities all around. On being told to *move out,* I thought, "My God! What now?"

I never stopped being amazed at how quickly a company of men could transform itself from a quietly sleeping camp into an organized group on a forced march. Within minutes after awaking, we were humping as fast and as hard as is humanly possible. As usual, the men started griping.

"What the shit's goin' on?"

"I dunno. Maybe some new type of torture they've invented."

"Anybody got a watch?"

"Hell! It's two o'clock in the morning!"

"Two o'clock? Fuck it. Have they got Vietcong hoot owls or something?"

"No. I think Dracula is a Vietcong suspect."

But soon all talking stopped. We needed our wind. It was pitch-black. We marched in a staggered column of two lines, within ten feet of each other, because visibility was so poor.

It was hot. There were no breaks. If a man wanted a drink, he had to take one on the move. It was torture. My legs hurt with every step, and soon my whole body hurt. I could dimly see the man in front of me keep moving, so I kept telling myself if he could do it, so could I. I sympathized with the radiomen with their thirty pounds of extra weight on top of their packs, and wondered how in hell they survived.

I heard a moan behind me as someone dropped. A sergeant told a private to stay with him and for everyone else to keep moving. How many men collapsed on that forced march, I will never know.

On and on we went. Would the torture never end? My brain grew numb. An eternity later, we stopped. It was still dark. The words *stage your gear* was passed around. This meant to put packs and ponchos in one small area to be picked up after the battle. A jolt of electricity passed through the men.

Suddenly I wasn't tired; I was scared. Officers and noncoms got men lined up for an assault. Even though I couldn't see for more than ten feet, I knew a village was near—the stench from open toilets and domestic animals was unmistakable.

As we lined up, the captain smiled at me and said, "Okay, Mac. You're a grunt today."

As we moved forward, I became, if that was possible, even more terrified. The darkness only added to my fear.

The firing started, but I couldn't see a thing to shoot at. Quickly the scattered firing became heavy and steady from all directions except from our rear.

I froze at the first pop! pop! pop! of M-16s and the crack of AK-47s. Men on the right and left kept moving forward and were about ten feet ahead of me when someone grabbed my shoulder and shook me.

"Stand there," the captain said, "and you're dead. Keep moving."

I hurriedly caught up with the rest of the line. Muzzle blasts and screaming from the wounded came from every-where. It was still too dark for me to see a target, but just then I saw a muzzle blast to the right and front of me. I aimed my M-16 and emptied a twenty-round magazine at the spot the shots had come from. I moved forward as in a dream. I stepped on something that felt like a sack of rice. I smelled the dead North Vietnamese soldier and kept going.

In the slowly creeping light I caught a glimpse of the terror in the eyes of the man to my right. He moved closer to me. He was new, a grunt from one of the rifle squads. He knew I had lived through Badger Tooth, and I knew he needed my encouragement. What he didn't know was that I needed support as much as he did. But he looked so young! He had discovered that war is terror, a terror that cannot be described in words. Maybe he now knew that there is no glory in dying on a battlefield.

In the dim light the grunt and I could make out a grass hut and bunker just ahead. We rushed to the bunker and crouched at its base. I patted his shoulder and whispered, "Well, you survived this one. You're home free now. Just stay put until you can get back with your squad." He just stared at me, but he did as I told him and he survived.

By daylight I could assess the situation a little better. Shooting was still going on all around, and now we could identify our men from those of the NVA. I chanced to stick my head up and saw several marines crouched behind covers of various kinds. Occasionally one would fire a burst from his rifle or rush up to throw a grenade into a bunker or hut. The battle would continue like this for hours, but this time the NVA did not have us trapped in a creek or in an open area where they could mow us down at their leisure. We had caught them with their pants down.

The grunt and I were hunkered beside an NVA bunker that no other marine had assaulted. I told him that we needed to throw grenades into the bunker to make sure there wasn't anyone in it. He just stared at me with a blank expression. So it was up to me. I certainly didn't feel heroic, and I didn't want to do it, but I realized the situation and knew what had to be done.

The bunker was large enough to hold twenty NVA soldiers, and I had already seen what a bunker that size could do to unsuspecting troops. It had to be destroyed, and a frightened Kentucky hillbilly was the only one around to do it.

As I cautiously stuck my head around to peep inside the entrance, I heard something move and glimpsed a brown-trousered leg disappear back inside. I thought, "Okay, you bastards. Payback time!" I was no longer afraid. I was thinking of all my dead buddies. Before December 27 they had been family to me. Now they were just cold meat rotting away in body bags.

I threw a grenade into the bunker. It exploded and I heard movement and muffled screams. I threw another and then another. I had four grenades, and I threw them all. Moaning and screaming still came from the inside. I felt, I suppose, like a wolf feels when it kills a flock of sheep just for the sheer joy of killing.

I looked up to see the white face of my partner. He looked at me as if I were some kind of savage beast, and I guess I was. I demanded his grenades, and he shakily gave me two, and I threw them into the bunker. By now the screaming had stopped, but I still heard an occasional moan. I felt drained. No energy was left in my body.

After a few more hours of the same kind of fighting, the battle wound down. The dreamlike quality was back. Officers and noncoms moved about, getting the wounded taken care of and rounding up NVA prisoners of war. When the bunker I had thrown the six grenades into was cleared, three dead NVA soldiers and a woman and child, both mortally wounded, were found inside.

The NVA had done what they usually did—taken a

woman with them inside a bunker, possibly as a companion, but more likely the woman had gone at gunpoint and had taken her small child with her. She was pretty, with long black hair, and was about twenty. Both she and the child were dying. I was sorry, very sorry, about what had happened.

I sat on my helmet with my face in my hands. What had I become? The grunt (did he ever say a word to me?) was long gone and had found his squad. Probably he told them stories about the crazy forward observer who had survived Badger Tooth and now wanted to kill every gook he saw.

Captain Hempel was exuberant. He was like a kid who had hit his first home run. Our casualties had been very light, and by moving so fast during the forced marches, we had taken the enemy completely by surprise and had destroyed an NVA battalion. Most of the NVA had been killed, but we had taken prisoners, some of them ranking officers. Also we had captured their weapons.

The captain filled me in on the overall picture of what had taken place, the route we had taken on our march and how we had taken the enemy by surprise. I was impressed by his telling a private about it all, and tried to pretend I was paying close attention. But actually none of his joy rubbed off on me. I just could not get into his holiday spirit. Just as soon as he started talking with some lieutenants, I eased away and lost myself in the hubbub around us.

I found Shultz, the radioman, and together we checked things out. We first looked at the captured weapons. In a hundred-foot-square area, closely guarded by grunts, were heavy machine guns, mortars, RPGs (Rocket Propelled Grenades), recoilless rifles, and piles of AK-47s. There were countless rounds and boxes of ammunition. Apparently the recoilless rifles were new, and I was thankful they had not had them at Badger Tooth. These NVA troops, as well as all units we were to meet later, were well armed.

Shultz and I, after getting our fill at looking at the weapons, made our way to the place where guards were herding the captives. On the way we passed an individual surrounded by radiomen and officers. He glanced at me, and for a second I saw a hint of recognition. He was dressed in jungle utilities like the rest of us and had his .45 drawn.

Like the rest of us, he was covered with dirt, mud, and blood. It was Colonel McCown! The man I once thought was God Himself, the man I had invited to warm his hands by my forbidden fire.

I stopped a marine attached to battalion headquarters and asked him to fill me in. According to him, the colonel had force-marched with the rest of us and had been with the troops during the assault. The story was that Colonel McCown had caught an NVA officer hiding during the fight and had killed him with the .45 he was now holding.

By the thousand-yard stare in his eyes and the blood on him, I had no doubt that he had been in on the fight. We hoped and half believed that he had personally killed the commanding officer of the NVA battalion. We all felt sure that with men like Colonel McCown and Captain Hempel leading us, we could march right on into Hanoi. The war would soon be over. Even today I'm overcome with sorrow when I think about how American politicians lost the war, and in doing so, caused thousands of unnecessary deaths.

Shultz and I went on to find the captives. There were about forty of them, huddled together and trembling with fear. They avoided our eyes, not wanting people to see their humiliation at having lost and being captured. I caught a glimpse into the eye of one prisoner and saw the look of a cold killer. They were veteran soldiers.

As I watched the prisoners, a cold hatred took hold of me. I thought of how hard these men had tried to kill me and the rest of L Company. They had succeeded in killing most. If the survivors had tried to surrender, they would have killed us, for the NVA took, with few exception, only officers as prisoners.

A cordon of watchful marines with loaded rifles guarded them. They were not as worried about their escaping as they were about what survivors of Badger Tooth would do if they had a chance to get at them. Luckily the officers and noncoms kept strict control over the situation. I would not want to live with what would have happened had some of us been able to get at them.

Shultz was a better man than me. I saw him get close to a prisoner and give him a cigarette. The shaking North Vietnamese seemed grateful, and he and Shultz had a short conversation. I would later admire Shultz for that. At the time, most of us were not that understanding.

What eventually happened to the prisoners, I never knew, but while they were in our hands, none were mistreated. I thought it ironic that they were treated much better than we marines had been at Parris Island, South Carolina. If any guard had treated a prisoner as we were treated in boot camp, he would have been court-martialed. This is just fact, not a complaint. Our tough training was necessary: without it, I would have been rotting in a body bag at that very moment.

From the prisoners, we moved on to where NVA dead soldiers were stacked like firewood. I guess that was a convenient way to put the dead together. At least in every firefight I was in, that was the way the dead, American or enemy, were handled.

Close by were the dead and wounded civilians. The wounded moaned pitifully as corpsmen tried to ease their suffering. There was little they could do. The NVA, as always, had kept civilians close to them in battle. They wanted as many South Vietnamese civilians killed as possible.

This battle had ended in one of the most complete victories U.S. troops had in Vietnam. The NVA were seasoned veterans, were well equipped, well rested, and had villagers do the hard work for them. But they had been outmaneuvered in the field by Colonel McCown and Captain Hempel, and outfought by individual marines.

After the battle I became better acquainted with Captain Hempel, partly because of the way I had performed on battlefields and partly because I was a forward observer. From that time on, I was always informed about our larger actions and was told beforehand where we were going and what to expect when we got there. I found out that in the Marine Corps, rank is not as important as action in the field. For the first time in my life I was to feel like an important part of a group.

6
R and R

ABOARD SHIP WE LEARNED WE WERE GOING TO HAVE A ONE-day R and R at a beach near Da Nang. It was the first one for most of us, and we deserved it. Cold beer, good food, no brutal NVA, and a great time ahead! It was good to be alive!

The trip to Da Nang was routine but pleasant. When the ship docked, we went ashore carrying our loaded rifles and plenty of ammunition. We were still field marines in jungle utilities. Trucks took us directly to a closed beach guarded by military police. Authorities wanted to keep Vietcong snipers out, and they wanted to keep us in. They didn't want us to mingle with the citizens of Da Nang. It would be too dangerous!

The beach was beautiful: white sand as far as the eye could see, brilliant sunshine, blue skies, and the South China Sea sparkling in the sun. I felt young again.

We spread our towels on the sand and lay our rifles on them. We stripped and hit the water. It was great! We were like a bunch of high school kids on a senior class outing. The men played games, thought up stunts, played good-natured tricks on one another, and laughed like carefree youngsters. In no way did we resemble the killers of the week before.

Booths set up on the beach featured ice-cold beer or soda pop, whichever you preferred. Naturally, most of us preferred beer. Boy, that beer was cold! After a couple of cold ones, two friends from the FAC team and I drifted toward a nearby open-air bar.

Novak, one of my companions, was a huge blond from

Michigan and looked like a football player. He was a survivor of Badger Tooth. The other, Private Nash, was tall, wiry, had brown hair, and was also a survivor. In the open-air bar we had a choice of beer or any kind of mixed drink imaginable. Soon we were feeling pretty good, drinking too much, and getting pretty loud. Just then I looked up to see five knuckles heading for my jaw.

The next thing I knew, I was lying under the bar, my barstool was turned over, and First Sergeant Michelle was laughing and helping me to my feet. I was so happy to see him that I forgot to get mad. Smiling, he said, "Mac, you son of a bitch! Don't you know you're supposed to be calling in artillery, not playing grunt? What do you think you went to school for? I warned you not to try to be a damn hero."

Now, First Sergeant Michelle and I went back a long way. When I arrived in Vietnam, he was the top NCO in C Battery, Third Battalion, First Marines. He had been through Korea and was a small, thin man who looked very much like a toy bulldog. He was one of the toughest men I ever knew, and as I had just found out, he had a good punch. Although close to forty, he often organized and participated in games of football for the men in C Battery.

For some reason, First Sergeant Michelle liked me. He had no family, no wife, or any close relation that anyone knew of. The Marine Corps was his life, and he treated the Marine Corps as his family.

As soon as I arrived at C Battery, I reported to the first sergeant and was given orientation by him. He was sitting behind his desk in his bunker and looked at me as if thinking, "My God, son, you're not even out of high school. What are you doing here?" What he actually said was, "Private Mac, your MOS is 0846. That is an artillery scout observer. It means that you call in artillery on the enemy. You're too damn young for that. I've never seen that before. Hell, that is for officers or NCOs who have been here for a while."

He then added, "We'll keep you here with us and let you learn the Fire Direction Control System and work in that. Besides, you have a wife in the States. You need to go back home alive."

41

I was surprised that he knew that much about me. I found out later that he knew all his men, knew about their families, and knew the good marines from the bad ones. He was a remarkable man. All the men respected him, and when he said jump, you jumped.

You learn early in the Marine Corps that you can punch an officer in the nose and you might get a few days in jail and busted to private, but you would soon get your stripes back and the jail sentence would be forgotten. However, you also learn early that whatever you do, don't piss off the first sergeant. If he says, "Shit!" you ask, "What color?"

I put up with Fire Direction Control, humping ammunition and burning shitters for about two weeks. I decided I wanted to go to the field with the grunts. It wasn't that I wanted to be a hero. It was just that it was my job to call in artillery on the enemy, and that was what I wanted to do.

I requested mast to see First Sergeant Michelle. "Request mast" is a military procedure where an enlisted man can go through the chain of command to get a request or grievance heard. If one of the men of higher rank sympathizes with the enlisted man or thinks he is right, then there is a good chance his request will be granted. I had asked my squad leader if I could be assigned to the grunts, and he refused. I requested mast. The platoon sergeant refused. Again I requested mast, and the gunnery sergeant refused. Finally I requested mast once more, and there I was in front of First Sergeant Michelle. His decision would be final. No officer would go against it.

I saw a hint of a smile on his face when I first entered the bunker and stood in front of him. This quickly changed to a look of strictly business.

"I know what's on your mind, Mac. You wanna play John Wayne," he said.

"I'd like to go to the field with the grunts, sir."

For some reason, I could hardly suppress a smile. I knew he was going to let me go. Somehow I felt on the same level with him. It is hard for even a first sergeant to scare you when you are asking to die anyhow. I felt the excitement of starting a new challenge and being free of the harassment and petty things in the rear.

"So you think life out there will be more pleasant than this chicken-shit stuff back here, huh?" he asked. "Let me tell you something, Mac, getting shot at is no fun. Forget the John Wayne crap. Out there the good guys get killed, too. I know what I'm talking about. I was a grunt in Korea. I've got enough lead in me to set off a metal detector now, so I'll tell you it won't be any fun."

He paused with an expectant look on his face. This was my chance. If I really wanted to live, all I had to do was change my mind now. I said nothing.

His face softened. For the slightest instant I thought I saw a look of indecision, then it was gone. He had made his decision.

"Mac," he said, "I knew you would have to go. You had to see what it was like. You have to see the elephant, don't you?"

He paused again. I had another chance to change my mind, but said nothing.

He half smiled again, as if he was remembering something. Perhaps he remembered when another young marine wanted to play John Wayne and see the elephant. Perhaps he had seen several young marines who wanted to play John Wayne. Whatever he was thinking, the faraway look quickly vanished.

He looked at me with a half-sad, half-mystified expression. "You know, Mac," he said, "ninety percent of the men in Vietnam would love to get out of the bush and stay in the rear for their tour of duty, and here you are asking to go the other way. I knew from the first time I saw you that you danced to a little different drummer than most of us. You know you will never have any close friends. You'll always be a little off the beaten path."

He looked me right in the eye and said, "Well, Mac, I'll see what I can do. You can go now."

As I turned to leave, he reached and stopped me with his left hand. He was smiling, and reached out his right hand to shake mine. "Good luck," he said, "and don't try to be a hero. Just do your job."

A week later I was humping a radio in the bush and wishing I had used a little better judgment. I had not seen much of First Sergeant Michelle after that, but I remember that he really cared whether I lived or died.

In the hellhole of a war, with mostly poor kids thrown together to fight a tough, well-supplied, and well-led enemy, people found time to care for one another. I suppose we had to. Our world was much different from the one back in the States. But in the States most people are too wrapped up with making money, accomplishing goals, making good impressions, or following some other sort of personal aggrandizement that they actually don't have much time to care one way or the other.

But now, back on the beach near Da Nang, I sat back up to the bar, and all of us had several more rounds of beer, told jokes, and related our experiences. It was good to be alive, and it was good to see First Sergeant Michelle again.

After leaving the bar, Novak, Nash, and I were soon back in the water and were having a great time when suddenly someone yelled, "Shark!" There was a big splash between Novak and me. We headed for shore, completely sober—for the moment. We three stood with the other marines on the beach and watched a dark shadow of death cruise around spots wherever it heard splashing sounds.

Eventually there was a stir around the entrance to the beach. A truck had backed up to the gate, and several marines were unloading a boat from it. They were going to rid the area of the shark.

During the confusion, I looked at Nash. Nash looked at Novak. Both looked at me. "Oh, no!" they exclaimed. "We know what you're up to, and we're not about to go along."

Nobody paid any attention to the three young marines, pockets stuffed with beer, as they slipped out the gate.

We were home free! Loose in Da Nang again! Nobody paid us any attention as we drifted into the outlying suburbs. We were walking down a hot, dusty road lined with tin-can shacks and grass huts when an ARVN officer stopped and gave us a lift in his jeep. We had no idea where we were going. But it wasn't long before we heard someone yelling, "Stop and talk, marines."

We motioned the driver to stop, and we bailed out into

the midst of five smiling kids. We were in front of a nice French villa which had a high stone wall enclosing a small yard. I smiled at the kids, and they smiled back, seeming to recognize the kinship I felt toward them. Back in Kentucky I had been used to seeing barefoot kids in worn clothes. Seeing the smiling eyes of these kids made me think of home. Children are pretty much the same everywhere.

We went inside the yard and, to my surprise, found it nice and cool there. The high walls and the shade trees did their job well. I offered a C ration cigarette to a black-haired boy, the oldest and the leader of the group. Smiling, he took it. Instantly all the kids were bumming cigarettes. We obliged them, and for a few minutes we stood around laughing and kidding.

The older boy, about fifteen, took a liking to me. When I offered him a beer, he accepted it. We sipped warm beer, and the boy, who was both intelligent and curious, asked about my home, listened to what I said, but after a few minutes he spoke the magic words: "You marines want Buku boom-boom?"

We had hit the jackpot! "Buku boom-boom" meant that this was a whorehouse and that the boy could get us a *siklo* girl (prostitute). At the moment I wasn't interested in Buku boom-boom, but Nash and Kovac started foaming at the mouth. They sent the boy for the girl.

While waiting for his return, he kept kidding and laughing with the other kids. They giggled in delight. They kept playing soldier and having many battles.

"How many VC you kill, marine?" a child would ask.

"Oh," Novak would answer, "about a hundred on the last operation."

Laughing, another kid would say, "You buku bad marine! You marine grunts. You fight in jungle and kill VC. You numbah one. VC numbah ten."

It was not surprising to find innocent children playing around and living in a whorehouse in South Vietnam. To these children, what adults did behind closed doors was just something to giggle about. They had never been taught shame, and they didn't feel any. While the older boy was gone, the other children told us that the mama-san fed them and kept them in clothing, that she never mistreated them.

So these kids were often happy in a country that was a living hell for many others.

The boy returned with the *siklo* girl. I couldn't believe it! She was prettier than anything I had ever seen in *Playboy,* or any number of other girlie magazines. She had black hair down past her waist, and she was wearing one of those white, tight dresses that emphasize the beauty of Oriental girls. The boy must have brought us the cream of the crop.

I was about to ask her to go to the prom with me when one of my buddies asked the price of her favors. Before I could interrupt and say that no girl so beautiful could be a prostitute, she answered, and they started arguing prices.

Was I shocked! But when I thought about it, I started laughing. If a girl is not beautiful, she cannot get very far selling her body. This young lady just had a good business head and knew what assets to put on the market. Novak, Nash, and the girl came to an agreement, and after much laughing, kissing, and playing around, they disappeared.

The older boy spoke English very well. He told me his parents and the parents of all the children in the compound had been killed by the Vietcong when the children were very young. He saw more beer in my pockets and asked for one, and I handed a can over. After we drank beer for a few minutes, he motioned for me to follow him. He seemed secretive and acted as if he wanted to share some great secret with me.

We followed a path that led to the top of the house. There, a couple of feet below the roof, was a hole in a side wall. By crouching back, we could see inside while those inside could not see us. In the room was a crude bed, and on the bed was Private Novak locked in embrace with the beautiful prostitute. Now, here was a girl who thoroughly enjoyed her work. I've always heard that prostitutes were expert at faking enjoyment, but I don't think this one was putting on an act. I know Novak wasn't.

The boy had let me in on one of his best secrets. While we sat there watching sweaty bodies, we continued to sip beer. After a few minutes we tired of this and went back to the courtyard.

Private Novak and Private Nash, with the girl between

them, soon returned. To this day the men don't know that their buddy spied on them. I didn't, and I still don't, have the nerve to tell them.

After laughing and talking for a few minutes, we marines started to leave. But the girl motioned for us to come with her.

"Oh, what the hell?" I thought. "What have we got to lose?"

We followed her through two rooms of the villa before reaching a dining area where an old Vietnamese man and an old Vietnamese woman sat. In the center of the room was a large bowl of steaming rice.

While the girl and the old couple talked for a few minutes, the boy explained the situation to us. According to him, the old people were the girl's aunt and uncle. Her parents, who had been high officials in the South Vietnamese government, had been assassinated by the Vietcong. The girl had been taken care of by her aunt and uncle. By the time the aunt and uncle had become too old to work, the girl had grown into a beautiful woman. With her intelligence, charm, and beauty, her relatives knew the easiest way for her to make a living.

She had gone to the mama-san of the villa we were in and offered her services, but only if her aunt and uncle would be cared for. The mama-san, a respectable businesswoman, agreed, and it had worked out for the good of all. In Vietnam at that time, a prostitute, like the geisha girls in old Japan, were simply thought of as working girls. They were not looked down upon, nor was it disgraceful to marry a girl who had been a prostitute.

When the girl finished talking to the old couple, the man turned to us with a gracious smile. He got out a bowl for each man and handed us some chopsticks. Ignoring stern looks from his wife, he then got each of us a large bottle of Tiger beer, a local beer that tasted good warm and would curl your hair if you drank very much. The man then got a beer for himself while his wife gave him even sterner looks. But he had guests, a good excuse for him to indulge.

The rice, with tiny crabs cooked in it, was served with the usual fish sauce. It was delicious. "Are you men back at the beach enjoying your C rations?" I thought, smiling to myself. The beer loosened the old man's tongue, and though we could understand only a little of what he said, we enjoyed the meal, enjoyed seeing him so happy, and were happy we were affording him a rare treat.

The girl was delightful. She sat between Novak and Nash, and they all were smiles and happiness. All too soon it was time for farewells.

On leaving, I gave the boy all of my C ration cigarettes while the other guys bade farewell to the girl. As I was about to leave, the boy told me that the old couple were on the VC hit list and would be killed if the Vietcong found them.

Outside, the hot tropical air didn't do much to help us back to reality. After all the Tiger beer, it would be a while before we got back all our senses. We staggered back to the dirt road, not really knowing where we were nor where we were going. But they say that God watches over fools and drunk Irishmen, and at the time, I guess we were a little of both.

Unbelievably, at about the same time that we got to the road, the South Vietnamese officer who had brought us to the villa came back from the other way. He recognized us, stopped, and picked us up again. We went back to the beach in good spirits. We were totally unprepared for what happened next.

7

Routed by Orphans

As soon as Novak, Nash, and I arrived back at the beach, a hubbub erupted. This time Novak and Nash shared in the black looks and angry stares.

"You damn dummies are going to get killed or court-martialed or both, if you don't get in step," one guy admonished.

"The lieutenant was looking for you, but he's so drunk, he forgot what he was looking for."

"Hell! Don't you know better than to go anywhere with that damn hillbilly?"

We quietly melted into the crowd without answering. We felt a little guilty for causing them concern, and we knew that if we had gotten caught, it would have been big shit. But what the hell? We were United States Marines in Vietnam. We were already in a world of shit.

Just before dark, trucks to pick us up and take us back to the ship pulled up to within five hundred feet of the gate and fanned out to hasten landing. Unfortunately, we had to pass a large orphanage to get to the trucks. As we passed the orphanage, at least a hundred children from the ages of six to ten converged on us, every one of them shouting at the same time.

"Marines numbah one. VC numbah ten."

"You souvenir me, marine?"

"What you got for me, marine?"

They wanted anything at all, and we had nothing at all to give. Marines with three-day R and Rs often visited this beach and had been very generous with the kids. The kids *knew* we were loaded also, but nothing we could say would

49

convince them that we had nothing to give. We did have a little MPC (military paper currency), but that would have been worthless to them. Later on we realized the kids knew very well how to use the black market, where they could have exchanged the military currency for money they could use.

The situation got rowdy. A kid grabbed for a marine's rifle, and the marine had trouble keeping the kid's hands off it. The children got mad. A hundred kids were screaming all at the same time.

"Marines numbah ten!"

"Tight-ass muthas!"

"Why you not souvenir me, marine?"

A small child threw a rock; another hit a marine with a stick. Mass confusion reigned as rocks and sticks started coming in from all directions. The kids grabbed at our jungle fatigues, tried to get their hands into our pockets, and tried to grab guns. I didn't know whether to laugh or what, I was so confused, when I saw a huge gunnery sergeant— big enough to whip three ordinary men—chasing a kid who had stolen his hat. That kid was having a ball, and the others were jumping up and down and laughing at the show. Finally realizing there was no hope of success in getting his hat back, the gunnery sergeant gave up the chase.

Where was the military bearing—of the men and of the officers? The noncoms and officers were at a loss. It was the first time they and their troops had been assaulted by small orphans. For the first time since I met him, Captain Hempel didn't know what to do.

We were in a dilemma. What do three hundred drunk marines do with a hundred attacking children? We couldn't hurt them, and we were too wobbly on our feet to catch them. We didn't have a chance.

Finally the captain yelled, "To the trucks, men!"

It was a rout: three hundred battle-hardened marines in full flight from rock-throwing, stick-wielding, laughing and screaming children.

As we jumped into trucks, a rock hit one marine right in the mouth, breaking a tooth. He flipped the safety off his rifle, but men near him quickly disarmed him. Not one, not even the angry marine, wanted to hurt the kids.

Someone aboard my truck yelled, "Give me General Giap anytime!"

We burst out laughing. It was a good trip back to the ship. We drank beer and yelled at girls all the way. But most important, there was a wonderful feeling of good fellowship.

It was good to be alive!

8

Headquarters Platoon

MOST OF THE PEOPLE I WAS ASSOCIATED WITH AND FOUGHT beside during the next several months were members of Headquarters Platoon in L Company, Third Battalion, First Marines.

Lieutenant Callahan was in charge of the artillery Forward Observer team, and as ranking officer, was the platoon commander. He was lean, sharp, and eager. All he needed was experience to become an excellent officer, and he was going to get plenty of that. His radioman, Private Shultz, had been with me during Operation Badger Tooth.

I had a new radioman, O. E. Jones, a black man with big-city soul-brother talk. He carried a picture of his wife and child with him all the time. When O.E. got up each morning, he would comb his hair, tell himself how beautiful he was, and kiss the picture of his wife and son. At first he was quiet, but as he grew accustomed to the bush, he became more open and talkative. He was one of the bravest men I ever saw. He took care of me both in and out of combat. For this I will ever be grateful.

Private Hays was the acknowledged leader and core of

the Forward Air Control (FAC) team. He had dark hair, was nineteen, and had a calm in combat that we all envied. He could endure anything with a smile.

Novak and Nash were the other two members of the FAC team. Hays, Novak, and Nash had volunteered to come to the field to call in air support. These brave men helped carry me through the worst of times. Without them, I could not have made it through the bad times.

Another close friend was Corporal Cizek. He was a volunteer whose job was to call in the marines' 81-mm mortars. Cizek was lean, black-haired, and had a pockmarked face. His good mood and excellence as a soldier made him a pleasure to be around. He was relatively new to the field, but was an exceptionally good soldier.

Another member of Headquarters Platoon was Private David Brown, another hillbilly from eastern Kentucky. He was six foot four and as strong as two ordinary men. He loved to fight, whether in the rear areas in a bar or in the jungle against the NVA.

Private Brown was the company runner or message carrier. Since he loved to drink and raise hell and had a background similar to mine, we quickly became friends. He moved through the jungle like a big cat and with the grace of a natural woodsman. He could handle a rifle as well as any Daniel Boone. He was a good man to have on your side in a fight, in a bar or in a battle. Before the battles along the Cua Viet River were through Private Brown was assigned to a grunt platoon and left headquarters platoon. He survived, only being wounded once, and probably is today still fighting and raising hell.

Two of my close friends were in K Company. Lieutenant Michaels was another officer trained to be an artillery forward observer. He was much better than I in calling in artillery fire, and I was happy he was around. He seemed amused by me, both at my ways and my talk. I often caught him smiling at my dialect when he thought I didn't see him.

Lieutenant Michaels's radioman, Private Binge, was yet another eastern Kentuckian. We, too, quickly made friends and joked that everybody but us talked funny. We would sit and talk about home for hours. Binge was stocky, dark-haired, and just eighteen. He never cursed nor drank. Despite his youth, he showed a lot of maturity and seemed totally without fear. A person didn't necessarily have to drink and raise hell to be a good friend of mine.

9

The Beginning of Hell

THE NEXT MORNING ABOARD SHIP WE ALL HAD HANGOVERS, but it was back to business—cleaning rifles and getting combat gear ready. We were headed for the Cua Viet River, one of the main supply routes leading to Khe Sanh, a remote outpost in the northernmost part of South Vietnam. Khe Sanh became an American household word during the first half of 1968.

Khe Sanh! Even now the name means endurance. It reminds veterans of incessant mortar and artillery attacks, of blood, of death, or wounded marines being carried to helicopters. The marines at Khe Sanh were completely surrounded by the very best troops General Giap had. During the Tet Offensive, Giap planned to defeat the marines in exactly the same way he had defeated the French at Dien Bien Phu. But he failed to realize one thing: Marines do not sit back and wait for an attack. They do the attacking.

The Cua Viet River connects an inlet of the South China Sea to Highway 1 and Highway 9. These two highways are the main arteries of transportation in Quangtri Province, and therefore the lifeline to the American bases at Dong Ha and Khe Sanh.

At the time, crack NVA troops occupied the countryside and every village around both Dong Ha and Khe Sanh. If these two towns fell, the whole northern section of I Corps would be in communist hands.

The normal supply route to Khe Sanh and Dong Ha began with the Cua Viet River. Goods were landed by sea at a small supply base right on the South China Sea on the northern shore of an inlet into which the Cua Viet flowed. From the base, supplies were shipped inland to Highway 1, and along Highway 1 to Dong Ha. From Dong Ha the supplies traveled along Highway 9 to Khe Sanh.

Highway 1 to the south had been completely cut off by the invading NVA forces, and thus the only way to supply Dong Ha and Khe Sanh was by the Cua Viet River. Each village from Dong Ha to the sea was occupied by the enemy. It was about twenty miles from the supply base to Dong Ha, and strung out along the banks of the river were four small villages, one on the south bank and three on the north.

Under usual circumstances, the river supply route met Highway 1 at a large town called Mai Xai Ti. This town, in effect, controlled the supply route by both water and land. A small river, about sixty yards wide where it divided the town into Mai Xai Ti east and Mai Xai Ti west, formed a line of battle between our marines and the NVA. It was this small river that kept us, after we had taken all the villages along the Cua Viet River, from totally defeating the North Vietnamese in our first assault on Mai Xai Ti.

Khe Sanh, Dong Ha, and the entire supply route were in range of the NVA heavy artillery from North Vietnam and Laos. These heavy guns have a range of about thirty miles, and we were bombarded periodically throughout our entire campaign. Apparently no effort, by those who had the capability, was ever made to silence those weapons.

Ironically, at the time, North Vietnam was virtually defenseless, for all its crack troops had been sent into South Vietnam. The Americans could easily have invaded and defeated, militarily, North Vietnam. But American troops were forbidden to invade. Anyway, although we enlisted men did not know it at the time, the question that confronted us when we arrived in the area was "Can the United States Marines break the communist stranglehold and regain possession of Quangtri Province?"

When our troopship finally reached the mouth of the Cua

Viet River, we were all ready to disembark. It seemed only yesterday that we had just finished Operation Badger Catch, and now we were expecting another big operation.

As we went down the rope ladders to the landing crafts, I felt a fatalistic terror, and there was nothing I could do about it. No matter what some people say, battle experience does not make the next battle easier. A soldier knows that every time he goes down that ladder and prepares to hit the beach, his odds of survival get less and less. It never got easier for me. Maybe I'm not brave.

The enlisted men of the Third Battalion, First Marines, did not know that General Giap had stationed a great number of troops in areas all around us. We never suspected what lay ahead. All we knew was that the doors of hell were opening and that we were going in.

I got a hint of the size of our operation when I saw the amount and kinds of arms and equipment we had: 106-mm recoilless rifles, huge supplies of all kinds of ammunition, tanks, LAWs, plenty of machine guns, and amphibious light tanks to transport troops across rivers. We called the tanks floating coffins, because anyone inside one when it sank was doomed. These tanks are commonly called amtracs.

Except for sentries on duty, the men at the supply base were swimming and apparently enjoying their stay in Vietnam. They had not taken any excessive hostile fire and were completely unaware they were surrounded by NVA forces. I suspect that not even our leaders in Vietnam actually knew the enormous size and strength of the forces we were up against.

The marines at the base looked shocked on seeing the landing crafts and hardened combat veterans disembark with full combat gear. They grabbed their towels and left the beach, saying such things as, "What the hell's going on?" "Boy, you guys are expecting action!" "Shit's gonna hit the fan!" "You guys are loaded for bear!"

Our seriousness and businesslike attitude told them we had been there before and that this was no picnic, nor a practice drill.

After we got unloaded and had set up camp, Captain Hempel invited me over to a briefing in his tent that night. At the briefing we went over plans for the next day. We would cross the river on the floating coffins next morning and, without warning, assault the village south of the river. It would be a battalion-sized operation, with L Company, I Company, and M Company being the assault companies, and K Company being the reserve. The enemy strength was unknown.

Later that night I pinpointed landmarks on my map and got the grids and geographical data I needed to call in artillery. No doubt Lieutenant Callahan was doing the same, but we worked independently. I was more than happy for him to run the show, but I never knew when I would be needed. Too, I would be the forward observer in platoon-sized patrols or incursions. It was a lifesaving measure that we both be familiar with the terrain and be able to call in artillery at a moment's notice.

10

Contact

BEFORE DAYLIGHT THE NEXT MORNING, WE WERE ABOARD floating coffins (amtracs), ready to cross the wide Cua Viet River. From atop one of the tanks I watched the activities, paying special attention to the men, most of whom had been in only one battle, Badger Catch. These men were excited, expecting another easy victory.

Scattered among the enthusiastic newcomers were the survivors of Operation Badger Tooth. We were grim and humorless, knowing all too well what NVA machine guns and mortars could do to young men. We just could not look forward to what was about to happen. To us, war had lost its thrill on that day when almost all our companions had been either killed or wounded. Surviving in war is a whole lot of luck, and in every battle the odds are stacked more and more against the combat soldier.

As we rode into the river, I was almost overcome with fear and was sick to my stomach. I could see my mangled body with eyes rolled back in my head. The carefree attitude of the new men only added to my depression: they were so totally unaware of what awaited them.

We came ashore east of the sleeping village, dropped our packs and all excess equipment, and carried only our M-16s, ammunition, grenades, and radios. As the infantry spread out to sweep the village, Lieutenant Callahan and I checked our landmarks and the terrain and prepared to call in artillery if it was needed. Then the sweep began. It was still dark. The FO team moved through the center of the village right behind the grunts.

We caught the enemy by complete surprise. Suddenly I heard shouting and movements all around, but as yet no rifle fire. This village was large and had the usual well-kept grass buildings and a lot of bamboo and underbrush growing in patches throughout the area. We moved along the main road but had enough brush and bamboo on each side to keep us pretty well covered. About halfway through the village, I heard a shout.

"There goes one!" Then came the familiar crack of an AK-47. A man screamed.

"Corpsman up!" someone yelled. American M-16s opened fire, and men were shouting.

"Do you see him?"

"I got the son of a bitch!"

"Corpsman up!"

"Dammit!"

My team crouched beside the road. The bitter taste of fear filled my mouth. Rifle smoke filled my nostrils. Colors got very bright. All my senses became acute. The adrenaline was flowing. I heard shouted orders and listened to people running about, and watched as a wounded marine was carried past in a poncho.

We kept just behind the infantry. Captain Hempel told us to be ready to call in the 105-mm howitzers, our main artillery support, if needed, and to let the infantry do the work this time. They were good at it.

The marines had come upon a platoon or company of NVA forces in the middle of the village. As it turned out, the enemy had not finished occupying the last village, before their final assault on the marine supply depot at the mouth of the Cua Viet River. Had the NVA destroyed our supply depot, all supplies to Dong Ha and Khe Sanh would have been sealed off, and in all probability General Giap would have had his victory.

As the tempo of the battle increased, I felt a strong urge to join the grunts. Fortunately, the NVA, realizing they were both outmanned and outgunned, fled. The fierce fighting was brief, but shouting and firing continued for an hour. The marines were on a rabbit hunt. The only problem was that the rabbits shot back.

The enemy managed to cross an open rice paddy, taking their wounded with them, and had gotten to a tree line with thick brush. From there they laid down murderous automatic weapons fire and wounded two more marines before Colonel McCown called for artillery to blast them out of the trees and brush.

I was originally happy that Lieutenant Callahan was there and eager to take over. His presence should have taken a big load off my shoulders, but as it turned out, the Lieutenant made a mistake and the men, Captain Hempel and I were not happy in the end. Callahan called for a first round of white phosphorus, which landed about one hundred yards east of the tree line. I was shocked when, rather than calling for a fire-for-effect, he called in another adjustment round. I wasn't sure what they taught forward observers in training back in the States, but in combat I knew one adjustment round was all you usually got. "Fire-for-effect" means exactly what it says: Fire to effectively destroy the enemy—usually 18 rounds of high explosive artillery shells. A second adjustment round gave the NVA a chance to escape, as happened here.

Captain Hempel was furious. He came charging toward us, yelling, "What the hell's going on? Why wasn't there a fire-for-effect? They're getting away!"

Immediately the lieutenant called for a fire-for-effect. It was too late. It simply served as a screen to help the enemy escape.

"Dammit to hell!" a nearby staff sergeant cursed. "That dumb-ass FO let the little bastards git away."

Had the correct call come at the right moment, the chances are we would have captured or destroyed the whole lot of them. As it was, only five remained, killed in the first firefight.

Combat veterans glared at the lieutenant, but he refused to meet their eyes. They glared just as harshly at me and saw the shame and guilt reflected in my own eyes. They didn't say a word. They didn't have to.

Captain Hempel took Lieutenant Callahan aside, out of earshot. But I didn't have to hear, I knew damn well what he was saying. The dejected slump of the lieutenant's shoulders and the look on his face showed his humiliation and feelings of guilt, and showed he would rather have been shot himself than to have made the mistake he had. He knew only too well that some, perhaps many, of our own forces would be killed as a consequence of his act.

I was wanting desperately to be a grunt. Then I could blame someone else if anything went wrong, and could either have lived or died without having other lives depending on me so much. I felt as guilty as hell. I should have spoken up and told the lieutenant to fire for effect after the spotter round.

I had learned an important lesson: When it comes to human lives, you speak up, no matter if it is to a lieutenant, a general, or anyone else. Also I learned not to assume that another person has the knowledge or experience to do a job. And I learned that a nineteen-year-old is too young and inexperienced to have so much responsibility.

When the two officers came back, Lieutenant Callahan refused to look at me. But Captain Hempel stopped and looked me straight in the eye. I expected the worst.

"Dammit, Mac," he said. "You knew better."

He never mentioned the subject again. But he was right. I knew better.

Looking at the lieutenant, I thought, "I hope I never see that look on a man's face again." He was going through his own private hell. He was a deeply sensitive man and always tried his damnedest to do a good job, to do his best.

Now he knew that in the bush, a man has to learn quickly—there is no room for mistakes.

The village was quiet as we moved back through it along the main road. The newcomers, who really did not yet understand all that was involved, were still giving us dirty looks. But the veterans knew worse things would happen, and happen soon. We had made it together through many firefights only because of artillery support. They knew me and I knew them. Together, I hoped, we would survive again.

Lying in the middle of the road were the bodies of five young North Vietnamese soldiers killed in the brief battle. We stopped and examined them. One was lying to the side by himself, apparently an officer. Half his head had been blown off. The others were piled together and were beginning to stiffen. Intelligence people had already gone over them.

By this time, seeing dead people did not fill me with the horror it once did. All the same, looking at these corpses, so recently vibrant young men, filled me with sadness. I noticed how fit they had been, how well fed, and I knew they had trained long and hard. And I also knew that the NVA forces were always well equipped and taken good care of by General Giap. In contrast, sometimes we got supplies and replacements, and sometimes we didn't. Before the upcoming battles were over, I would know very well how poorly the Americans, at times, supported their troops in the field.

I looked about at the newcomers. They had had a brief taste of fire, but did they have any idea about what lay ahead? I suspected a great number of NVA forces were in the neighborhood, and I knew we would find them wherever they were. I just wished I had the confidence in ourselves that Captain Hempel and Colonel Mac did. Maybe it was battle fatigue or just plain cowardice, but at the moment I was not at all sure we would win.

The villagers were happy to see us and were anxious to tell how the NVA had treated them. They told the same stories we had heard before: the killing, the bullying, the forced labor, and on and on.

While the officers and staff sergeants were planning and

talking, we privates had some time to ourselves. Men rushed to the only barber in town, and that barber probably got more money that day than he had seen before in his whole life.

Some of us were attracted to beautiful pagodas with their beautiful artwork. The buildings were very old but were kept in excellent condition. The dominant colors were blue and white. Many figures of dragons and of Buddhas were in and just outside the buildings.

I soon knew my way around the village. O.E., a couple of other guys, and I found an old man, probably the village chief, who had a wife, a beautiful daughter, and several small children. The beautiful daughter stayed away from us, and I don't blame her, but the old man enjoyed talking with us. We bought some rice candy and learned he owned the village beer store. What did we do? Promptly bought a quart of rice wine. I proceeded to get bombed.

Being from the Kentucky hills, I was well qualified to compare mountain dew with the local brew. They were pretty much alike. The wine was colorless, but the taste and smell would knock down a water buffalo. Nobody liked the stuff, but we drank it anyway.

About dusk Captain Hempel called a meeting to go over what would happen the next day. I was invited to attend. Lordy, Lordy! I was in Irish heaven, and like all good Irish drunks, was in the mood to sing. But O.E. was not happy at the idea of my going to the meeting.

"You crazy muddafuckah," he said, "you gotta go to the captain's meeting, and would you stop singin' that damn grit song?"

O.E. had drunk some rice wine, but as I had noticed before, he had more common sense than I, and unlike me, he hadn't gotten plastered. I was God's own drunk and a fearless man, and I knew beyond a shadow of a doubt that the captain, the other officers, and the noncoms were dying to hear my song. O.E. knew beyond a shadow of a doubt that I would get court-martialed and sent to the brig or worse.

"Okay," O.E. said. "If you gotta go, I go with you, you fool. Just to keep you from breaking your fool neck. But

61

promise me one thing, that you'll keep quiet and not sing that stupid grit song.''

I made a solemn promise to behave.

I half staggered and O.E. half carried me to the captain's tent. I still had a fair amount of rice wine hidden in my jungle shirt. We smelled like a brewery, a cheap one at that.

As we went inside, everyone stared at us, and a staff sergeant exclaimed, "Whew!" They knew we were zonked, at least that I was, but as long as we behaved, no one was going to say anything. But that did not keep some sergeants from throwing dirty looks our way. Maybe they were just peeved, for they could have used a drink themselves.

Well, O.E. kept me sitting upright by holding my arm while the captain went over plans for the next day. The battalion was going to hit the village across the river at dawn. Our company, L Company, was to be held in reserve. The other three, Company K, Company I, and Company M, were to conduct the assault with two tanks for support. The road was good to the village, and tanks could be used. The artillery forward observers, Lieutenant Callahan and I, were to be on the alert from the beginning of the assault in case artillery was needed. Company L would not cross the river unless needed. The enemy strength was unknown.

Members of our team felt good; probably we wouldn't be killed tomorrow. Captain Hempel, though, was a trifle disappointed that we were not one of the assault companies. He need not have worried, for we would get plenty of practice in assault attacks later.

After a few questions from some of the officers and noncoms, the captain asked whether anyone else had comments or questions. No one spoke up. I saw my chance. Lurching to my feet before O.E. could grab me, I said, "Yeah, I got a little song I know everybody wants to hear before they leave."

It was like somebody had made time stand still. Total silence reigned.

The staff sergeants (many of them Korea and World War II veterans) looked on in disbelief. The young officers were speechless. O.E. covered his face and muttered, "Oh,

God!" I looked around, and the shocked faces made me feel wonderful. The wine had destroyed my inhibitions, and this was my audience. I had a good idea I would not die tomorrow, but probably would in a week or so. Why not sing?

To everyone's surprise, the captain laughed and said, "Okay, Mac. Give us one, but after that, you've got to share whatever you're drinking."

Everybody relaxed, and a good spirit filled the room. So I sang, way off-key, an old song from the Kentucky hills. The song was called "That's My Pa" and is about a man who went to town and got drunk, and his two young sons had to go fetch him. In the song, one of the boys describes his father in action.

One stanza goes:

> He climbed right up in that wagon seat
> And said, "Boys, I'm hard to beat.
> I'm tough as steel and twice as hard.
> Now, I can dive deeper and come up drier
> Than anyone else in the whole durn holler."
> And that he did, right off the wagon seat.
> Though it shook him up when he hit the ground,
> He just stood up and looked around
> And said, "I can whup anybody fer miles around."
> But there wasn't anybody there
> Except me and little Ted.

The song had several verses, and I sang every one I could think of. The song had appeal to veteran soldiers, especially to old sergeants who had hillbilly origins. I think they enjoyed the song. I know I did.

Anyway, by the time the song ended, the captain was laughing, almost everyone was smiling, the whole camp was wondering what was going on, and O.E. Jones was mortified.

Still standing in the middle of my audience, I got out the jar of wine, took a long drink, and handed the jar to the captain. The last thing I remember was a grizzled sergeant taking a drink and smiling before I fell into O.E.'s arms.

I just half remember O.E. dragging me home. But I remember his fury. "You damn drunk fool. You embarrassed me to death. We could have both been court-martialed. That was the stupidest damn song! You're gonna have to straighten up."

11

The Onslaught Begins

BEFORE DAYLIGHT THE NEXT MORNING, WE WERE ABOARD amphibious tanks and stationed on the river's edge, ready to cross in case we were needed. The first hour, I felt so bad, I hoped a mortar or an artillery round would fall on top of the tank and end it all. Just a whiff of rice wine would have nauseated me. I was still in a half stupor from my spree last night. But eventually I became conscious of a lot of shooting from across the river. The assault companies were in a world of shit.

There was steady firing, and in the dark I saw tracers from machine-gun fire from both sides. I heard the pop, pop, pop of M-16s and American machine guns, exploding grenades, and rocket launchers going off, and the lighter roar of Chi-Com machine guns. Occasionally I heard the dull thug of a Soviet RPG. The enemy was well armed and more than willing to fight.

The battle was still raging at daybreak. While we remained poised to join in the fray, I got my binoculars and found I could get a good view of most of the village. I watched as one marine company's assault was stopped by

NVA machine-gun and rifle fire coming from two brick French-style houses.

I watched as several marines fell and the rest faded into the rubble that yesterday had been stone buildings. Both sides kept up a withering fire, the NVA fire keeping the marines at bay.

Then I saw a marine start a stealthy approach on one of the buildings. He would run swiftly from one pile of rubble to another, getting ever closer to the house. He ran fast and with the grace of a cat. But I knew how he felt. With all the adrenaline and fear in him, I knew that to him, everything was in slow motion. In a situation like that, the whole earth slows down. A person sees every little movement, and his senses are tuned to the utmost. His attempted assault took only a few minutes, but I know to him it seemed like years.

With the steady fire from marines keeping them busy, the NVA had not as yet spotted the advancing marine. He was now crouched within grenade-throwing distance of one of the houses. I could feel his tension. When a marine sees a comrade in extreme danger, he feels as his comrade does. When a marine gets wounded, his friend flinches as he flinches, because he feels the same pain.

As the young man crouched, I felt as he felt. He was tasting death the same as I had tasted it at Badger Tooth and Badger Catch. His next move would bring him on top of the enemy.

Just then the rubble erupted as if someone had thrown a hundred packs of firecrackers at it. The NVA had spotted him and were trying to get him before he got inside their fortress, or close enough to drop a grenade in.

The soldier remained behind the rubble for just a second. Then he leaped out toward the enemy. His arm flew backward, carrying the rest of his body with it. It was as if his arm were rocket-propelled, or had a mind of its own. God! I jumped when he was hit.

He lay at the bottom of a pile of rubble. I thought he was dead.

I continued watching through the binoculars. When I again glanced at the marine I thought killed, I was surprised to see him move. He lay in a half-curled position and occasionally moved an arm or leg slightly. A navy corpsman tried to crawl to him and was promptly shot. Marines succeeded in dragging the corpsman back under cover.

Another marine tried to assault the enemy position from another angle but was spotted and shot instantly. He slumped to the ground and never moved.

Why did we not pull out and let the artillery and naval gunfire finish the village off? Well, by this time the marines were so close to the enemy that if they tried to pull back, they would be destroyed by the machine guns. And we had learned from experience that the North Vietnamese would be dug in so deeply that no amount of artillery fire could have driven them out. Even after several days of shelling, the enemy would have put up a stiff resistance to any ground attack. And on this day low cloud cover prevented any help from the air, except from limited helicopter support.

We did not have time to wait. Khe Sanh would fall if the supply route was not opened soon. We did not have the luxury of being able to wait for help. We had to take these villages now.

As the battle continued, I felt the rage and frustration of my fellow marines pinned down on the other side of the river. They could not help their wounded, and if they tried to overrun the enemy, they all would be killed in the attempt. But one marine got into position to fire a LAW. He was hit before he got the rocket off, but even so, he managed to aim and fire. The rocket slammed into the side of one of the houses but caused only superficial damage and interrupted enemy fire for only a second. At least the NVA were learning they were in for a fight, that the marines were not about to retreat or surrender.

Word passed back to us to get ready to go in. We were poised, ready to start. As much as I wanted to help the men, I couldn't keep from being terrified. It was obvious what my company was getting into.

Just before we moved, like a juggernaut moving to turn the tide of battle, one of the huge tanks that we had brought ashore arrived. I cheered. The tank moved toward the enemy positions, firing its 90-mm cannon and its machine guns as it moved.

The devastation was wonderful. The cannon fired repeatedly into the buildings, and the machine guns and the rifle fire from the infantry turned the two buildings into hell. I sensed the great excitement on our side. A round from an NVA RPG (the NVA version of a bazooka, greatly feared by tanks and American armor) was fired, but the rocket went wide and slammed into a pile of rubble, because the soldier manning it had been cut down by infantry fire.

The tank continued its advance and slammed into the wall of one of the French houses. Much of the wall collapsed and the tank backed up, still firing point-blank at the NVA positions. It rammed the wall again and took the rest of it down. The infantry erupted!

The NVA were doomed. Like madmen, the marines swarmed over rubble and on into what was left of the French houses. They were now doing what they excelled at: close-up-bayonet and hand-to-hand combat.

I watched one marine charge into the rubble beside the tank and start bayoneting something in the corner of the house. He was obsessed. The rifle and bayonet rose and fell like a machine. It was a savage and merciless assault. The enemy had stalled our attack, and the conditions, in effect, had temporarily made madmen of the marines. Very few prisoners were taken.

Word came back that we could relax. The NVA had broken, and victory was assured. It looked as if I would live another day.

As I continued to watch, I saw the infantry, accompanied by their tank, move on through the village and out of sight. None stopped to mutilate the dead or take trophies. They were dedicated soldiers with a job to do, and they did it well.

As I saw wounded marines being taken to the rear, I hoped the hero I had watched first, the man who had almost made it to the houses, was among them. But I never knew whether he lived or died. I just hoped he lived.

Through the binoculars I saw dead NVA troops and soldiers lying everywhere. I thought, "This is the real thing. This is war. Surely the people back home will get behind us now and we will get plenty of help." I did notice, however, that there were no television cameras nor newspaper reporters around. It was so real to me that I thought surely everybody knew what was going on.

I would not have believed at that time that people in the United States were burning our flag and that some were actively sending aid to the North Vietnamese. It makes me sad to think of it today; back then it would have broken my heart.

Realizing now that this was an all-out invasion of South Vietnam, I expected, at any time, to see fresh American troops, along with new equipment: tanks, artillery, all the works. This never happened.

12

Communist Brutality

THAT NIGHT L COMPANY MOVED ACROSS THE RIVER AND ON into the village. I will never forget my distress at the dismal scene that awaited me. All permanent buildings had been reduced to rubble, all grass and bamboo buildings had been burned, but saddest of all, bodies of young men lay scattered all about the place. Both American and enemy dead still lay where they had fallen.

As usual, the marines had taken most of their losses in the initial attack. Once NVA lines were broken, the communists had had little chance. The basic Marine Corps style of combat in the field is to take a calculated percentage of losses until an enemy's defenses are cracked. Once that break occurs, the marines' aggressive charge results, most of the time, in total victory. The great rate of success justifies the high losses. This type of combat is emphasized over and over in boot camp. And now I saw firsthand just how effective such tactics are. We had suffered many casualties, but the NVA had suffered more, and they had been routed.

Surviving civilians had been herded into small, shivering, terrified groups, and were guarded by two or three rifle-wielding infantrymen. The communists had painted graphic pictures of atrocities supposedly committed by Americans, and these natives feared the worst. On seeing their eyes, I quickly turned my head: I couldn't bear the pain and despair I saw there. Since sporadic firing was still going on in the outskirts, any stray villager could be taken for a North Vietnamese and shot. As yet, the natives did not realize we were protecting them.

As Headquarters Platoon moved through the village, our attention was caught by the screaming and gesturing of a woman of about thirty. Traces of her beauty showed through her dirty and disheveled appearance. She had recognized Captain Hempel as leader of our group and was trying desperately to get him to come over and talk with her. Guards were restraining her.

The captain called for Meades, his interpreter, and we all gathered around while the three of them talked. I could understand the gist of her story, and later Meades filled me in with details. They talked for a while, and frequently the woman pointed in one direction.

According to her, one day a platoon of NVA troops had swaggered into the village at daybreak. They forbade anyone to leave. The soldiers had been arrogant, bullying, and had ordered everyone around as if the villagers were slaves. Guards with machine guns were placed around the village. Soon the main body of NVA soldiers had come. They moved into the houses and grass huts and ate the people's food. Not long after arriving, the NVA leaders called a council. A list of 10 names, made up mostly of old men but also of a few women, was produced and read aloud. Those whose names were on the list were marched to the edge of the village and shot.

The woman telling the story told of the horrified silence, of the muffled sobs, and then of being forced to dig a large grave for those murdered. The remaining 500 villagers were then forced to dig bunkers and erect fortifications. A woman whose husband had been shot refused to obey. She cursed the killers and was calling them every dirty name in the Vietnamese language when a rifle shot silenced her. No one else refused orders. Our informant was the daughter of one of the men shot.

Finally the talking was over and we all followed the woman to the edge of the village, where we saw a twenty-foot square area of freshly dug earth. I knew what was coming and dreaded it. We privates got out our entrenching tools and started digging. The captain called some of the newer men to help. It was not long before we knew the woman's story was true.

I did not dig long. I had dug up the decomposing body of one victim when the captain called for more new men to finish the job. I was grateful, for the stench was overpowering. Unearthing the bodies was like opening the gates to a Hades located in a hot, tropical tomb. During the 1968 Tet Offensive, graves like this one were found all over South Vietnam.

As the grave was being covered, I looked at the woman who had brought us here. She was crouched and sobbing uncontrollably. Any triumph she may have felt at exposing the communist atrocity was gone. I helped lead her back to a group of civilians huddled together. She looked at us with the saddest, the most lost, eyes I have ever seen. Her eyes seemed to be asking us, Whatever in the world am I going to do?

At that moment I recognized another dimension, an even greater horror, of war. In South Vietnam guerrilla warfare had taken a backseat to a devastating scorched-earth policy. As usual, the ones who suffered most were those most innocent.

No words can describe the anguish in that woman's eyes and in the eyes of the small groups of terrified civilians. They had lost everything. They didn't even have a change of clothing. Their food was gone. What were they to do?

The marines had leveled the village, reducing it to rubble and burned grass buildings. The NVA had fought from behind every possible structure, and we had had no choice but to destroy every place that a communist might hide. But whoever was most to blame, the villagers paid the highest price.

13

Patrol West

AT DUSK WE SETTLED IN FOR THE NIGHT. I LOOKED AROUND at the site filled with poncho tents. Some of the men were doing the same thing I was—cooking a meal of C rations over a heat tab; others were writing letters; some were just talking. Rain was falling. Smoke from smoldering grass huts emphasized the eeriness.

Members of forward observer teams have long periods of being alone, at times just sitting and waiting. On this night, as I sat and waited, I thought of the natives who had just lost everything they had, and I began to think I could not go on with this war. On this night the war and our tactics made no sense to me. We were supposed to be helping the South Vietnamese, but it was them, and not their enemy, who had to endure most of the suffering, see most of the horrors. In my mind, we could just as easily have been fighting in North Vietnam. That would have made much more sense because, obviously, our chances of winning and ending the war quickly would be multiplied many times. Why did politicians send troops to war and then undermine their efforts by cowardly or stupid political decisions?

After thinking for some time, I decided I'd better think of something else. Frustrations and tensions can often be worked out in physical actions, but if a person sits alone for too long, he does too much soul-searching: about home, about heroic actions of dead buddies and of their bodies being put into body bags for choppers to pick up, about Jane Fonda and others of her ilk, and on and on. Thoughts of home brought loneliness, thoughts of dead friends brought grief, thoughts of Jane Fonda brought bitterness, and thoughts of political leaders brought questions, frustrations, and, eventually, cynicism.

The next morning we were up before daybreak. Platoon-sized patrols scouted the outskirts of the village, checking for snipers or any stray survivor from yesterday's battle. Other patrols were sent out in all directions to check the terrain, and to look for artillery landmarks and enemy movements.

O.E. and I were assigned to Third Platoon which at the time numbered about 40 men. Our patrol was to travel four miles, to the outskirts of the next major village directly to the west. The captain asked me to go so I could get the lay of the land and to familiarize myself with landmarks that could be used to call in the artillery on future operations. Of course, our platoon was sent primarily to check any enemy movements.

After a grueling forced march, we were approaching our destination. Ahead was a tree line on a small hill. Our maps told us there was a large cemetery overlooking the village, our ordered destination.

We had been very lucky. Evidently the enemy had not sighted us yet, but we still had to attain our objectives. Reaching that tree line and occupying that hill were imperative in getting information about the village itself.

"We'd better finish our job quick and git the hell out of here," the platoon sergeant whispered to me, "or our ass is mud. We're a long way from home."

The sergeant was a career man in his thirties. He seemed to know exactly what he was doing at all times, and at this moment he was concerned about the safety of his grunts. The lieutenant, our commander, fresh out of college and officers candidate school, seemed competent but had limited combat experience. He wisely leaned heavily on the sergeant for advice.

"What do you think, Sergeant?" the lieutenant asked.

"Charlie's not stupid," the sergeant replied. "I'll guarantee you that someone's in that tree line. We just don't know how many or what they're there for. I don't think they'll try to hold the hill. They're probably just scouts put there to report anyone approaching the village."

Both men looked at me. "I'll call in the artillery if you want, but if nobody's there, we'll warn the whole neighborhood that we're in the area."

Tough decisions had to be made. So far we had been lucky. No doubt a large NVA force occupied the village, and we could be discovered at any minute, or we could walk into an ambush. Either way, we were much too far from our battalion to expect any help. In an emergency we could call in artillery.

No doubt a few NVA survivors from yesterday's battle had reached the village and told the commander there to expect a battalion-sized attack. At the moment the communists were not expecting anything as small as a platoon.

The lieutenant and sergeant talked in agitated whispers, trying to figure out some way to accomplish our mission without being wiped out.

The sergeant turned to me and said they had decided to send a squad of ten men to approach the tree line. If no one was there, the platoon with O.E. and me would occupy it, observe the village, and get all the information we were looking for, including coordinates for possible artillery fire. At the first sign of enemy fire or movement, the squad would get back to our lines and I would call in the artillery. Occupying that tree line was a necessity.

I quickly plotted the tree line on my map and called the coordinates in to the artillery battery. It was time for the infantry to move. Not a word was said. I noted the sweat on the lieutenant's brow and the concern in the sergeant's eyes. What if we were wrong? What if we were already surrounded? What if there was a company-sized force in the tree line? I knew one thing: If we were going to be wiped out, I would have all the artillery at my disposal coming down on top of us. Our artillery was our ace in the hole.

I felt for the lieutenant. He was worried, and I was conscious of his self-doubts. This was the real thing. If he was wrong, the whole platoon was doomed, and he was feeling the weight of responsibility.

The grunts spread out, hiding behind bamboo, behind paddy dikes, or behind anything else available. No matter how many times I saw it, I was always amazed at how quickly the grunts could become, and how long they could remain, invisible. They were superb in every way. The lieutenant, sergeant, O.E., and I crouched behind a fallen tree and watched. Occasionally I caught a fleeting glimpse of a marine or heard a muffled splash as the men made their way toward the hill.

Finally, on the last run before the men gained the hill, we came alive at the crack of AK-47 rifles. The point man in the squad went down, and the other men instantly returned fire. After a sharp firefight, the sergeant nodded at me and said, "Okay, arty. Earn your pay."

Since I already had the coordinates of the hill plotted exactly, and since the marines were under cover, I fired for effect immediately. I called for Battery 3 (eighteen rounds of high explosives). The guns answered almost immediately, and 105-mm rounds hit before the sounds of guns reached our ears. There must have been a terrible stink on that hill, for if those artillery rounds did not scare the shit out of the North Vietnamese, then nothing would. We had taken them by complete surprise.

The enemy was saved by the rounds hitting slightly behind their position. I immediately called for drop fifty Victor Tango (variable-time high-explosive shells). The Victor Tango explodes twelve to fifteen feet above ground and sprays an area with shrapnel killing men even in fighting holes.

The lieutenant, taking a dangerous gamble, called for the full platoon to assault the hill after our artillery barrage was over. The gamble paid off, for the enemy fled. The lieutenant and I got busy finishing the job we had set out to do. While he was checking out the village and sketching the formidable breastworks of felled trees, networks of strong bunkers, and anything else that might be useful to know about in an assault, I was plotting coordinates for possible artillery attacks and taking note of the whole village and area around it, paying attention to any details that might be useful later.

I thought the village was invincible: only fools or marines would assault it! Tanks would be useless here, low clouds would prevent help from the air, an attacking force would have to cross a wide, open rice paddy. I had a sinking feeling when I thought of tomorrow.

The lieutenant was still sketching and the sergeant was perched like an eagle overseeing its brood when a single artillery round landed a hundred yards west of our position.

The lieutenant was furious. "What the hell was that round for? I didn't call in any artillery!" he stormed at me.

I looked at the sergeant; he looked at me. We grinned. But the situation wasn't funny, to say the least.

"Lieutenant," the sergeant drawled, "I hope you're through drawin', 'cause if we don't git the hell out of here fast, we're going to git blown to hell."

At that instant a communist 130-mm artillery shell that sounded like a freight train roared overhead and exploded about fifty yards west of us, showering us with mud and water. The lieutenant stood with mouth agape, eyes wide, and a startled expression on his face. He had seen the light!

The sergeant got his men moving and we rushed hell-bent toward battalion headquarters. As we hurried along in a forced march, I was thankful the NVA had made the same mistake that Lieutenant Callahan had made earlier, that is, calling in a second adjustment round. Just as Callahan's mistake had allowed the enemy to escape, the enemy's mistake allowed us to escape. Maybe things even out.

We arrived at battalion headquarters after dark, and I had a quick conference with the captain. Hempel was relieved to hear the day's mission went off without a single casualty—even the point man who was shot on the initial assault on the hill was saved by his flak jacket. He wasn't even wounded, as he and the others found safety in the hill itself, which was homeycombed with tunnels and fighting holes. Tomorrow those tunnels and holes would save O.E., me, and numerous other marines.

14

Another Assault

KEEPING ALL OUR GEAR ON, O.E. AND I GOT READY TO sleep, which meant mostly that we lay down on the ground. We kept on our flak jackets, helmets, ammunition, ponchos, and grenades. As I began to doze, I looked over at O.E., his head resting against his radio as if it were a pillow. "That guy took every step I took on that patrol today with a radio on his back," I thought, and then smiled to myself. "Thank God I don't have to carry that damn heavy radio!"

We slept only a couple of hours before wake-up, when we were ordered to move out. Lieutenant Callahan acted like an all-state basketball coach before a big game. Captain Hempel was everywhere, yelling encouragement and making sure every man was ready. The sergeants were keyed up also, but they were businesslike and somber. They had seen a lot of battles and knew what to expect. They gave words of encouragement and pats on the backs to the men while making sure that everything was in order.

As for O.E., me, and many other enlisted men, we were just plain tired, so tired that we just mechanically went through the motions necessary to get started. We already had all our gear on and had plenty of ammo and grenades. It was going to take all our effort just to put one foot in front of the other.

Where the officers and noncoms, many in their thirties, got the energy to inspect the troops and get us all moving, I will never know. Most of them had covered as much or more ground than we had the day before, and as little as it was, we had had more sleep than they.

When we started marching westward, I was aching all over: my feet hurt, my arms hurt, my back hurt. To me, my poncho and rifle weighed two hundred pounds. But after a while I walked in a daze, unconscious of just about everything. When I jerked awake, it was getting daylight! I felt refreshed. Maybe I had discovered a secret: Sleeping on a forced march can renew a person. The march that had taken our patrol so long yesterday had passed in what seemed like minutes today.

We reached the cemetery on the hill. The view took my breath: Lined along the top of the hill, in full view from the village below, was a battalion of marines, combat gear on and rifles at the ready. I thought of cowboy movies when all of a sudden Indians appeared on the horizon. That is probably how we looked to the NVA. If these marines could not break the enemy's stronghold, then Dong Ha and Khe Shan were doomed, and the Vietnam War would be lost then and there.

Low cloud cover prevented help from the air. Tanks would have been useless: there was no way they could get across the mined, muddy rice paddies. We would have to go it alone except for one ally—artillery. Suddenly loudspeakers boomed out from above the village and from behind our ranks. I understood enough Vietnamese to know that we were asking them to surrender to avoid further bloodshed and to allow civilians to leave the village. The only answer was silence. There would be no surrender nor release of any civilians. It would be kill or be killed.

Imprinted on my mind forever is the picture of the long lines of young, sunburned faces staring across the rice paddies. These were men in the prime of youth, men willing to die for what they believed in. For many, that fortified village would be the last thing they saw on this earth.

The captain was excited, animated, happy. He had the hunter's look. Lieutenant Callahan shared his enthusiasm. The sergeants were grim, as tense as steel springs. We enlisted men were looking across the paddy fields with that familiar hollow look in our eyes.

The scream of a heavy artillery round silenced the loudspeakers. The round exploded right behind the line of marines north of us. O.E. and I looked at each other and dove for the nearest hole, a fighting hole made earlier by the NVA. I landed on top of two marines already occupying the hole, and O.E. landed on top of me. He was barely in.

I lay with two warm bodies under me and one on top of me, and I was scared shitless. The barrage was extremely heavy, and rounds were exploding in every direction. All I could do was to pray that one didn't land directly on top of us. The noise was deafening: 130-mm shells like freight trains roared overhead, shrapnel whistled through the air, and the ground shook. After twenty minutes or so, the heavy barrage stopped.

As soon as the shelling stopped, we leaped from our holes and prepared to attack. We had learned a valuable lesson: All prominent landmarks, as this hill, along the Cua Viet River had already been targeted by the NVA for artillery attacks. Later, whenever we staged an assault or retreat, or whenever we camped, we avoided prominent landmarks whenever possible. It was a lesson that saved many lives.

Miraculously, because of the honeycombs dug into the hill by the NVA, there were only two casualties during the whole bombardment! O.E. Jones, who got a piece of shrapnel in his hand, and a marine from another company. O.E.'s hand was covered with blood, but the wound was not bad enough for him to leave the field. Starting with this battle, a marine did not leave the front except for life-threatening wounds. With no prospects for replacements, we simply did not have the men to do our job. Or so it seemed. We hadn't yet found out how much a few men could do.

As we started moving toward the village, Captain Hempel told me to stay behind with my radioman and to keep contact with our artillery in case the extra support was needed. I looked at the hill, still smoking from the bombardment, and then at the open rice paddy. I chose the paddy, not out of bravery but because I had had enough of being a sitting duck for Ho Chi Minh's artillery.

"I'm comin' in with you, Captain," I said.

He grinned. "Come on, then, Mac. Let's get 'em."

"You're crazy," O.E. growled at me.

O.E. had already put his radio down and was about to

relax when I told him to stay behind if he wanted. Shultz was with Lieutenant Callahan, and one radio was really all we needed. For a second a look of indecision flashed across his face. Then his eyes flashed, his jaw set, and he started cursing.

"You damn fool! If I don't go wid you, who the hell's gonna keep you alive? Well, let's go!"

O.E. was miserable. His hand was swollen twice its normal size and was still bleeding from the shrapnel. And he was mad at me.

"Git a chance to git a break and that damn fool has to go in with the captain. Crazy, crazy!" he grumbled as we started off.

From the time he arrived at the front line until the Tet Offensive was over, O.E. never shirked a responsibility. He griped and fussed at me a lot, with good reason, but he always did his job. He was a true friend and a true soldier.

After a brief conference among the lieutenant, the captain, and me, we agreed upon a distance from the hill to the North Vietnamese fortifications, and the lieutenant called in the first adjustment round. It was white phosphorous and hit right on target, in the middle of the NVA fortifications. The captain smiled, and the lieutenant called for fire-for-effect of Battery 6, and the line of marines started moving toward the village.

As we advanced, I noticed we had not taken a single round of enemy fire. General Giap's men knew what they were doing. They had excellent discipline and would wait until we were within range before they started their deadly fire.

I was content to let Lieutenant Callahan control the artillery fire. He did a great job. I sat back and watched the show as he kept the rounds coming in, blasting fortifications, houses, trees, and shrubs to bits. It was like some sort of pagan ritual: the artillery dancing up and down the enemy's lines, and the lines of marines moving forward with one intent—to break the NVA stranglehold on the Cua Viet River.

When a line of eighteen- and nineteen- and twenty-year-old marines moves right into the enemy's artillery and on into the inferno they know awaits them, that is discipline. I was watching a great display of raw courage.

A crowded battlefield is one of the loneliest places on earth. We all knew that if a marine got wounded to the point that he could no longer fight, all he could do was to lie where he fell and pray, for there were no doctors or ambulances. All a buddy could do, possibly, was to put a quick battle dressing on and keep on fighting, for if we stopped fighting, we all were dead. There was no choice.

Medevac choppers could land only if they had safe landing zones; otherwise they would be shot down. All during the battles on the Cua Viet River, there was never a safe landing area for helicopters on the front lines. If a man was dead, his body stayed put until the battle was over. If a man was wounded, he was carried by fellow marines in a poncho to a medevac chopper after the battle was over. In the battles along the Cua Viet River, a marine soon found out that the only thing he could depend on in a battle was himself and his fellow marines. He could never count on air support or armor or anything else.

As we drew closer, we saw the damage the artillery was doing. When we were within fifty yards of the village, the artillery was still coming in. Freight trains kept roaring, shrapnel kept screaming, the ground kept shaking, and exploding rounds blasted to shreds just about everything in sight. The marines kept advancing.

The village was an inferno. I wondered how anyone could survive. But in the back of my mind I was remembering how we had been blasted on the hill with guns more powerful than ours, and yet only two men had been wounded. Plenty of NVA men were alive, that was certain. We found out what we already knew: The only way to win battles is with infantry. A position can be bombed and shelled all day, but the only way to win is to go in and occupy it. And that was the toughest part.

We were within forty yards of the fortifications when the captain halted the artillery. It was then I noticed bullets hitting the rice paddy water all around us. I didn't know when they started firing, but they were certainly in earnest now.

Across the rice paddies I saw brown dots lying facedown

in the water, and on the dikes I saw many brown humps—marines dead or dying. I heard cries for help above the AK-47 and M-16 fire.

O.E. and I dashed for the nearest rice paddy dike and hit the ground behind it. We were there a few seconds before I heard a nearby M-16. I saw the look of disbelief on a youth's face as a bullet hit his arm. As he tried to get off another shot, a second bullet struck him. As he crumpled behind the dike, I saw a bone protruding from his shattered right arm. There was absolutely no way that O.E. and I could get to him. We had no choice but to listen to his moans and pleas for help.

As the marine moaned, I peeped over the dike. About twenty yards ahead of us, at the edge of the NVA fortifications, was a small group of marines pinned down. It was part of our headquarters platoon: Lieutenant Callahan and Shultz, his radioman; Corporal Cizek (the 81 mortar forward observer) and his radioman; Captain Hempel and his radioman; and three infantrymen. The core of our platoon had reached the edge of the enemy fortifications.

"We gotta git with them," I told O.E. "If we stay back here, we're dead." O.E. nodded.

Leaping over the dike, we zigzagged toward our friends and dived for the dike they were hiding behind. We made it! The dike rose about two feet above the ground level of the village. It was the last paddy dike before we would enter the village itself. Pushed to the side of us were two dead marines.

We were receiving bursts of machine-gun fire against the dike, and so I decided to fire back. Rising up, I fired a burst from my M-16 toward the point where the machine-gun fire was coming from and got a quick look at the scene ahead.

About twenty yards west of the dike, directly in front of us, was a large thatch hut with a grass roof. Lying around the hut were five dead marines, and lying close to the door was a marine still alive. He had been shot in his legs and hips so that he could not move them. In the door lay a dead North Vietnamese.

About fifteen feet from each side of the hut was a large bunker, made of bamboo framework and covered with about eight feet of dirt. The bunkers had entrances about eight feet long and three feet square, plenty big enough to crawl through and big enough to hold a Chi-Com machine gun. The entrances gave machine gunners a good field of fire both of the hut and the rice paddy beyond, without the gunners being exposed to view.

The cavity of such bunkers was like a large room, big enough to hold eight to twelve men comfortably, together with all their equipment and ammunition. A shorter entrance or exit led from the cavity to the rear.

Since the camouflaged entrances faced the hut, I knew instantly what had happened. The enemy had set a trap, and inexperienced marines had fallen for it. The NVA had placed a single sacrificial soldier in the hut to fire at the oncoming marines. It is the nature of attacking soldiers to assault the most prominent landmark ahead of them. When the squad of marines assaulted the hut, they were in the sights of the bunker machine gunners. Except for the one wounded man, the squad had been wiped out. It soon became clear why one man was left alive.

Hearing the wounded man's cries for help, we looked at one another, trying desperately to think of something we could do. We knew the man was bait, left there to draw others into the enemy's line of fire. To approach the man meant certain death.

On my left was a large, strong, blond infantryman who was one of the replacements after Badger Tooth. He had made it across the rice paddies, and being relatively inexperienced, thought he could do something. Listening to the pleas for help finally overcame him. He clenched his teeth, got a fierce look in his eyes, and turning to me, said, "I'm going after him."

His body tensed as he stood up, prepared to lunge. I heard the crack of the sniper's rifle. It's odd how a fierce hero can, in the blink of an eye, become just another corpse for the worms and scavengers.

He fell on top of me. I rolled him off and was about to apply some kind of first aid when I saw his sightless eyes and slack jaw. He was dead. I felt the warmth leaving his body. I looked at his helmet and saw the hole in the front and streams of blood coming down his neck and ears. I didn't take his helmet off. I simply rolled him aside.

Then I went insane.

I moved along the dike like a madman, screaming and cursing the North Vietnamese. I would rise up in one spot and fire a rifle burst, and then move to another spot and do the same. I never gave the enemy a chance to get me in their rifle sights. For about thirty minutes it was a stand-off. The NVA would fire short bursts of machine-gun rounds at me, and I kept up my attack. I was firing at the front entrance to the bunkers and randomly in front of the bunkers. I had no way of knowing if I was doing any damage but I was keeping the enemy off balance. Occasionally the sniper took a crack at hitting me. But they couldn't pinpoint me. Finally O.E. grabbed me and said, "Get down, Mac. You're not the only one here. Let somebody else do something."

As I dropped behind the dike, I looked at my companions. They were staring at me as if hypnotized. The captain and lieutenant tried, over the company radio, to locate the rest of the company. The platoon to our north had broken through the bunker complex but was pinned down by two snipers. The platoon to our south was stopped at the edge of the village, much the same as we were.

While the captain and lieutenant moved north of our position to a nearby platoon in an effort to get it past snipers, it was up to the rest of us to hold the enemy at bay. Cizek and I discussed the situation and realized that with the expert sniper, whom we hadn't even seen, and the gunners in the bunkers, we would have to stay pinned down until the platoon to the north could eliminate the snipers holding them down and help us by attacking the bunkers from the other side.

We kept exchanging fire with the NVA, with our feet in stinking water and our heads in the broiling sun. Once when I rose to fire a volley from my rifle, I saw a miraculous thing. The wounded marine by the thatch hut had pulled himself with his arms almost to the door of the hut. He was lying on his back and was shielded on his right and left by dead comrades. He had pulled the dead Vietnamese to his front as a shield. He had stopped screaming. He might make it!

Then I saw the smoke, and soon I would witness the most sadistic cruelty that I hope to ever see. Our men became nervous and fidgety, suspicious but not quite sure about what was going on.

Somebody yelled, "Good Lord! They're gonna burn that marine alive!"

It was the truth. We were going wild, crawling back and forth and hurling curses at the NVA. It still meant certain death to go over the wall. The heat from the burning hut was so intense that it was hot where we were. The man near the doorway was trying desperately to move away from the heat. He was screaming and again crying for help. The NVA, of course, had their guns trained toward us, ready to kill anyone who went to the man's aid. Maybe this time their bait wouldn't work. Dying for our comrade, under these circumstances, would accomplish only one thing: help the enemy.

Then I was shocked to see that one of the other marines from the doomed squad was not dead. He was close to the hut and was moving, but his head and the clothes on the upper part of his body were already smoking. His legs moved slowly back and forth.

The other wounded marine had curled up close to the doorway. His face was a blackened mess, and his hair and clothes were smoking also. The only sound coming from him was "Eeeeeeee!"

A grunt to my right went berserk, stood up, and tried to charge the bunkers but was killed instantly by the sniper. The bait had worked after all.

O.E. looked at me, his eyes wild. "What are we gonna do? They're burning alive. Can't you smell it?"

"Dammit," I answered, "there's nothing we can do. If we stand up, we're dead. We can't do anything."

One of our men began to cry. It was awful. The smell of burning flesh, the smoke, the cursing and crying, all combined with our helplessness, created an unbearable hell.

We continued to exchange fire with the bunkers, and Cizek and I ordered the others to stay down, not to charge the bunkers, for that was what the NVA wanted.

Smoke grenades on one of the dying men started going off, and soon afterward his ammunition began exploding. It seemed impossible, but the explosions seemed to revive him, for he started moving again. Maybe the movements were just reflex actions.

The macabre scene seemed to last forever. But in the end, all movements by the wounded men had stopped, and both bodies has been riddled with bullets. Certainly the bullets had not come from the NVA. One of our men had not been able to take it any longer and had mercifully ended the suffering of our comrades. Although I could never have done it myself, I think he did the right thing.

15

A Break

SUDDENLY THERE WAS A LULL IN THE FIRING. IT WAS AS IF both sides had decided on a coffee break at the same time. Captain Hempel came back from the position north of us and told us the marines to our north had killed one sniper but that the other one still kept them pinned down. I could hear sporadic firing both to the north and to the south.

We were at a stalemate. As yet no one had even seen the sniper firing at us. The bunkers remained as formidable as before. It was late morning, and the heat was sweltering. It was monsoon season, however, and clouds were coming in. Soon the rain would start.

During the lull we relaxed a bit and took a better look at ourselves and our surroundings. I was next to O.E. Jones. We were crouched with our legs and hips in the water. As O.E. moved his body to a more comfortable position, I noticed blood around his right ankle. He was already wounded in one hand, and I thought, "Oh, hell! He's hit in the foot, too."

"O.E.," I said, "check your ankle. There's something wrong."

He got a worried look on his face and raised his trouser leg above his jungle boot. There, attached to his leg, were five or six huge leeches gorging themselves on his blood. O.E. forgot about the NVA and started clawing at his leg.

"Stop it, O.E.," I said. "You can't tear them off."

His leg was a bloody mess and he was almost frantic.

"How the hell we gonna get them off?" he asked.

"Light a cigarette."

"What the hell you mean, light a cigarette? We got NVA in front of us. I got these bloodsuckin' mothafuckers all over me. We probably won't even be here tomorrow, and you say light a goddamn cigarette. You're even crazier than I thought."

I had never smoked nor even lighted a cigarette, but I got a cigarette off O.E.'s helmet, bummed a light from him, and lit up. O.E. stared at me as if I were crazy, still clawing at the leeches.

I moved his hand away and told him to hold still. His eyes got as big as saucers when I moved the cigarette toward his legs. Then it dawned on him what I was doing. He flinched as I touched the first leech. It curled up like a huge slug and dropped to the ground. I burned all the leeches off that leg and then checked the other. Two small leeches were on it, and we quickly dispatched them.

After this, we kept our legs out of the water. It was odd, but we were so absorbed with the leeches, we had forgotten our situation. Then I heard Cizek shout, "I saw the bastard!" He had spotted the sniper!

This electrified us all. "I just looked up and saw the son of a bitch running across in front of us. It was like he jumped right down into the ground."

It dawned on me what was going on. The sniper had two spider holes, one in front of each bunker. From either he had perfect fields of fire all along the dike. He could pick off any single marine, or he could alert the bunkers if we tried to move in force. The sniper moving from one hole to another had kept us from pinpointing his exact location.

The NVA commonly had snipers in front of bunkers to shoot their enemies and to alert forces inside bunkers. This sniper was especially good.

While the captain was trying to coordinate his other platoons, Cizek and I were trying to figure out what to do next. Just then a Chinese grenade sailed overhead. It hit in the paddy water about ten feet behind us. I do not know whether it was the water or whether it was just luck, but the grenade was a dud.

"Man, we've got to do something. We're just going to get wiped out here," Cizek said.

"Hell," I answered, "throw a grenade. You never know. You might get lucky."

What happened next was too miraculous to believe. Cizek pulled the pin from a grenade and, without looking, hurled it over the dike. Our thinking was "If we lob grenades over at them, it will keep their heads down and they can't lob them at us."

After the grenade exploded, Cizek looked over the dike. He stared a brief second before crouching back down with a look of disbelief on his face. "I got the bastard," he mumbled.

"What!" I exclaimed.

"I got the son of a bitch."

His eyes widened as he grinned his familiar grin. He started laughing. "I got the bastard."

My jaw dropped as I stared at him. I thought he had cracked up. We had fought this character all day, and Cizek blindly throws just one grenade and gets him. It was unbelievable.

To be sure Cizek hadn't gone crazy, I peeped over the dike. There, lying on his side, half-curled, was the sniper. One of his arms, badly mangled, was twisted backward. He had run smack into the grenade! Beside him, like a discarded stinger from a honeybee, lay his rifle. I had seen his fire kill two marines, and he had fought us to a standstill. But now he had met his doom.

What a miracle! The grenade had exploded at the exact time the sniper had decided to change holes, and he had run right into it. The chance of such a thing happening is almost beyond calculation.

I scurried to Captain Hempel, who was back with us. "Captain," I said, "Cizek killed the sniper!"

"You're kidding!"

"No, I'm not. Look over the dike."

After checking, the captain's eyes lit up and he grinned. Cizek was ecstatic. He was shaking and grinning at the same time. "God, I feel good," he said.

We all congratulated him. The whole ball game had changed. Although a frontal assault on the bunkers was still out of the question, killing the sniper had given us freedom of movement. Now we were the hunters and they were the hunted. What a difference!

We were still getting bursts of gunfire from the bunkers, but the gunners' fields of fire and their vision were limited. They could see to their front, but not to their sides or rear. Evidently no one in the bunkers had the nerve or skills to replace the dead sniper, or maybe they thought they were safe in their bunkers. They had wiped out an entire squad of marines at their leisure and would be more than happy to kill more.

As soon as he saw the sniper was dead, the captain started thinking. All the marines were ready for action. The sniper's death was the first positive thing that had happened to us that day. We had been trapped, and now we were ready to move. It was payback time again.

The captain pointed to a bamboo thicket and motioned for us to accompany him. We left two grunts behind the dike to fire occasionally to keep the enemy from knowing we were moving around to flank them.

We melted into the bamboo thicket, the captain leading the way. With his M-16 at the ready, he moved along, not making a sound. We were hungry for blood and we could smell our prey. At the moment I never gave dying a thought. Our eyes reflected blood lust. The Drill Instructors had done a good job on us in boot camp. Killing had become our nature.

We moved through the thicket to a point directly north of the northern bunkers. It was the closest we could get to them. On inspecting the bunkers, we saw they had rear exits. We checked carefully for a few minutes but could find no signs of a guard. For any of several reasons, I guess, the NVA did not think it necessary to protect their rear. Perhaps fire from the grunts we left behind convinced them that we were still behind the dike.

The captain, together with his radioman, again left us to rejoin the first platoon. His plan was to get rid of the sniper who kept them pinned down and then to bring what was left of them to join up with us. We would then begin our assault. But things don't always go as planned.

16

A Trip to Hell

WITH CAPTAIN HEMPEL AWAY, LIEUTENANT CALLAHAN was now in charge. Six of us were hiding in the bamboo thicket: Lieutenant Callahan, Cizek, and me, with our three radiomen—Shultz, Spacek, and O.E. Today had seen the first fighting for both Cizek and Spacek. Spacek was a tall blond who looked out of place on a battlefield. His smooth face looked as if it had never felt a razor. But he was trying to become a good marine, and with experience, he would make it.

I stared at the rear entrance to the bunker with many thoughts, including ones of John Wayne, going through my mind. That was it! Someone had to run up and throw a grenade into the bunker. That's what John Wayne did in *The Sands of Iwo Jima*. And that was the way marines did it. Marines did not stand and stare at bunkers. They attacked!

"Got any ideas?" the lieutenant asked.

"Somebody's got to get a grenade into that bunker. We've got to get them before they spot us."

The hole that was the rear entrance seemed to come

closer and closer. I swear I could have counted ants on that bunker. Suddenly I crouched and sped toward that hole, expecting bullets to hit me any second. I faintly heard, as I started, cursing from the lieutenant.

I made it safely and flattened against the enemy's bunker near the rear entrance. I could smell the earth and the grass mixed with it. I could smell the different minerals of the earth, the insects, the bamboo, the dead marines, and I could definitely smell the North Vietnamese inside.

I looked around and saw a grunt peep over his paddy dike. Our eyes met, and clearly he saw I was a marine. At least *he* would not shoot at me. I felt all alone, as if I were the only person in the world. Looking back toward the bamboo thicket, I saw five pairs of eyes riveted on me, eyes that glowed with a light that was not human. For a second I was afraid of them. But it was the main show, and I was the main attraction.

Coming back to reality, I slowly and silently pulled the pin out of a grenade. I flipped the explosive back into the rear entrance. I heard a muffled, excited voice just before the grenade went off. Either I did not get the grenade far enough back, or one of the NVA had started to throw it out, because it exploded in the tunnel.

I motioned for the men to join me, and in an instant they were there. The bunker was large enough for all of us to hide behind and effectively shielded us from enemy fire from the bunker to the south. The lieutenant stationed a man to watch both sides of the bunker while he and I quickly discussed our next move. The other bunker we needed to destroy was about fifteen yards south of this one, beyond the burned-out hut and the bodies of the squad of marines that had been wiped out.

The lieutenant looked at the rear entrance of the bunker we were flattened against. "You think anyone's alive in there now?" he asked.

"I don't know. We have to make sure," I answered.

I looked at the lieutenant, and he looked at me. We knew what had to be done. There was never a doubt about who was going inside. The lieutenant handed me his .45, and I took off my helmet and flak jacket. I took a last look at the men. They were staring at me with a funny light in their eyes. Again, the adrenaline had made the world into a dream.

I had no idea what to expect inside. I did not take time to think. I threw another grenade, and as soon as it exploded, I went in, my .45 loaded and cocked.

It is odd how many thoughts come to mind with no measurable passage of time when words are not used to express those thoughts. One of my thoughts now was of how we boys used to try to dig groundhogs out of their dens. We never got a groundhog, but we sure had fun trying. I remembered the sense of adventure when we would get the tunnel deep enough for all of us kids to get back into it. It was exciting to go back into the tunnel and feel the cool earth around us. The tunnel in the bunker reminded me of all this. It is strange the things a person thinks of when he is about to die.

I scurried through the tunnel and on into the main cavity. The back entrance was about six feet long and about three feet square, just big enough for a person to enter. It took a second for my eyes to adjust to the dim light coming from the front entrance. To my right I saw a dead NVA soldier lying on his side with his arm blown off. Then I saw another man lying on his back with his body peppered with shrapnel.

Something to my right moved. I turned and fired. It sounded like a cannon going off. Whoever I had fired at was slammed against a wall before crumpling to the floor. He had been hiding in a blanket. All I saw was a crumpled blanket with blood spraying out of it.

By now blood was all over me. And the smell of blood filled the room. Haze from the exploding grenade and the pistol shots hung in the air. Maybe the grenade blast had numbed the Vietnamese, for they had turned from merciless killers to sheep ready to be slaughtered. I was the wolf. I did not intend to stop.

I moved about three feet toward the main entrance. I sensed rather than saw another shape to my right. Then a North Vietnamese face was suddenly framed in the light from the front. I shoved the pistol in his face and pulled the trigger. He fell to the floor and did not move. Again I was showered with blood.

I kept moving toward the front entrance. I saw, outlined against the light, a human shape. I aimed the .45 and fired. The shape clutched its abdomen and folded over onto its knees. The man put his arms over his head and started moaning. I shot him again. I could see him clearly now. He jerked and started crying. He put his hand out toward me. I emptied the pistol into him, but he would not stop crying and moaning. I will never forget this. "Die! Damn you, die!" I yelled.

To this day I have nightmares about that man. I dream he is coming back after me, and I think that someday somebody will send me to the electric chair because of the way I killed him.

Today I would not hurt an insect, and cannot imagine how I could do what I did. But this is a true story. It happened exactly as I tell it. When I judge myself too harshly, I think of the young marines whom this man and his comrades had deliberately burned alive, and I don't feel as bad. War is not pleasant. Memories of war are sometimes worse.

I backed out of the bunker and into light. I was covered with blood from head to toe. I shook uncontrollably. I sat against the bunker, exhausted. I chuckled softly and looked around. The other men were staring at me in disbelief. For the moment I was, regardless of rank, the leader of the group. Shakily I handed the pistol to the lieutenant.

"What the hell happened in there?" he asked. "We heard shouts and shooting. It sounds like someone is crying in there now. They were all dead when you went in, weren't they?"

"No, Lieutenant. They weren't all dead when I went in there."

"You mean you found live men in there? Bullshit! They had to be dead. Why were you doing all that shooting?" Cizek's radioman asked. This from the kid too young to grow a beard.

I looked at all the men and saw their looks of doubt. They didn't believe me. To them, no human being could have survived doing what I had just told them I had done. The only logical explanation was that the grenades had killed the NVA and that I had emptied the pistol into dead bodies. This was what many of them thought. So I didn't argue.

"Well, they're dead now," I said. "There's another bunker to take, and this time somebody else can play John Wayne."

Turning to Cizek's radioman, I said, "Throw some more grenades back in there to make sure."

Three of the men threw grenades into the bunker, and that bunker was eliminated.

The men were looking to me, not to Lieutenant Callahan, for leadership now. The lieutenant seemed a little miffed, but a person cannot argue with success, so he let it go—for the time being.

Something kicked up dirt on the bunker just above my head. Wind whizzed past my face. Then came the familiar crack of a Chi-Com machine gun. The enemy had spotted us! We were in deep shit. That bunker would be hard to take, for they knew we were coming, and they would be ready.

The lieutenant, Cizek, and I were trying to figure out what to do while the three radiomen kept up their fire. Finally I looked at the lieutenant and said, "Well, we know what we've got to do. Somebody's got to get over there and throw grenades into that bunker."

"It'll be twice as dangerous this time, but I don't have any other suggestions. Damn! It'd be nice to have a flamethrower or some big guns."

I was thinking the same thing. The United States was the strongest nation in the world and had the most sophisticated weapons in existence. Surely there must be a better way to destroy enemy bunkers than to throw in grenades and go in shooting.

Cizek and the lieutenant looked at me. "You want to go in this time?" I asked Cizek.

Spacek, Cizek's radioman, broke in. He was excited and his eyes glowed. He wanted to be a hero! As I said, he was new to battle and had been lucky to survive this long.

"Let me try it. I know what to do." It was a kid's voice.

"No," said Cizek, "I'll go."

I knew that Spacek, like most young marines, wanted to

prove himself; to prove oneself in battle meant more to many marines than life itself.

"Let him go," I suggested to Cizek.

I reasoned that if Spacek survived, he could tell his story over and over again back home, and he would be a local hero. If he was killed, although it would be a terrible loss, it would not have been any worse than losing Cizek.

The lieutenant looked worried, but he made no objections. The decision was made. I signaled the grunts behind the dike what we were going to do. They nodded that they understood.

"When our man attacks the front, watch the back close and make sure no gooks come over right on top of him or throw grenades at us. Okay?" I said to the lieutenant.

His expression showed his resentment at my telling him what to do, but still, he could not argue with success. The men had been following my directions, and they were still alive.

Spacek's eyes were riveted on the front of our target. Every muscle was tense, and he seemed about to explode from excitement. His face was pale and clean, and his blond hair showed under his helmet. But it was his face that attracted my attention.

"He looks like an angel with that face glowing like that," I thought, and immediately continued, "Well, soon he might be one—if his luck runs out."

I turned to the men. "He's getting ready." I slapped him on the shoulder and yelled, "Go!"

He bolted across the clearing. The volume of our fire shifted to the back entrance and top of the bunker to keep the enemy down until Spacek reached the front.

He flattened himself on the left side near the front entrance. After a second he raised up and started to lob a grenade inside, but heavy fire from the communists prevented him from getting into position to throw.

Spacek was in a quandary. He was getting confused. He rose up and started to move away from the bunker, but quickly realized the NVA would see and kill him. Not knowing what to do, he turned and looked at us for guidance. I felt O. E. Jones's eyes boring into me.

Before I realized what I was doing, I found myself racing

across the space that separated the two bunkers. Bullets whistled overhead and on both sides of me. The grunts behind the dike had kept the enemy so busy that they could not get a good aim at me. The grunts had saved me.

Flattening myself against the bunker, I looked at Spacek. He was nervous and scared. The fire coming out of the front by the enemy and the cover fire hitting the top of the bunker and the back entrance left a very small area to stay without our being shot, by either friend or enemy. For an instant it seemed we were the only two people in the world.

"Get a grenade in there! Now!" I ordered.

He hesitated a split second, then pulled the pin from a grenade and threw the weapon back through the entrance. Since he had to throw from an angle, it hit the entrance walls and exploded without doing any real harm.

The NVA responded with increased fire. They now knew we were upon them. I glanced at Spacek and saw that his sleeve was covered with blood. He was hit! Damn! I could not tell how bad the wound was, but blood was all over one hand and was oozing from the one holding the .45. When he had thrown the grenade, he had been hit in the forearm.

I threw another grenade into the bunker, but again the communist fire caused the grenade to explode in the entrance. No harm done. Then came a familiar hissing sound. We both knew what that was, a Chinese grenade.

"Grenade!" I yelled, and flattened against the bunker, burying my face into the dirt on its side. I could feel shrapnel piercing my back and legs, and wondered whether this was the end. Had my luck run out? I kept waiting but heard no explosion. This grenade, too, was a dud! How could it be that two Chinese grenades thrown at us today had both been duds? Miracles happen. That's for sure.

Spacek and I looked at each other, our eyes big as saucers.

"What now?" he asked. "Do we try to go in the bunker?"

"Hell no! We git the hell out of here! You go first. Now!"

He flew across the thirty yards to the relative safety of the other bunker. He had his story. No matter how bad things got later or how low he felt, he could always think back to this experience when, for a moment, he was the star of the show, the king of the universe.

After Spacek left, I froze for just a second. I looked at the entrance. Should I go in? It would be suicide, but I was wondering how long I would live anyway. "Well, I might as well get it over with," I thought, and started to make a move. But that was insane: I would be committing suicide and gain absolutely nothing in return.

I looked toward my group. All the men were motioning for me to return. Quickly I flipped another grenade into the entrance and took off. A split second later I was back with my friends, comparatively safe for the time being.

All eyes were again focused on me. It was time for another plan. Spacek was leaning against the side of the bunker pale as a sheet. A marine used a battle dressing to bandage the wounded arm. The wound wasn't bad: a torn muscle in the forearm and no broken bones.

"You did great," I told him. "That wound looks like a ticket to swingin' doors and slant-eyed whores."

Another marine chipped in. "Lucky bastard."

Spacek didn't smile. He looked at us with pained, vacant eyes and clutched his arm. He said nothing. Maybe the reality of war was sinking in.

We remained in deep shit. The bunker was as formidable as ever. The captain was still north of us, and as far as we knew, First Platoon was still pinned down by the sniper.

Although none of us had a watch, we knew it was afternoon. Those old familiar low clouds had moved in, and already a few drops of rain had fallen. Soon there would be the everlasting steady rain.

While the lieutenant was watching the back entrance and the radiomen and the grunts behind the dike were watching the front, Cizek and I came up with a plan. We would run up to the front entrance of the bunker. We each would carry an illumination grenade, a smoke grenade, and three fragmentation grenades. When we reached the entrance, one would first throw in an illumination grenade and follow that with the smoke grenade. The first would blind anyone inside, and the second would add to the confusion. Between us we should be able to get all six grenades into the bunker. If one of us got shot, the other would finish the job.

Lieutenant Callahan, who had been listening, left off watching the back entrance and came over to us.

"I'm the ranking officer here, and I'm going with you. It's my responsibility, not yours," he told me.

"Keep watching the back entrance," I answered. "I'll go."

I was thinking that the lieutenant was intelligent, an excellent forward observer, had had excellent training, and that soon he would be an excellent commander, a commander who would not let a private get by with what I had been doing—usurping his authority.

Just as I was about to talk the lieutenant into staying behind and letting Cizek and me assault the bunker, something dawned on me. No one was watching the back entrance!

"Lieutenant!" I screamed. "Who's watching the back entrance?"

Then I heard it: the hissing of a Chinese grenade coming over the bunker we were hiding behind. I dived for the ground and screamed, "Grenade!" The last thing I saw was the lieutenant's startled look as he turned to look at the back entrance.

This Chinese grenade was no dud!

I was scuttling on my hands and knees away from the grenade when the world exploded. Again, I expected to feel shrapnel piercing my back and legs. But immediately I was in another world. I felt no pain. I was standing up, staggering toward an unknown destination. I felt wind whizzing past both sides of my head. Pesky insects buzzed around my face.

Just as I reached up to slap away the insects, I saw, as in a dream, an NVA soldier leaning out of the back of the bunker and firing an AK-47 at me. I felt no danger. I just kept weaving around the area.

Still in a daze, I saw to my right a squad of grunts moving toward us. The platoon to the north, I thought, must have finally made it past the sniper. Even in my semiconscious condition I recognized their leader: he was a minor legend who, allegedly, had killed twenty-six North Vietnamese himself. I did not know him personally, but I certainly knew about him.

He was carrying a sixteen-gauge shotgun with shells filled with small, pointed buckshot for maximum damage to anyone unlucky enough to get hit. He had been through Operation Badger Tooth and probably deserved at least two or three medals of honor. But usually the heroic actions of marine enlisted personnel are not rewarded with medals. Bravery and acts of valor are expected from grunts, and medals are not even thought of.

The shotgun seemed a part of the squad leader's body. It flew automatically to his shoulder and kicked twice as he fired. I did not hear the sound, but I saw the smoke and saw the shotgun jump. Suddenly the bugs stopped buzzing around my head, and on looking back at the bunker, I saw the NVA soldier slumped on the ground with his rifle lying nearby. An NVA soldier tried to run out the rear entrance and was instantly shot to pieces by the infantryman.

"Well, the man's killed twenty-eight now," I thought.

As always, the grunts moved in without a word being spoken, and they fanned out in a skirmish line. The fire from the enemy bunker picked up, and the squad leader decided against rushing it. He would wait them out. Now we had the superior numbers. Things were looking up.

Still feeling as though someone had shot me full of anesthesia, I tried to talk to a couple of infantrymen I knew. But they looked at me as if I were crazy and did not answer. I was still staggering around and had tried to engage them in silly small talk.

When I was able to focus my eyes a little better, I saw the lieutenant trying to pull himself forward with his arms. Obviously he was in great pain, and his face was deathly white. "At least," I thought, "he's alive."

Shultz was leaning back on what had been his radio. He had a battle dressing, oozing blood, on the back of his neck, but he seemed all right. A relieved look on his face indicated he was happy to be alive. I bet he was!

Why hadn't the NVA attacked? Four of us were wounded, and the other two in a stupor. We were helpless and easy targets. Had things been reversed, the marines would have attacked as soon as the grenade exploded. But throughout this great offensive, we found the communists made the same mistake over and over again. They were superior in guerrilla warfare, but in regular battles, they were no match for us, even when they had more men, better equipment, and more supplies.

I had just finished checking my body for possible wounds when I felt someone gently pulling me down. It was Captain Hempel.

"Are you okay?" he asked. "It looks like you all have been through a meat grinder."

He told me that First Platoon was still pinned down when he reached them, but they had started moving forward, first on one flank and then on the other. That sniper was good! He wounded two more marines, but the others kept moving. When they had him almost surrounded, he fled amidst heavy rifle fire. The last they saw of him, he was disappearing into brush outside the village. At least the marines could move out now.

As soon as possible, the captain had gotten a squad of infantry and come south to help us. As it turned out, they arrived just in time.

As I looked at the wounded and became even more conscious of their suffering, I was overcome with guilt. I had assumed the role of platoon leader, and look what happened. I had learned at least one thing—how real commanders must feel when their men are wounded or killed! I felt for them.

After telling me these things, the captain looked me closely in the face. He was concerned about us. No matter what happened, Captain Hempel was always concerned about his men. And he seemed to care whether I lived or died. At the moment he could see that I still wasn't all there, so he just smiled and said, "You rest a minute. We'll take care of this."

He turned to talk with the lieutenant and then went to each of the other men. His sorrow and concern about what happened to us was real. In the Marine Corps enlisted men seldom see a captain, and this was really something: to see a captain going among the wounded and not being ashamed to show his feelings.

After the captain left, I staggered over to the lieutenant

and squatted beside him. I'll never forget the anguish and feeling of guilt on his face. The shrapnel had shattered his legs and pelvis, and he could pull himself up only by his arms. Like all the wounded, he had to wait till the battle was over before he could be medevacked.

He looked at me with a gaze I cannot bear to think of even today. He could barely talk, but he reached for me and softly said, "I'm sorry, Mac. It was all my fault. I should have watched the bunker."

His words startled and confused me. "What's he sorry about? He couldn't help it. Things like this happen in a war. My God, he may not even live, and he's worried about it being his fault. I wish he'd quit looking at me like that."

The lieutenant, the captain, and many enlisted marines had something in them I could not understand. Maybe it could be called nobility or character or integrity. Whatever it is called, it is the essence of manhood. It is when a person does not worry about his own safety but worries about how he performs his duties and about the safety of others. Lieutenant Callahan was on the verge of dying and was worried because he thought he had not done his job well.

I didn't know what to say, but I knew I wanted to make him feel better. I took his hand, which was as cold as ice, and said, "It's okay, Lieutenant. You did fine. I should have let you take over, and I should have watched the bunker."

Feeling dazed again, I walked over to see Shultz. We discussed what happened. The grenade had hit on his radio, and that had saved his life. Shrapnel had only hit the lieutenant and Shultz, and he wasn't badly hurt, but he, too, was a little dazed.

My mind now came back to what was happening in the battle. The NVA were still holding out, though Cizek had rushed over and thrown two grenades. One had come back at him, and the other had exploded in the tunnel entrance.

Just then a wave of excitement went through our ranks. An ontos (a tracked vehicle that has six 105-mm howitzers mounted on it) had somehow made it to the battlefield, and the captain had gotten it over to help us. All six of the ontos pointed in the same direction and can be fired one at a time or all at once.

Apparently the bunker we were besieging was the last NVA stronghold in the village still holding out. Anyway, we were getting a lot of help now. The men on the ontos found they could not destroy the bunker, but they were able to cave in the front entrance. That was a great effort. Unable to help further, the ontos left.

Just as the ontos left, two marines with a flamethrower came up. Those two were very hesitant, but soon two grunts volunteered to burn the NVA alive. But before they could do so, the captain came up and put a stop to it. Even though the men in the bunker had purposely burned two of our comrades alive, the captain just could not do the same to them. He sent the flamethrower away.

By now the rain was falling, it was dusk, and I was still miserable. To make matters worse, a pimple behind my right ear had turned into a boil as big as my thumb, and it was beginning to be more than just an irritation. Besides, my head had not completely cleared.

There was little shooting going on except at the bunker we were trying to destroy. Bloodthirsty marines, eager for the kill, had it completely surrounded. For sure no NVA men were going to be left alive. The marines had left their feelings of mercy in that rice paddy we had crossed. They were going to avenge their dead comrades.

The battle continued until almost dark. The marines got close enough to blow the back entrance shut with plastic explosives. The front entrance had been closed by the ontos. Now no North Vietnamese could get out, if any were still alive. Any possible survivors would be dealt with tomorrow.

At dark, I leaned against the bunker we had secured earlier and fell into a troubled sleep. The battle must have been over, for I heard no shooting. Although I had been on the skirmish line with the infantry, I was not a member of the infantry and so did not have to stand guard duty. And for some reason, the captain did not use me that night for radio duty. Actually, I was sick from the boil and at times was still incoherent. I could see clearly, but when

I talked, the words didn't come out right. I didn't make sense.

It was a terrible night. It was raining, but nobody bothered to use a poncho tent. We just lay where we were—in the mud. We were too tired and too sick to care. I saw phantoms all night long. Dark shapes chased me, and I was too tired to run. I saw that human shape framed in the bunker door and fired the .45 over and over at it. The boil was a dead man gnawing through to my brain. I was smaller than the tiniest midget and more helpless than a newly born baby. At last I was living in a world of shit. Shadows swooped around me, and hell was a reality. Then I felt someone shaking me. It was breaking daylight. Time to get moving again. As I focused my eyes, I saw the captain. He looked fresh and happy again.

Our original headquarters platoon was all but gone. There was still the captain, but I felt alone. The lieutenant was gone, and I didn't know whether or not O.E. was still around. Cizek was okay but his radioman and Shultz were both wounded bad enough to leave the field. I realized the grunt platoons had been terribly decimated. But this was the time for marines to show what they were made of. No matter how few the men, we kept going. Only the severely wounded were sent to the rear; anyone who could lift a rifle stayed on the front line. If anyone had the nerve to complain, he was immediately answered by his comrades.

"You should have joined the army if you wanted to rest."

"What did you think you were in for? A cakewalk?"

Few complaints were heard.

The question still was, Would the five thousand marines at Khe Sanh be saved, or would they suffer the fate of the French at Dien Bien Phu? Either Khe Sanh would be saved, or the president would be sent a truckload of dog tags. That was the thinking of the marines in 1968.

17

The Next Day

By THE TIME I WAS HALF-AWAKE, TERROR HAD AGAIN seized me. I turned over on my side, curled up, and grabbed my knees. A North Vietnamese was firing his AK-47 at me, and the hissing of a Chinese grenade filled my ears.

Captain Hempel knew what I needed, knew what I had to do to overcome this panic. "Come on, Mac," he urged. "We've got to finish this."

I rose to a crouching position, rifle in my right hand.

That rifle was an extension of my body. I was vaguely aware that O.E. had not left with the wounded. He was awake and staring at me. God! I was scared.

"Come on, Mac. The village is secured. We just have to clean up the mess. Get moving!" the captain insisted.

Somehow I got up enough nerve to stand straight, and before long I was moving with the rest of the men. If O.E. with his badly swollen and painful hand had not complained, I certainly wouldn't mention my neck.

The grunts moved slowly through the village like hunting dogs sniffing for scents of their prey. NVA members were the prey the grunts wanted. I was too woozy to care whether or not we found any. We swept the entire village but found no more resistance. If any of the enemy had survived, they apparently had escaped during the night.

During this sweep a man created a stir by appearing with a German shepherd. The dog belonged, I guessed, to the K-9 Corps and had been trained to kill at the command of his handler. A German shepherd in Vietnam was an oddity indeed.

After the sweep, marines gathered around the man and his dog. To them the German shepherd was a bit of home amid this desolate landscape of burned-out huts, destroyed bunkers, and the dead NVA lying about everywhere. Many of us took pictures, but we were careful to keep our distance, for a wrong move could result in someone getting hurt.

As I looked at the dog and his handler, a slow rage built up in me. My rage was irrational, for I did not know where the pair had been nor what they had done before coming here. But the experiences I had gone through yesterday made me so tense, I was ripe for anger and resentment.

"What the hell are you doing coming here now and acting like big shots? You're like a couple of vultures or hyenas, showing up after the killing is done to hunt down any survivors or to kill the wounded. Where were you when the real battle was going on?" Happily I never uttered these thoughts aloud. I knew I was being unfair, but I just had to criticize someone or something.

Seeing the pleasure of the grunts and their admiration of our unexpected visitors who were strutting around, showing their stuff, increased my anger and disgust and resentment. It was the grunts who, with the ground forces of the army, bore the brunt in all wars. It was they who had the most casualties, endured the prolonged suffering under the most horrible conditions. The grunts, not the man and his dog, should have been the objects of admiration.

"Well, that is true enough," I thought. But every group in the service has its place and does the job it's supposed to. I was being unfair. But at the moment I was thinking, "You and your damn dog aren't worth a pimple on a grunt's ass." The dog and its handler soon left.

The village was secured, and our next job was to count the dead, to see what weapons we had captured, and to see whether there were any prisoners. I was slowly getting over my terror, and as usual after a village is secured, I had relative freedom and could wander about as I pleased.

I stuck fairly close to the captain and his interpreter. Our headquarters platoon did not have many men left, and I wanted to stay close to our survivors. Also, if anything of interest was learned, the captain would be told, and I had regained my curiosity.

The remains of dead marines were gathered up and sent to the rear to be identified and then sent home.

To get as accurate a body count as possible, we opened all bunkers, checking both for dead and possible survivors. Navy intelligence needed all the information it could get in order to get some idea of enemy strength. At times, surprising discoveries were made.

Being an artillery forward observer and one of the most senior enlisted men in the field by this time, I was spared the digging. I had little work to do and relative freedom within the village. With the lieutenant gone, the only bosses I had were Captain Hempel and the gunnery sergeant. In following battles I had good chances to check out battlefields and see many things probably unnoticed by grunts who were kept busy digging up bunkers, collecting American bodies, and sorting weapons.

As we moved through the village, we heard a clamor at one of the bunkers. When the captain hurried over, I tagged along. There, lying outside the bunker, was a dead Chinese. The grunts had a rope around his leg and had just pulled him out of a destroyed bunker. He probably had been killed early in the battle, for he was swollen and had started to smell.

The captain seemed in deep thought. We enlisted men were excited. The Chinese had entered the war, and now the United States would go all out! North Vietnam would be invaded, we would defeat General Giap, and all over the United States young men would be volunteering for the armed forces.

Just then a marine ran up and told the captain that another Chinese had been found in the same bunker. Captain Hempel looked worried. I do not know what was called in over the radio, but soon afterward some Americans and South Vietnamese arrived. They, the captain, and other officers talked for a while. The visitors did a lot of laughing and smiling. They soon left.

I never heard the Chinese mentioned again, but if we had found two in one bunker, how many had been elsewhere in the village and had managed to escape when the village was besieged?

A change came over Captain Hempel. He seldom smiled or laughed. He stayed tense, and his eyes smoldered with rage. What the American and South Vietnamese policies were about the Chinese, I'll never know.

As I looked around, I saw that the surviving marines—about six or seven hundred left in the battalion—were becoming more and more at home in a setting like this: burned-out huts, destroyed stone buildings, ruined bunkers, filthy and bloody clothes, enemy dead all about, leeches, mud, and monsoon rains. All we needed now were ammo and C rations. Everything else was incidental.

As the day wore on, the men became even busier. We had one sorry bit of luck. We had used up almost all of our battle dressings during the battle. Every marine was to carry two, but now we were about out, and no new ones had come in. If we did not get some before the next battle, lives would be lost unnecessarily, for those bandages had made it possible to save countless lives throughout the years. But the lack of resources was not to last.

We soon found out how to resupply ourselves: The NVA had plenty, and all were marked *Made in the U.S.A.!* We replenished our supply by taking exactly the same kind as our own from dead NVA soldiers. And then we hit the jackpot. We found a field hospital! In it were syringes, cotton, gauze, and various kinds of medicine. All came from the United States.

We assumed the enemy had gotten their supplies on the black market. Little did we know that some Americans were actively sending medical supplies to North Vietnam and that the supplies were going directly to their troops in the field.

I still had faith in the United States and expected to see fresh troops arrive at any time, with all kinds of big guns and war machines that could walk through these villages. No more having to destroy bunkers with hand grenades. But uppermost in our minds right then was to help save the five thousand marines trapped at Khe Sanh.

It seemed a thousand years since I had entered that bunker with Lieutenant Callahan's .45 and shot up the place.

A morbid curiosity drew me back there now. The grunts had found seven dead North Vietnamese in the second bunker we had taken and had moved to the one I had invaded. Suddenly there was a great commotion. One of the NVA soldiers was alive! Needless to say, I was fascinated.

No doubt the grunts would have killed the prisoner, but the captain rushed over and stopped them. As the North Vietnamese face came into view, I recognized him. He had the face that I had put the .45 to and pulled the trigger. Either the concussion knocked him out, or he had played dead. Part of his left cheek was blown away, but other than that, he seemed healthy. He had, evidently, lain in the bunker all night.

As two grunts led him past me, our eyes locked. He recognized me, and a look of terror and defiance flashed across his face. He stopped and stared at me, pleading for help. But there was nothing I could do. As he was led away to a landing zone, I knew he would be taken to the rear, questioned intensely, and then shot. It probably would have been better had my shot in the bunker killed him. He was a good-looking young man, and under different circumstances we could have shared beers. But war made us enemies. I would have helped him, but I could not.

Seeing that man reminded me of how prisoners were treated when I first came to Vietnam. Then, prisoners were locked up for two days, and either a teacher or a South Vietnamese army officer gave them a few lectures. This "rehabilitated" them and they were set free. The American government paid for all this. Everyone—the Vietcong, the North Vietnamese, and the South Vietnamese—got a laugh out of this racket. The Vietcong and the North Vietnamese because it gave them a few square meals and then set them free. The South Vietnamese because it allowed them to sell the extra food. When I was stationed at Marble Mountain, I saw this program firsthand. After the Tet Offensive started in 1968, the rehabilitation program was dropped. The few prisoners taken in combat were either executed or taken far to the rear away from the combat zone.

The rest of the day was dingy, rainy, miserable. My neck was sore and stiff, and the outlook for my future seemed bleak. But one happy thing happened: The FAC team got back with us. How wonderful to see the healthy, smiling faces of Novak, Hays, and Nash. Their good spirits were heartening, and it was a joy to talk with them. We exchanged war stories and talked for a long time.

One story they told has stayed with me. It seems there was a likable, popular, strong squad leader who had built up a reputation for himself and had become widely known. One day he had picked up a burnt skull in a bunker and had kept it. The skull still had brains in it, but the outside was burnt so badly, a person couldn't tell whether it was American or North Vietnamese. It had a terrible stench, maybe from the brains.

The squad leader carried the skull with him wherever he went. When he ate, he set the skull beside him and talked to it. He said that since it still had its brain, it could probably hear and understand what he said.

"Hell," he would say, "who knows? It might be a woman. If it is, it might be the last woman I ever talk to."

He carried the skull with him all through the Tet Offensive. Maybe it brought him good luck, for he made it through safely. Later I met him and saw his skull. When the Tet Offensive ended, we were allowed R and R, and the marine took the skull with him. I don't know whether or not he took it back to the States with him.

It had been a long day, one filled with activities, and many of them interesting. When I had awakened that morning, I never suspected I would be able to take part in anything again.

After dark, word came that early the next morning we would move against another village. The boil on my neck was now as big as my fist. I had chills and fever and I could not turn my head. Going to a doctor was out of the question. Doctors did not come to the front, and corpsmen were often scarce. So I did not complain. The night, again, was filled with nightmares. I knew that tomorrow I would die.

18

Assault on Mai Xai Ti

LONG BEFORE DAYLIGHT THE NEXT MORNING, SOMEONE WAS waking me. I was chilling and feverish but managed to get my gear together. We staged our packs in one area, took all the ammo and grenades we could carry, and prepared to move out. I was still terrified, at the edge of the breaking point. I would be killed this time. There was no doubt.

O.E. and I were with the FAC team. The captain told us we would be used as infantry, but for O.E. to keep his radio with him for artillery support.

The town we were to assault straddled a small river that ran south into the Cua Viet River. The small river divided the town into Mai Xai Ti east and Mai Xai Ti west. We were to attack Mai Xai Ti east. Across the Cua Viet River from Mai Xai Ti east was Highway 1 into Dong Ha. From Dong Ha supplies could get to Khe Sanh by either chopper or convoy on Highway 9. We had to take and hold Mai Xai Ti east long enough for supplies to get by the water route to Dong Ha, or both Dong Ha and Khe Sanh were doomed.

Enlisted men are not paid to think. We didn't bother to compare the formidable forces we were up against and our own ragged, exhausted, decimated ranks. It is a good thing we did not think: we would have been defeated before we tried.

The NVA knew we were on our way and were waiting behind strong breastworks with the most modern weapons, and of course, there were the open rice paddies that left us exposed to their fire when we began the assault. Too, they were well fed, had excellent uniforms and other supplies, and were rested.

Lucky for us we had Colonel McCown and Captain Hempel on our side. They were sure we could do anything. As Colonel Mac would say, "I would rather have one squad of grunts than the whole damn air force." These officers, together with the staff sergeants, had unconquerable wills. They would not let us quit.

When we moved out, no one said a word. I became a very selfish person. I don't know why my life seemed so important to me that day, but I just didn't want to die. My life was no more important than that of anyone else's. Maybe it was the fever from the boil, maybe it was the pressure and weariness, maybe I didn't have the guts I should have had, and maybe it was a combination of all these factors, but I was more frightened than I had ever been.

As we force-marched west through bamboo thickets and rice paddies, I could barely make out the back of the man in front of me. It was that dark. I kept telling myself that if the other men could do it, I could, too. If the other men hadn't been there, I would have broken and run.

After we had marched forty-five minutes or so, we were ordered to stop. We sat down on a rice paddy dike. I could dimly make out the faces of a few friends. We all knew that some of us would not be seeing anything after the next few hours.

Soon the attack started. It was still very dark when artillery started coming in on the town, first with a lot of illumination rounds along with high-explosive and white phosphorous rounds. By the light of the flares I saw the open rice paddies and got the general lay of the land in my head. I also saw that the breastworks looked much like those in the village we had just destroyed.

The artillery was doing its job well. Whoever was calling it in was doing a great job. Then I heard the rapid thumps of chopper rotors and saw rockets hitting the town. My hopes soared. The fly-boys were getting into the act! Three gunships were overhead firing rockets and machine guns at NVA positions. I had heard about helicopter gunships but had not seen them. For a moment it looked as though they were going to really work out on the town. I felt like cheering.

As the lead chopper fired a salvo of rockets, I heard a heavy whump! whump! whump! in rapid fire coming from the center of the town. The tracers from the 50-caliber machine gun seemed like a long, terrible claw from some long-forgotten prehistoric monster reaching out to claim its prey.

Stunned, we watched as men in the helicopters fired their rockets into the town and raked the town with machine-gun fire. But they could not find the huge antiaircraft gun. But the gun was finding them. The first burst hit the lead helicopter, which seemed to hesitate in midair. After that the rocket and machine-gun fire from the choppers became erratic.

Heavy machine-gun tracers again zeroed in on the lead chopper. A second burst hit its target. This time the helicopter stopped and wavered. I wanted to scream, "Go back! Go back! It's going to kill you!" The same craft was hit a third time. It burst into flames and dropped into a rice paddy. A terrible realization dawned on me: There were Americans in that helicopter, and now they were all dead. There was no chance of anyone surviving.

The other two helicopters kept firing at the bunkers, but the heavy volume of small-arms fire coming from the town dwarfed their efforts. The choppers were beaten. They had done some damage but had not come close to seriously harming the NVA defenses.

A burst from the 50-caliber machine gun hit a second chopper, stopping it in midair. The craft faltered, shuddered, then turned and headed toward the rear. The other helicopter, though buffeted by small-arms fire, laid down a cover fire for the retreating one, and then turned toward the rear also.

"Well, so much for the fly-boys," I thought.

We were still sitting there, waiting, each man with his own thoughts. This time mine were different from those I had had in the past. I was thinking only of myself and what was going to happen to me, of the dead bodies I would soon be seeing all around; and the heavy antiaircraft machine gun had become an unseen monster that would soon be turned on the ground troops. Not knowing where it was located increased the tension, and knowing that eventually we would have to find and destroy it brought me to the breaking point. Suddenly I cracked.

I looked up and broke the silence. "Boys, I'm gonna git killed tonight."

They looked toward me, and I imagined them thinking, "Hell, don't tell us your problems. We've got plenty of our own." But they said nothing.

"Seriously," I continued, "tonight's my last night. My luck has run out."

Then in the light of the flares I caught Novak's eyes looking at me. His look of concern and understanding flabbergasted me. It was funny. We were about the same age, but now he seemed like a father or a big brother. Maybe that was what I was looking for—comfort and encouragement, someone to tell me I was doing a good job. I wanted to scream, to cry. There was no fight left in me.

"We all could get killed tonight," Novak answered softly. "Your chance is as good as any of the rest of us."

He was not being a smart aleck, he just said it in a gentle, matter-of-fact way.

"We're all in this together," Hays said, just as softly and gently. "Besides, there's no use worrying about it. What choice do we have? Come on, Mac, you'll make it all right."

The words of my friends should have comforted me, but they didn't. If anything, my dread increased and I started shaking. Heavy firing continued in the town. Word drifted back in that invisible way that it does in the services that the antiaircraft gun had been located and that an entire squad of marines had been wiped out attacking its position.

Above the sounds of artillery rounds exploding, of rifle fire, of light antitank weapons (LAWS, also called disposable bazookas), of grenades going off, was the terrifying thump, thump, thump of the antiaircraft gun.

After an eternity, word came back for us to move out. We got up. No one spoke as we formed into a single column and marched into hell. Bullets whistled overhead but were too high to hurt us. My thoughts were still on myself. I was not thinking of victory, of the welfare of my comrades, and I certainly had stopped thinking what a great honor it was to die for my country. I just wanted to live.

We moved along a paddy dike toward the breastworks. The sergeant told us to spread out and we immediately fanned out into a skirmish line, keeping abreast of the marine to our left and right, careful not to get in front of him. Not paying attention to military discipline in this situation was a good way to get shot by friendly fire and with headquarters platoon now down to seven men, not including the captain, the gunnery sergeant and their radiomen, any such casualty could ill be afforded.

Just as we got fanned out, the thump, thump, thump of the heavy machine gun started up again, and this time its fire was directed at us. Some rounds hit the paddy dike, others went overhead. We were trapped behind the dike in a foot of water. The gun raked the area for a few minutes, then abruptly shifted its fire to another area.

Now I knew what was happening. We were attacking the gun's position. While the gunner attacked one group of marines, another group would move forward. This would go on until the marines had finally achieved their purpose— silencing the gun.

We now ran forward and reached the enemy breastworks. I threw myself against a large bunker and froze there, panting. O.E. was beside me. The NVA had quickly abandoned the breastworks and moved back farther into the town.

By now my neck and shoulders were so stiff from the boil that I had to expose myself from the waist up to get a look over the bunker. I looked over to see confusion and death. I hunkered back down and leaned sideways against the bunker. O.E.'s eyes were glowing. He wanted to get in the fight, but the captain had told him to stay with me in case we needed help from the artillery.

Suddenly a familiar figure sprinted toward us. The captain had an uncanny ability to find his men no matter where they were.

"Mac," he said, "we need artillery support now."

We had reached a crisis situation. The infantry had fought its way into the enemy breastworks, but had stalled at the edge of the town. Casualties had been heavy, and the men were now pinned down. Artillery was still coming in toward the middle of the town, searching for the antiaircraft gun and giving us illumination rounds, but we needed close support if we were to advance.

I risked another look over the bunker and did my best to locate targets for the artillery. I got out my map, but my hands shook so badly, I could not hold it. The captain gave me a funny look but said nothing. O.E. held the map while I found where I thought we were and got a location for us. Then I got a direction and called in the first artillery round. Lieutenant Michaels was directing all rounds to the center of town, seeking out the antiaircraft gun, and I had to scream into the radio that we had to have some support right then. They reluctantly let me have two guns.

With no hot phosphorous rounds left, we had to do with high explosive for a spotter round. This was hard to see in the dark. I called for one adjustment round and prayed it would not hit us. The round hit, but I couldn't see it. It exploded too far to the west. I needed another adjustment round, but the captain ordered me to call for fire-for-effect. I requested six rounds of high-explosive shells dropped one hundred yards closer to us. In seconds fifty yards ahead of us, the town erupted like a volcanic reaction as the 105-mm shells tore through bamboo and stunted evergreens.

O.E. looked at me. "Get some, Mac!" he encouraged.

I called for another fire-for-effect, this time ten rounds of high explosives. Again bits of bamboo and other debris flew overhead as the artillery did its awesome work. As soon as the last round hit, the captain ordered the marines to move out. The attack resumed. I quickly thanked the artillery battery and moved out with the captain.

I stayed with the captain. Grunts were attacking viciously all around. This time I had no urge to be a hero, and besides, we had to keep the artillery support handy if it was needed. I was relegated to being an observer.

By now daylight was breaking. The savage battle was short-lived. I noticed something: The antiaircraft gun had been silenced! From here on, it was a rout. I continued along with the captain behind the line of grunts as they moved forward.

We had broken the enemy lines, and now the only question was, Did we have enough men left to deliver the knock-out blow? As it turned out, we did. Rifle and machine-gun fire were still heavy as we moved into the center of Mai Xai Ti. But the NVA retreated, and the firing became just an occasional burst as a few North Vietnamese fought a suicidal delaying action, and others were simply trapped by the rapidly advancing marines.

19

Digging In

WE HAD WON MAI XAI TI EAST, BUT THE ENEMY STILL HAD a stronghold just across the small river. One thing was certain: We would hold this territory until we were ordered out or we died.

The grunts stayed on the front lines. One man remained on constant alert, while others rested or joined in a reconnaissance and search of the town. As we searched for wounded marines and surviving NVA, one thing was uppermost in my mind. "Where is that terrible antiaircraft gun?" I had to see it.

We moved through the town, walking around dead marines and dead NVA, when we came to a bamboo thicket. As I pushed through it, I stopped, startled. There it was, its fifteen-foot barrel pointed at the sky. It was mounted on a revolving platform, on a raised area surrounded by a moat about forty feet in diameter.

The gunner had died at his post. He was hanging in his shoulder straps, slumped over the gun with his arms hanging straight and useless. In and around the gun and moat were twelve dead North Vietnamese.

Surrounding the moat on all sides were dead marines,

looking pathetic in their torn, faded jungle fatigues. On looking at them, I remembered something a Medal of Honor winner once said: "I am not the best man who was on that battlefield. The best men are still there, lying dead."

He was telling the truth.

O.E. and a few marines not busy collecting marine bodies were with me. Just then we heard a commotion and looked toward a small group of grunts. They had found a survivor from the platoon that had been wiped out by the antiaircraft weapon. They had found him curled up under the dead bodies of his comrades. Now he was crying, his eyes were wild, and he kept shaking his head. Saliva ran down his chin, and he was talking gibberish. He was shell-shocked. It was a tall, blond sergeant, one of our best men. Two grunts took him gently by the arms and led him toward the rear.

We were all shocked and subdued to see a man we admired so much in such a condition. A sergeant nearby told me what had probably happened. At the beginning of the assault the blond sergeant's platoon was out in front. He had somehow gotten his platoon through the enemy breastworks and had pinpointed the antiaircraft gun.

He and his platoon had worked their way across the main street of the town and were lined up for the final assault on the weapon when they were spotted by the gun crew. The NVA, seeing their main defensive weapon was in grave danger, concentrated all available firepower on this one platoon. The platoon had been cut to ribbons, and apparently every man had been killed.

The sergeant telling me the story continued. "The platoon sergeant, seeing all his men being killed and not being able to do anything about it, had gone into shock. His mind just couldn't take it. He had fallen, and several of his men had fallen on top of him. He had stayed locked in shock and under his dead men for the rest of the battle."

It is very possible the enemy had deliberately let that platoon creep close to the antiaircraft weapon so that the entire unit could be easily wiped out. In later battles the NVA forces used this kind of trick many times.

A light monsoon rain had started, and by now all was wet and soggy. We moved like ghosts through the town.

Cautiously we entered the thatch huts and searched the bunkers. The infantry had done its job well.

O.E. and I were alone as we approached an unusually large thatch hut. I felt queasy, like being alone in a graveyard at night. We approached cautiously, ready to fire our M-16s at any movement. The door to the hut was partly open, and I carefully looked inside. I saw a dead NVA soldier sitting with his chest and head slumped over into his lap.

I looked at O.E. and found him looking at me. Without saying anything, we burst through the doorway. The inside of the hut was a slaughterhouse. Talk about doing a job well! The grunts were perfect.

Some of the dead were backed against a wall, their eyes wide open and reflecting terror; some were lying at the windows and wall near the front and had been killed while fighting back; some were strewn about the floor where they had been bayoneted or shot while trying to flee.

O.E. and I looked at each other and shook our heads. The looks of terror on several faces and the various positions of the dead reflected the ferocity of the attack. I thought back to my experience in a bunker a few days before.

The scene indicated the marines had hit at the height of the momentum of the assault. No doubt they had fired a heavy volume of fire at the hut, probably killing a few of the men inside and scaring the shit out of the others. Then the grunts had charged just when their lust for blood was at its highest pitch, and the only way they could be stopped was to kill them. In assaults like this, a soldier showed no mercy and took no prisoners. The momentum of the attack could not be slowed down or disaster could result. There was no time to take prisoners.

We continued our search and found huge quantities of rice and other supplies. Also we saw a few dead Chinese. One large bunker turned out to be a field hospital with bamboo beds, bottles for plasma and IVs, syringes, cotton, battle dressings, antibiotics, and other medicines. One thing no longer surprised me: All unopened crates and boxes were labeled *Made in the U.S.A.* One thing did surprise me, though. Very much. A recent copy of *Playboy!* Hell, our enemy had a better supply route to the States than we did! At the time we could get no mail, no newspapers, nothing, and the communists could get copies of *Playboy!*

Later in the day, during lulls in the firing from the NVA in Mai Xai Ti west, I was able to check out more of Mai Xai Ti east. It was a large, sprawling town with numerous thatch huts on the outskirts, in back of which were either rice paddies or the other half of the city across the small river that divided the town. Large thatch buildings, many of them stores with foldout doors, lined the main thoroughfare. But there also were many stone buildings of French design. The centerpiece of midtown was an old but beautiful Catholic church.

The NVA had put barricades of stone and bamboo in the main road to slow down our armor. I smiled at this: We had no armor! The enemy had wasted his time and money. Now the street was pocked with shell holes and littered with dead bodies and debris. Mai Xai Ti, so recently a beautiful place, was now devastated.

After the town was secured, we set up our camp. We had no idea how long we would stay, but I felt pretty sure we were too short of men to attack the NVA forces across the river.

Most men used holes and bunkers built by the NVA or, more likely, by natives of the town who were forced to build them. Some grunts dug and lived in their own fighting holes. Others used trenches and bunkers already in place. The captain set up his command post in a large bunker about thirty yards behind the front lines. The rest of headquarters platoon, the FAC team, the interpreter, and the artillery FO team (O.E. and I) found a large bunker that opened into a large, but heavily damaged, brick building.

The west wall of the building was mostly intact. This was hog heaven! We could come out of the bunker and eat and move around in the building without being exposed to sniper or mortar fire. And it was only about fifteen feet from the captain's bunker. It was an excellent place to spread our maps and plot targets and locations for calling in artillery and mortar fire. I looked at the map so much in the following days that I knew it by heart. The building had an upstairs that was usable, and although it exposed us to enemy fire, we used it occasionally to call in artillery fire.

The FAC team and Meades (the interpreter) set up in the bunker that opened into the house. With O.E. and me, the bunker would have been a little too crowded, so we looked for another home. It was raining every day now, and living outside a bunker would expose us to the weather. But what the hell? We would take the rain and live away from the rest of the group. Besides, I was afraid to live in bunkers.

There was a small creek, its banks lined with bamboo thickets, about ten feet west of the brick building. The two-foot-wide stream was bordered on each side by three feet of level, comparatively dry, ground. A three-foot wall rose from the dry area next to the creek. It was like this all the way to the river. We had natural cover and an ideal fighting trench. It was much more inviting than a bunker. O.E. and I selected a bamboo thicket on the creek's bank near the brick building, and there we made our home. We were well camouflaged, and after spreading our ponchos over our spot, we were protected from rain. We were exposed to enemy artillery and mortar fire, but you can't have everything. Apparently word had spread that we would stay here at least for the night, for I saw the other marines making similar camps. We all wanted a good night of sleep.

Actually, I expected a counterattack, and I believe the captain did, too. It would have been an ideal time for one. We had no air support, they had as much artillery as we did, and they greatly outnumbered us in troops. An attack never came.

We had taken Mai Xai Ti east, and for the present, the water route to Highway 1 was open and Khe Sanh could get supplies, but we were at a stalemate. We had roughly five hundred men left out of a battalion of eleven hundred when the assault had started. We simply could not counterattack, and the only thing to do was to hold on desperately and hope help would come soon.

20

Patrol North

THE MONSOON RAIN WAS FALLING STEADILY AS O.E. AND I got our poncho camp made and our sleeping mats laid out. My neck was throbbing and I was looking forward to lying down for a few minutes to see if the fever and pain would subside a little. That tent and sleeping mat looked like a room in a Miami Beach hotel. It looked so cozy that I was just about to lie down when I glanced toward the brick building where the rest of headquarters platoon was located.

We had set up camp without telling anybody where we were. I guess I subconsciously planned this, thinking that if nobody knew where we were, we would at least have time to get a few minutes of rest. I was wrong.

Our buddies in the brick building seemed agitated and seemed to be looking for someone. I knew damn well what they wanted. I gave O.E. a look that said, Oh well, something's up. We might as well find out what.

I knew that whatever was going on, it was not good for our friendly FO team. I strolled up to the building and walked in casually as if I were walking into a store or a classroom back in the States. Everyone froze.

"Where the hell have you been?" Novak asked. "The captain wants to see you. *Now.*"

Every member of the FAC team was talking at once. I needed to understand only a couple of words from the garbled talk to know I had better get my radioman and go see the captain immediately.

I wanted to say, "Hell, I'm sick. Let the captain get someone else."

I wanted to say, "I was in the same assault as you, and you get to rest while I have to see the captain. Isn't anyone else in this damn war but me?"

What I said was, "Okay."

I hurried back to tell O.E. to saddle up and get ready to go. Then we went to see the captain.

The captain was in earnest conference with a staff sergeant. This sergeant was tall, thin, tough as wire, and judging from his past actions and words, he wasn't particularly in love with me.

The staff sergeant gave me a cold look, and the captain turned toward me and said, "Mac, get ready to go. There's a small village north of us. You can find it on your map. We don't know if it's occupied or not, but we assume it is.

"You're going with a squad of eight men from the staff sergeant's platoon to scout north of Mai Xai Ti to see if there's any movement in the village."

I thought, "A squad of men! I have to go outside our lines with a squad of men. I wouldn't feel safe outside our lines with a company of men, and he wants to send me with a squad! Well, I'm dead now."

"If there's any unfriendly movement, blow it all to hell. Good luck." He said "good luck" as if he never expected to be able to say that to me again.

I knew what he was doing. Instead of risking a platoon or company on a very dangerous scouting mission, he was sending a squad. The captain reasoned correctly that a platoon or company would also no doubt be outnumbered and that whatever the size unit he sent to scout the village, they would have to escape, under cover of artillery fire. Since the survival of any size unit depended on escaping under cover of artillery, I had to go regardless. So I went.

Meades volunteered to go along. He knew I was sick and couldn't move my neck and shoulders. He said he would help me with the artillery if I needed it. I would need it.

The staff sergeant also volunteered to go. He said he didn't want any damn crazy headquarters pogue to get his men killed. I was surprised by these men volunteering. At the time I would have loved to rest just for an hour or so. My neck was throbbing, I was shaking, my head was hurting, and I was scared silly. It seemed like every time there was something I would have liked to get out of, there were people volunteering to go.

I didn't have to go over the map with the captain. I knew the area by heart, but the captain showed me the route we would take. Directly three miles north of Mai Xai Ti east was the small village we were going to scout. Northward, Mai Xai Ti east petered out into isolated farmhouses. The battalion's defensive lines ended with the main city. Once we left the defensive lines and got to the isolated farmhouses, we were on our own.

We were taking this scouting mission because the village had to be taken soon. It was almost right on the DMZ and was a direct link with North Vietnam and the NVA heavy artillery. Also, from this village the NVA could observe any troop movement going to or coming from Mai Xai Ti east, and it made an excellent observation post for calling in enemy artillery on top of us.

Our mission now, however, was just a probe to try to gauge the enemy's positions. The time to attack and take the village would be decided by Colonel Mac, along with his staff and the grunt commanders. They made the battle plans. We just fought the battles. With O.E. and me were the staff sergeant, Meades, and five infantrymen. The grunts looked young, very young, but their faces were smoke-blackened, and their eyes had that thousand-yard stare.

A dirt road leading north to the village would have made for easy traveling, but since it would have been an excellent place for an ambush, we decided to go through rice paddies and bamboo thickets. On the road, one claymore mine or well-placed machine gun could have wiped out our whole squad in seconds. The sergeant was much too jungle-wise to take the easy way.

The country north of Mai Xai Ti was a little different from the land we had traversed close to the river. There were still the ever-present rice paddies, but there were more brush and bamboo thickets. The brush consisted of small evergreens, palm trees, shrubs, and vines. This growth helped keep us from being spotted by the enemy. There were also small patches of sand, cactus, and graveyards.

As we left the battalion perimeter, I had the old uneasy feeling that we were on another planet or in another dimension. We were leaving the relative safety of the marine lines and venturing into no-man's-land. Except for artillery, we had no one but ourselves to turn to in case of an attack.

We were just going outside our lines when an NVA shell that sounded like a freight train roared overhead, and an instant later an NVA artillery shell exploded close to the middle of Mai Xai Ti east. As we moved farther into the unknown, we continued to hear the NVA artillery from North Vietnam blasting our encampment. Safe from American ground attack, the enemy was giving the marines at Mai Xai Ti east a greeting.

We were silent and almost invisible as we kept to the brushy areas and hurried toward our objective. Three infantrymen led the way, with two infantrymen behind us for security. I felt as if we were on a safari and that O.E. and I were the hunters.

We stayed in the middle of the grunts and kept our eyes on the terrain. I checked my map periodically. We had to know exactly where we were at all times in case we needed artillery.

The pressure was great. We didn't know where the NVA were, but we knew they were close and that at any second we might hear the crack of an AK-47. We kept moving fast until we came to two thatch huts close together, with a huge family bunker built next to the hut on the west. Palm trees and bamboo thickets offered good concealment around the huts, and in order to see quite a distance, we would need to get on top of the family bunker.

But first we had to make sure these huts and the bunkers were not occupied. We were tense and nervous as we approached them. The grunts, from long practice, moved like jungle cats up to the doors and dived inside, ready to fire at anything that moved. The huts and bunker were not occupied. The grunts, with no commands given, took up defensive positions around the bunker. They were as tense and taut as coiled springs. They were ready to kill anything that moved.

We climbed partway up the bunker and looked over the top. There in front of us was the northern village. In the center of grass huts scattered about were two large French buildings. The two-story brick buildings would be ideal observation posts for calling in artillery on top of our men in Mai Xai Ti east. Across a small river from the village were two large thatch huts, probably homes of farmers who tended rice fields on the west side of the river.

The absence of any movement in the village made me suspicious. I was certain the NVA were there and that they knew marines were on the move. Just then came the crack of an AK-47. The enemy had spotted us, but they had no idea of our strength. Not using the main road had allowed us to get right on top of them without being seen, but they had spotted us on the bunker. The fire we were receiving was coming from too far away to be accurate, but we kept our heads down in case of a lucky shot.

In just a moment we had our bearings and realized all the firing was coming from two huts across the village. I was undecided for an instant about whether to call in artillery as the weak attack called into question whether the village itself was occupied. The staff sergeant, Meades, and I all agreed not to call in artillery on the whole village.

The sergeant made all decisions, and he decided we should destroy the two grass huts from which the fire was coming. I called in artillery until eventually both huts burned even though they were soaked from the monsoon rains.

I felt sure the artillery had either killed or wounded the men who had fired at us, but there was no way to be certain unless we assaulted the huts. The sergeant wisely decided not to do that, for, as we later found out, surrounding the village were brick buildings and bunkers filled with NVA troops. Had we assaulted the huts, we would have walked into a trap and been completely wiped out. And so I did not call in any WIAs or KIAs. We couldn't confirm casualties.

Both sides could have done better if they had known more about each other. The NVA could have wiped us out had they known how few we were, and we could have saved many marines later had we known definitely the brick buildings were occupied and destroyed them. But that is part of war.

After we obtained the information we needed for pinpointing artillery fire if needed for the future, collected information about the terrain, checked out enemy movement, and noted any other information the captain might be interested in, the sergeant gave the order to move out. We all sighed in relief. We had been very lucky.

Taking a last look at the burning buildings, I knew we would be back, and when we were, it would be for all the marbles, not just a scouting mission. I had a bad feeling about it. The boil was extremely painful and I had a fever, but that was not the cause of the bad feeling. I knew the village was full of the enemy and that they were not about to run.

The trip back was hurried but uneventful. This patrol gave me great respect for the staff sergeant who led the grunts. He was a lifer. He was tall, thin, in his late thirties, and had a face carved from granite. The men obeyed him without hesitation. He made excellent decisions on the patrol, and the only boner we made was in not destroying the two large buildings in the village.

On reentering our lines, we found very little movement inside the perimeter defense. For the most part marines had disappeared either underground or into camouflaged bunkers.

As we worked our way back to L Company's command post, I saw many fresh shell craters. Some were still smoking. No wonder the men were wary! These craters were six and seven feet across and about three feet deep. And there was a ten-foot round hole blown out of the side of the Catholic church in the middle of town. The marines had taken a heavy bombardment. Many more such bombardments were to come.

Even though I knew the NVA could shell us whenever they pleased, being inside our lines was like being in a haven of rest. All things are relative, and being outside in enemy territory had put us in mortal danger.

We quickly found the captain and reported in. The sergeant gave him all the information he could. I mostly just listened and waited to be dismissed.

After we left the captain's bunker, the sergeant said he would send a corpsman to look at the boil on my neck. I didn't actually think he would remember to do so. One thing I learned in the Marine Corps was not to complain (at least out loud), and I had not complained about the boil. But it was obvious I was sick and that if I was going to do my job effectively, something had to be done about that damn boil.

21

Back in Mai Xai Ti

MEN IN HEADQUARTERS PLATOON, AS WELL AS THE OTHER men, were shaken up. They had been subjected to heavy artillery and mortar attack for two hours. Again, everyone had expected an attack from the NVA forces in Mai Xai Ti west. The grunts would have welcomed an attack; it would be a change from their always doing the attacking. Enemy troops crossing the creek would have been easy targets, and the slaughter would have been terrible. Anyway, no attack came.

After leaving the captain's office, O.E. and I headed for our ditch. Although a light rain was falling, it was surprisingly dry under our ponchos. We oiled our rifles, cleaned the radio, and then settled down to a C ration meal heated over heat tabs. We were starved. Damn! That food tasted better than any served in the finest southern mansion. O.E. fell asleep just as soon as we finished eating, but the boil was burning and felt as big as a baseball. I joined our friends in the brick building.

Soon a tall, nervous corpsman walked in and said he wanted to check out the boil on my neck. I bent my head over and took off a battle dressing I was using to keep the boil from being touched.

"Lord!" the corpsman exclaimed. "I can't treat that. You have to see a doctor." He turned a little green. That must have been some boil!

I went along with him to see the captain, but I already knew I could not see a doctor. Doctors lived in another universe. I had as much chance of seeing a doctor as of finding Brigitte Bardot waiting for me when I returned to my tent.

"You've got to get professional help for that boil, or you're liable to die. If the infection gets any worse, you won't be able to beat it. I'm going to see to it that you get to see a doctor."

I smiled to myself: For sure the corpsman was regular navy. He had a lot to learn about the marines.

When we entered the captain's quarters, I sat down just inside the door. I couldn't hear what was being said, but I saw the corpsman getting agitated. The captain was quiet for a minute and then shook his head. I knew it! Any man who could walk could not be spared.

Captain Hempel gave me a hard look. I looked back, trying to say with my eyes, I know no doctor's available. I was just humoring the corpsman.

On leaving the captain's office, the corpsman's look of exasperation changed to one of defeat. "Well," he said, shrugging his shoulders, "I guess we'll have to do the best we can." He seemed at odds with himself. He was going to have to diagnose and treat a condition he didn't even want to touch. Left untreated, the boil would kill me. He decided to see what he could do.

The corpsman had a pack full of medical materials. I didn't know what he was going to do, but anything was better than putting up with the pain I'd gone through for several days. I took off the battle dressing and bent my head forward. The corpsman asked one of the men to hold a flashlight on the boil while he worked. I soon felt a small prick behind an ear. He had given me a local anesthesia.

"I'm going to lance it, drain it, and put an antiseptic on it," he told me. "The salve will draw the infection out, and I will open and drain it again in about a week."

That sounded fine to me. The anesthetic was working, and for the first time in days, I felt no pain in my neck. I did feel the pressure of the scalpel and of his fingers as he pushed and kneaded the infection out. After wiping the pus and corruption off with clean gauze, he again washed the boil with alcohol, applied a heavy layer of salve, and tied the whole thing securely with a battle dressing. I looked like a walking casualty with the battle dressing wrapped around my head. When it was over, the corpsman looked relieved but still worried.

As for me, I felt as if someone had taken a hundred-pound weight off my neck. The corpsman cautioned me again to be sure to see him in a week. I said I would if I could. I thanked him and went on to my tent.

Damn! I had a two-hour radio watch that night, but that couldn't be helped. I felt weak and light-headed and soon drifted into a fitful sleep.

Some time later, I was awakened. Time for duty. I stumbled through the dark to my post, hardly noticing the stench from the dead NVA. Strange how a man can get so used to the smell of dead people that he can eat while sitting next to a dead man or sleep beside a rotting corpse and think nothing about it.

In combat areas, radio contact is maintained twenty-four hours a day. Every twenty minutes the man on duty locally will hear something like "Lima Company, Radio Check. Over." The local man will set the handset twice to indicate everything is all right.

It was a long two hours that night, but every twenty minutes when I heard that voice say "Lima Company, Radio Check. Over," I felt as if I had just had a nice visit from a friend. I was that lonely.

When my duty was up and I woke up my relief, I went directly to my tent. I lay down on what seemed like a feather bed and fell asleep instantly.

22

The River Belongs to the Marines

I HAD SLEPT FOR ONLY A COUPLE OF HOURS WHEN SOMEONE shook me awake. It was the captain himself. I rose up feeling rested and refreshed, the first time I had felt like that in a long time.

The captain's eyes shone. He was excited! "Come on, Mac," he said. "I've got to show you something."

We went to the roof of the building where the FAC men stayed. We both had our binoculars. What a sight! Coming up the Cua Viet River were six large ships, loaded to the hilt with supplies for the men at Dong Ha and Khe Sanh.

Upon taking Mai Xai Ti east we marines opened the Cua Viet River to supply boats. While Mai Xai Ti west was still under communist occupation, the supply boats were sheltered from this part of the town by a large, swampy, jungle island in the middle of the Cua Viet. The jungle island was quicksand and too soft for the North Vietnamese to mount a gun heavy enough to hurt the supply boats. North Vietnamese artillery from 30 miles away or from the village itself was not accurate enough to hit unseeable, moving targets—ships that were sailing south of the jungle island.

Just beyond the swampy island, the Cua Viet turned south, into territory held by marines, leaving the entire river supply route open to Dong Ha.

I realized that we were only one group out of many involved in getting supplies to our beleaguered troops, but that didn't take away from the importance of what we had done. Without us, those ships would not be going up the river. I felt like shouting.

I glanced around and saw marines perched on any high spot they could find. They, too, were enjoying the sight. A feeling of triumph was in the air. All our misery had not been in vain. Tears came to my eyes.

The NVA had spotted the ships, for soon a freight train sailed overhead and hit in the middle of our town. The marines disappeared instantly, but I remained long enough to see two shells hit the water. They were not even close. Only a lucky shot would hit a ship, but I bet a few sailors had to change their underwear before getting off that river.

Small-arms fire grew in intensity, and artillery shells came down all over the town. Bunkers shook from rounds exploding close by. The captain screamed for air support. Then I noticed something. In the time it took our planes to get to the guns from aircraft carriers, the shelling stopped. The NVA forces were not stupid! They knew the American planes could not find their guns through the heavy cloud cover unless they were firing when the planes arrived.

Since they knew exactly how long it took the planes to reach their positions, they knew how long to shell before stopping for a while. If only our leaders would let us cross over into North Vietnam, we could silence those guns forever. But we were not allowed to do that.

After the shelling stopped, men emerged from their bunkers, and as usual after such an attack, all were shaky. There were surprisingly few casualties considering the intensity of the bombardment: two marines were wounded badly enough to be medevacked out.

Now the captain, the FAC team, and I started trying to figure out a way to pinpoint enemy artillery to the north. First we tried to judge the distance by calculating the time between the shells hit and the reports of the guns firing. Then we would calculate the direction from which the shots came. We did our best at this but did not succeed in pinpointing the guns.

We also tried, occasionally, to spot the muzzle flashes to the north and then determine the time from muzzle flash until the shell hit. This way we could get a better direction because we could see the flash, but also we had to expose ourselves to artillery fire, and that was risky.

The coming day saw a duel between marines in Mai Xai Ti east and the NVA. They had heavy artillery: mortars, recoilless rifles, and small arms. We had our 105-mm artillery, 4.2 and 81 mortars, LAWs, and small-arms fire. We worked desperately twelve and fourteen hours a day trying to determine a way to silence those guns from across the border, but at best, we were only partly successful.

One day a grunt burst into the building. I recognized him and knew which squad he was with.

23

Dueling with the NVA

THE EYES AND FACE OF THE EIGHTEEN-YEAR-OLD GRUNT REflected the strain of prolonged combat. He was out of breath and seemed a bit nervous to be in the headquarters bunker. He came directly to me and said, "The snipers are giving us hell. The lieutenant's hit, and another man's wounded. The sergeant said to come and get you and try some artillery. We can't spot them."

The battle between the NVA in Mai Xai Ti west and the marines in Mai Xai Ti east was getting hotter.

I grabbed my helmet, compass, rifle, ammunition, map, notebook, and binoculars, and followed him out the door. Without looking, I knew O.E. was right behind me with his radio and gear. It takes only seconds to gather up the tools for killing.

We headed for the front lines, on the river facing Mai Xai Ti west, staying close to the ground. When the enemy is firing, it can take only a second of exposure to be killed.

The marine led us to a partly destroyed thatch hut close by the river. Half the roof was still standing, and the marines had dug in under the roof. This made an ideal bunker, what with a roof to keep the rain off and a wall of dirt between the marines and their enemies.

The platoon sergeant and three squad leaders were in the bunker. In a nearby bunker I saw a corpsman tending to the lieutenant and the other wounded man. The lieutenant had been lucky: A bullet had gone through both legs without hitting either bones or major blood vessels. The grunt was not seriously injured, but both men were in a great deal of pain.

The likable young platoon sergeant, Sergeant Havelok, filled me in. After the artillery barrage earlier, small-arms fire had slacked off a great deal. During a relative lull, marines had moved about a little. Then sniper fire started. The first volley had wounded the grunt, and the lieutenant had been wounded when he was going over to check the man's wound. As yet none of the men had been able to spot the snipers. Needless to say, the grunts stayed in place, for every moment brought forth AK-47 fire.

The Americans had fired grenade launchers and volleys of small-arms fire into the opposite side, with no luck. Sergeant Havelok wanted me to try artillery before someone was killed.

The other side of the river was an easy target to find on my map. I decided I would either blow the snipers to bits or make it so hot for them, they would have to set up housekeeping elsewhere.

I risked a close look at the other side of the river and saw a lot of bamboo cover and some thatch huts near the bank. Also I saw some large trees, palms, and what looked like elms. I decided there was an excellent chance that some of the snipers were in the trees.

The artillery battery was located over 10 miles east of us at the mouth of the Cua Viet River at the supply depot. It was a long range for 105-mm howitzers, but the gunners were good and I had full confidence in them. We would give the snipers hell.

I called in the fire mission with one white phosphorous round for adjustment. I noticed the excitement of the grunts, and was feeling excited myself. The round whistled overhead and exploded close to one of the elm trees. It was right on target! A volley of AK-47 fire came back in answer, and it riddled the roof of our bunker. The grunts laughed, and I grinned at them.

"Fire for effect, Battery 6, danger close, fifty meters."

Thirty-six rounds of high-explosive 105-mm artillery rounds hit right on the opposite bank. Debris flew into the water, and shrapnel whistled overhead. The opposite side of the river looked like a hell.

In the other bunkers, marines were plastered against the walls of their fighting holes. The artillery rounds had hit about forty-five yards from our own lines, and we could feel the concussion and hear the shrapnel overhead.

To a person who had never been in combat or had never seen an artillery barrage, it would have seemed we had wiped out every man across the river. But we knew that if the snipers were well dug in, they, or most of them, had survived.

The sniper fire ceased, but the marines were too jungle-wise to expose themselves. "You think they're still there?" Sergeant Havelok asked.

"I'd bet my bottom dollar they are. We probably scared the shit out of them and maybe wounded some, but they're still there. I can feel it."

"I know what you mean," the bearlike sergeant answered.

Just then came the crack and whine of an AK-47. At least one sniper was still alive. The men in the bunker looked at me as if to say, It's your show, Mac. See if you can get 'em. And from here on in, it was my ball game, me against the unseen killers across the river.

It was very possible that some snipers had been hidden in the trees, and it was also possible the firing had come from two thatch huts on the riverbank. I decided to try a mixture of high explosives and variable-time rounds to cover the treetops and the bank. So I called, "Repeat Hotel Echo (high explosive) and Victor Tango (variable time), danger close, fifty meters."

The shells came immediately and landed on target. The variable-time shells showered the trees with shrapnel, and the high explosives shook the earth.

"There goes the little bastard!" the sergeant yelled, and pointed.

There, not ten feet from the water and crawling slowly up the bank, was an NVA soldier.

He was hurt badly and was pulling himself by his arms, dragging the rest of his body along. He had bandoliers of ammo around him, but had dropped his rifle. He had had an excellent sniper hole at the very edge of the river, which he had probably moved into at night.

By now all the marines had spotted him. You could smell murder. I knew they were going to kill him, and I didn't blame them. He had shot two of their own and had kept them pinned down all day. They were not in a forgiving mood.

Sergeant Havelok shot first when the wounded man was halfway up the bank. The bullet hit about a foot in front of the man. He started crawling desperately, trying to reach the top of the bank. Then all the grunts started firing. The first several rounds hit the struggling man in the back, and he humped up and remained motionless until dozens of other bullets caused his body to jump and jerk. Finally he slid down the bank and stopped as he scooted against some brush next to the river.

I watched the show but did not fire myself. This was the grunts' revenge, and I let them have it. I felt neither sorrow nor hate for the dead man. He had taken his chances just as our dead had taken theirs.

The grunts started to relax just a little, but the sergeants were still wary. Then we heard the familiar crack! crack! crack! AK-47s again. "Corpsman! Corpsman!" I heard somebody yell. Another marine was wounded.

I decided the firing had to be coming from the grass huts. Despite the wet weather, I knew those huts would burn. I called for a repeat of the fire mission with white phosphorous and high-explosive shells mixed. Again the rounds were right on target: eighteen rounds of high explosives and eighteen rounds of white phosphorous.

On the other side of the river was an inferno. The grunts laughed, grinned, and yelled, "Get 'em, Mac." One grass hut was burning, and the other was smoking.

Anyone who has called in a great amount of artillery fire

will tell you that the fireworks can hypnotize a man. Maybe it is in part because of the intense concentration of the forward observer. When a person calls for rounds to drop only fifty yards from the observer himself, he has to concentrate. But there is something else. The person calling in the fire gets the feeling that he is God, that the artillery explosions are his creations, that he has the power of life and death over others. And another thing: the beauty. If a person enjoys fireworks at Fourth of July celebrations, then he would enjoy watching the artillery do its work. Just watching the fireworks themselves can be mesmerizing.

I was now in such a state. Without being conscious of it, I had moved away from the protection of the bunker. I was exposed to shrapnel that was whizzing all around me. I just kept saying, "Repeat, variable time, white phosphorous, and high explosives, danger close, fifty meters . . ."

The grunts were awed. I paid no attention to O.E., who kept motioning me to come back to the bunker, nor to the sergeants and others who urged me inside. I kept calling the artillery in even though shrapnel continued to hit all around me. I was in my own world. I had created the explosions, and the artillery would not hurt me.

Then a whistle in the air caught my attention, and I felt something hit my hand resting on my right thigh. I looked slowly down. The top of my hand was a mess of blood. Instantly O.E. and Sergeant Havelok were on top of me, dragging me back to the bunker.

While the platoon sergeant was wrapping my hand in a battle dressing, O.E. was lecturing. "You crazy mothafucker. You almost blew yourself up. We tried to git you back in here. You just ain't got sense enough to learn." I had to listen to this kind of talk for the next thirty minutes. I didn't have enough sense to learn, and O.E. didn't have enough sense to realize he was wasting his words.

For a moment I was shocked when I stared at the bloody battle dressing on my hand. But I was lucky at that. The shrapnel had hit only five inches from my private parts. If I had been as well endowed as some of the Romeos in the company claimed they were, it would have been a disaster.

Back at the headquarters bunker, one of the men said, "You can get a Purple Heart for that."

I guess my eyes widened a little: getting a Purple Heart for an injury I had brought upon myself! I would never live that down. No, I was not about to accept a Purple Heart.

Anyway, the platoon sergeant had told me I had done a good job and we could leave off the artillery for a while. No more sniper fire came that day, so maybe the artillery had killed all the snipers, or at least had put them out of business for a while.

We found a corpsman in a nearby bunker. He was just finishing dressing the wound of another marine, and when he saw me, his eyes lit up. The last time I had seen him, he had broken up a fight between another marine and me, a fight in which I had received the worst of it.

I was happy to see him; it was kind of like a link to a happier time when, in comparison to now, we were both babies. He was regular navy, friendly, and easy to get along with. He was always telling marines we were stupid. "Why would anybody put up with all the bullshit and then get stuck right out in the thick of it when fighting breaks out? You marines go to more trouble to get killed than anyone else in the world."

By now he had been in the field so long that he could have gone back to the ship at any time. But he stayed on the front, doing whatever he could to help the wounded.

"Well," he said now, "I see you haven't learned your lesson. Anyway, you're still in one piece."

"Well, I'm still needing you to pull me out of it, Doc," I answered.

He laughed when he learned how I had gotten hit by shrapnel. "Well, you finally got a taste of your own medicine. This should make an interesting Purple Heart."

A Purple Heart would be nice, and I hesitated before answering, "No, don't put me down for a Purple Heart."

He thought I was crazy and insisted he would do so, and said that the report would only say the wound was from shrapnel. But I would not go along. I could hear all the guys laughing and kidding me about going to all that trouble to wound myself just so I could be a hero. I finally convinced the corpsman not to write me up for the award.

"You damn jarheads are crazy. You go through hell for

all the glory, and when you get it, you turn it down. Okay. No damn Heart."

After he had cleansed the wound, which extended all the way down to the bone, and taped the skin back together, I thanked him and left. It would have been nice to talk awhile, but he looked exhausted.

I almost turned back to tell him I would like the Purple Heart after all. But thinking of the soldiers in many wars who had been so seriously injured, I felt totally unworthy of such an award. So I left the bunker knowing I would not be receiving a Purple Heart.

24

Attempted NVA Counterattack

I FINISHED MY RADIO WATCH AND WAS SOUND ASLEEP WHEN I felt someone shaking me. "The gooks are trying to cross the bridge," a voice whispered.

O.E. and I grabbed our gear and were quickly on the way to the bunker from which I had called in artillery the day before. The grunts were illuminating the bridge with hand flares, and in the vague light I could see what was going on. It was a footbridge with heavy bamboo rails, and the marines were raking it with heavy small-arms fire.

The bearlike platoon sergeant told me that one of his men had spotted a shape on the bridge moving our way. After checking the report, the sergeant saw a moving shadow himself. The bridge was the best way for snipers and sappers to sneak into our lines, and thus any movement on it could easily mean a major threat.

The sergeant had alerted all squads within shooting distance of the bridge, and instantly all available M-16s and machine guns were trained on the target. Also the sergeant alerted headquarters platoon. It was feared the long-awaited counterattack was about to start. In the light of hand flares, the sergeant saw several moving dark shapes. Once we started firing, the shapes ran toward the other side, but the sergeant heard a few splashes in the water, indicating that some men had either been shot or had dived off the bridge.

With all the firepower hitting it, I doubted anyone could still be alive on that bridge. But as dawn started to break and the bridge became gradually more visible, I saw a moving figure. Grunts saw it at the same time and opened fire. Apparently the NVA soldier had flattened out on the bridge while waiting for a chance to scurry back to his lines.

How he made it across to the other side, I will never know. He seemed to have been wounded, but he managed to dive into some brushes. With daylight we could see that although the railings had been damaged, the bridge itself was in excellent order. About a hundred yards downstream I saw an NVA soldier, facedown, in the stream. His body slowly bouncing up and down in the water seemed to calm the marines a little.

Whether or not the NVA had planned a counterattack, we never knew. There was a very real possibility the men on the bridge were sappers and snipers sent to destroy the command centers and throw the defense into confusion in preparation for the main assault. Possibly our sending the men running back to their lines and foiling their plans saved us. At any rate, a counterattack never came.

As soon as we chased the enemy from the bridge, I took out my map and pinpointed artillery targets. I told the platoon sergeant I would like to catch some of the fleeing men and perhaps make the NVA think twice about mounting an all-out attack. "A good idea," he agreed.

As always, the artillery replied instantly and plastered the areas I called in with high-explosive 105-mm rounds. I continued calling in targets and walked the artillery up and down the opposite riverbank. The grunts enjoyed the show.

While still absorbed with the artillery, I felt somebody shake my shoulder. It was Sergeant Havelok. "Let's try to get the bridge," he suggested.

The bridge certainly needed to be destroyed. If I could get two or three artillery rounds to hit it, the bridge might be damaged so much, it would be impassable. But it would be dangerous: The slightest miscalculation on my part or the slightest mistake or malfunction in artillery could bring hell and chaos on top of us. But what the hell! We were still teenagers and maybe a little reckless. There was only a small chance of our getting out of Vietnam alive anyway. I started adjusting the artillery for the bridge.

Now, that was close! We could feel the wind from the shells' trajectory before they hit not thirty yards from us in the water around the bridge. The earth shook around us, and the grunts were getting nervous. I continued calling in, hoping for direct hits, and one shell did explode on a railing but did no substantial damage to the deck. Bamboo is tough, and it takes a lot to hurt a well-built bamboo structure.

I decided to try some white phosphorous rounds to try to set the bridge afire. This was a fateful decision. I called in for nine high-explosive rounds and nine white phosphorous ones. All the high explosives hit where they were supposed to, but only two or three white phosphorous made it to the assigned target. Something was terribly wrong.

Just then I heard screaming from the lines. I looked around and saw a haze of white smoke over our lines where the white phosphorous rounds had fallen short.

"Oh, God!" I thought. "I can't believe it. We've shot our own men, and I'm to blame."

I called for a hold on the fire mission immediately. I was terrified, worried, and sorry all at the same time. My brain told me that one of the guns must have been out of adjustment or a gunner had put the wrong adjustment on a gun. All the shells had hit on target except three, and they had hit directly on our front lines. I just could not believe that. It had to be my fault.

The sergeant and the men faced me with accusing eyes. How could I explain? My confidence was shattered. I felt that never again would I feel competent to do anything right. For sure, I would never play God again.

I still heard screaming down the line. A lieutenant was waving his arms angrily at me. Everything had become dreamlike. The mind has a defense mechanism that keeps it from going insane. When something happens that is just too much to bear, everything becomes dreamlike. It is like you are looking through unclear glass.

I was in this state of mind. What had happened was too terrible for me to accept. I could not talk. I wanted a place to hide, a cave where I could call down the rocks on myself.

Sergeant Havelok, who thought more quickly than I, said, "You better get to the captain before that lieutenant does, or your ass is really in a sling."

I nodded dumbly, and O.E. and I took off to find the captain. For once, O.E. was speechless.

When we got to the captain, the lieutenant was already there, shouting and waving his arms. I did not hear what was said, but at least the captain's voice was calm. Finally the lieutenant stomped off. He had not taken ten steps before a high-explosive round hit on our side of the river, close to the lines. The lieutenant wheeled around, gestured toward me, and yelled: "Dammit! Tell him to put a hold on the artillery."

The captain looked at me just as another high explosive hit, this one in the middle of town.

"That's not me, Captain," I said. "That's incoming."

Finally it dawned on the lieutenant that this was NVA fire. He ran toward his lines, shouting, "Incoming!"

We ran to the headquarters bunkers as the enemy barrage intensified. By now it was a full-scale bombardment with 130-mm shells hitting all over the town. As we crouched in the bunker, I asked the captain what had happened. He told me that three white phosphorous rounds had fallen short and had injured three marines. That sickened me.

"How bad?" I asked.

He said that two had received minor burns and would remain on duty but that the third had a badly burnt leg and would be sent to the rear for treatment. I was relieved that no one had been killed, but was terribly worried about the man sent to the rear. If he was sent off the front line, his injury had to be very serious.

Another thing that bothered me was the pain the men were undergoing. White phosphorous just won't stop burning until it burns itself out. The pain from such burns must be almost unbearable. I was about to lose touch with things.

"Well, he won't lose his leg, will he?" I asked. "It's just a minor wound, isn't it?"

The captain looked at me, his eyes reflecting sympathy and understanding. "Don't worry," he said. "It was just a minor wound. Mostly it was the pain. He won't lose a leg. You probably did him a favor getting him out of here. Hell, Mac, a gun screwed up, that's all. There's nothing to be done about it."

His words helped a lot. But could he be belittling the injuries just to spare my feelings?

"The lieutenant just had to have somebody to blame for his men getting hurt," the captain went on. "You were available. Sometimes a man has to lash out and hit something or he goes crazy. Just hang in there and watch that white phosphorous. It's heavier than high explosive, and there's more danger of a short round. But it wasn't your fault."

No wonder I liked the captain so much!

But I still felt guilty and was afraid the marine would lose a leg.

"Captain," I said, "I don't want to call in any more artillery. Hell, it had to be my fault. Why can't I just carry a radio and let somebody else call the guns in? I just don't think I can do it."

I would have quit then and there if the captain had let me.

He looked at me and said, "Mac, you're the only artillery FO in the company. You can and will continue to call in artillery fire when it's needed."

That settled it. I would continue to call in artillery fire, even though, at the moment, it was the last thing in the world I wanted to do.

25

Artillery Up!

THE ARTILLERY BARRAGE FROM THE NVA ACROSS THE BORder got worse. It was the worst yet. The captain screamed into the phone, asking where the hell air cover was. But no planes were available. We were getting blown apart and had no defense.

For over an hour we sat huddled in our bunkers and prayed we would not get a direct hit. Finally someone from battalion headquarters called in for naval gunfire. We soon heard the flat trajectory of the naval shells as they went from the South China Sea toward the direction of the NVA forces. The naval gunfire was totally ineffective so far as damaging the communists was concerned, but it helped us feel less alone.

The bombardment continued for another hour, with shells exploding all around us. We were miserable. Then I saw the captain smile. American jets were on the way! By listening very closely, I could hear the approaching planes. I wanted to cheer.

The communists knew about the incoming planes, too, and the bombardment stopped quickly. We emerged, shaky, into the gloomy afternoon rain. We walked around to look at things as if we had never seen them before. Everything was new, and death had been so close that it just felt good to be alive.

About twenty feet from our bunker was a ten-by-eightfoot crater. It was still smoking. Similar craters were all over town. How close to death we had been!

I never knew the exact number of casualties we suffered,

but there must have been many, judging from the number of choppers that came in to pick up the dead and wounded.

Seeing some excitement over at the medevacs, I hurried over and saw fifteen new men had arrived to help us. These had been clerks and other rear-area personnel. Everybody was getting into the act.

One of the newcomers was the blond sergeant who had been shell-shocked and had survived buried under the dead bodies of his men. He looked fine now, his color was back, he was not nervous, and he seemed to be in complete control. After sending the men with him to serve in various grunt squads, he stopped and talked to the rest of us, men he knew so well. It was great. After leaving us, he talked briefly with the captain, who told him to go back to his old platoon.

We had just finished talking with the sergeant when I heard, "Artillery up! Artillery up!"

O.E. and I grabbed our equipment and hurried toward the cry from the far northwestern part of town. We saw four marines serving as lookouts from the top of a large brick house with a green roof.

As we approached the building, a lieutenant came to meet us. "Are you that hotshot FO I've been hearing so much about?" He was sneering!

I was surprised, to say the least. Was it my imagination that detected a little jealousy in his voice? He did not know me except for things he had heard. No doubt he had heard about the phosphorous accident, and who knows what else? He may have heard about my wild goings-on when I was on R and R. Perhaps, also, he resented a private doing a job usually reserved for officers.

O.E. and I ignored him and rushed to the rooftop. Four marines, veterans of Operation Badger Tooth, filled us in on what happened. They had spotted five young Vietnamese west of the river moving south. These men were either NVA replacements or messengers. Whatever their function, they were now in deep shit.

I looked through the binoculars and noticed that the terrain was typical: rice paddies, bamboo thickets, and brush of different kinds. There was a particularly long stretch of sand on the west side of the river, with two small grass huts and a haystack in its middle. Anyone going south would have to cross that stretch of sand.

I scanned the horizon and saw the unbelievable: In plain view, walking as if on a Sunday stroll, were the North Vietnamese soldiers. I called the artillery battery and told them that it was NVA in the open.

I watched the soldiers walk stiffly toward the sandy area. "Do something, arty. They'll get away!' the lieutenant was getting excited.

I intended to so something. I would wait until the men got to that stretch of sand and were in the open before I fired; otherwise, they would disappear into the brush and be gone.

The lieutenant was now jumping up and down. "Dammit, do something! They'll get away!"

I waited until the NVA got well into the open, and when they were about halfway from the brush to the two huts, I prepared to call in, even though I was still feeling the effects of my mistake about the phosphorous shells.

I called for one round of adjustment with a high explosive. I was still a little distrustful of white phosphorous. The round hit about two hundred yards northwest of the three men. The soldiers tensed a little and walked a little faster. The spotter round was so far away, they could not be sure it was meant for them.

Meanwhile, the lieutenant was going crazy. "You're not even close! They're just walking away! I need a sniper."

He ran through the town yelling for a sniper. I was glad to get rid of him for a while. I called in more fire, but the NVA pretended to ignore what was happening until high explosives started going off all around them. One of them clutched his side and fell. One of his companions grabbed him, and they hurried toward the two huts. A leg of the third man seemed to spin around, evidently hit by shrapnel. He half limped, half ran toward the huts.

Things were going according to plan. Of course, the sniper-hunting lieutenant was not around to see. If I had fired when he first asked me to, the men would have been long gone.

I looked at the other men on the roof, and they grinned at me. They knew what I had done. They gave me the thumbs-up, and I got a lot of confidence back. I would rather have the confidence and approval of guys like these than of a dozen lieutenants like their commander.

For some reason, one of the men dashed from one hut to the other just as artillery hit. He doubled over and lurched into the large haystack and disappeared.

I had them now. I knew what I had to do. I felt no guilt or elation. Marine boot camp prepares men to kill. If a person makes it through boot camp, he will have no qualms about killing. But I felt no joy about what I was doing. These NVA men had to be destroyed.

I called for a repeat with white phosphorous and high explosives. Nothing was moving now in the huts or haystack. They had all caught fire and were blazing. I called in three confirmed WIAs and three possible KIAs, NVA army soldiers.

As O.E. and I left the observation post, the lieutenant came storming back. He had two scared-looking snipers with large rifles with scopes on them and a platoon of 60-mm mortars with him.

He pointed at me and screamed, "You can't do shit! You let them get away."

Turning to the men with him, he yelled, "Set those mortars up! Snipers, get on that roof!"

O.E. and I grinned, waved at the men on the roof. They waved back, and we eased on back to L Company headquarters. We glanced back and saw that the lieutenant had the snipers on the roof and was pointing toward the sandy area. I doubt whether our friends on the roof even told him what had happened. They probably had to put up with his shit every day.

It was almost dark when we reached the company headquarters. The captain stopped me.

"Mac, did you call in three WIAs and three possible KIAs?"

"Yes, sir."

"The lieutenant said there were no KIAs nor WIAs. You know we don't send in false information."

"But, Captain," I protested, "I saw the men drop. The artillery hit all around them. I know we wounded some, and I believe we killed some, probably all of them. I saw it, Captain.''

"We don't count a KIA unless we can put a foot on his chest and say, 'You're dead.' ''

"Well, I couldn't do that, Captain.''

"You'll have to amend your report to the battery to say three possible WIAs.''

"Aye, aye, sir.''

He grinned. "I know what really happened. Good job, Mac.''

I grinned back and went back to our poncho home for a supper of C rations. The captain had made me feel good. He had had to take care of a fellow officer, but at the same time he had let me know that he knew what was going on.

Were those two frightened snipers the lieutenant had tracked down and brought to his post afraid of the enemy? You can bet your bottom dollar they were not. It had been the insults and gesturings of the lieutenant that bothered them. He made people feel bad.

26

Fooled by the NVA

THAT NIGHT, THOUGH I COULD BARELY STAY AWAKE, WE pored over maps and plotted Harassment and Interception Fire Missions, missions of artillery rounds fired at periodic intervals throughout the night on enemy supply and travel routes. The chances of these rounds killing anyone were remote, but who knows? Maybe we got lucky a few times. The captain was particularly interested in routes to the north that led to a village we were soon to attack.

The night was quiet, and we were up before daylight the

next morning expecting the usual heavy artillery barrage. We had our maps out and again studied the area to the north. When a barrage came, we always hoped our knowledge of the terrain would help us pinpoint NVA guns.

Everything was tense on the front lines, the marines quiet and invisible as they awaited an attack. They waited and waited, and for the first time since we had taken Mai Xai Ti east, no attack came.

About nine that morning an amazing thing happened. The clouds parted, and hot, beautiful sunshine hit us. Men who had been cold, wet, and miserable for days took off their boots and dried their feet. A carnival atmosphere sprang up. It is amazing how young men can go from complete misery to happiness in seconds. By now we appreciated small comforts, but that sunshine was not a small comfort: it was a godsend. Up front, men laughed, horsed around, played jokes on one another, and occasionally someone whooped just for the hell of it.

The captain came walking toward the front lines with a puzzled look. He half smiled as he passed me. "Hey," he said, "this is okay." Evidently the good feeling affected him, too.

Marines on the front line had become visible in enemy territory! A strict taboo. They moved about, broke out shaving gear, and fetched water from the creek. Shirts came off, and soon men were shaving and washing their bodies for the first time since leaving the troopship. It was unreal, dreamlike. They had forgotten war. They were supposed to be quiet and invisible!

I had a bad feeling, a premonition. I stayed close to our poncho tent, careful about exposing myself. A voice kept saying, "Where the hell are the North Vietnamese? I know they just didn't go home." Some of the older staff sergeants, I noticed, looked worried as they hurried about the lines.

Word came that after everyone was cleaned up, we would bury the dead gooks. Things would get civilized again. I heard all this but was still uneasy. Then I thought, "What the hell? I must be paranoid. Everyone else is happy. I must be a stick-in-the-mud."

I found a razor and washcloth, filled my steel pot with

water, and started out to the creek bed, still uneasy. Then I heard it. Above the noise of the playful marines I heard what sounded like small firecrackers going off one at a time in a garbage can. I froze for what seemed like minutes but which could not have been over a microsecond before it registered in my brain just what those sounds were. Flinging aside my water, I ran to the creek screaming, "Incoming! Incoming!"

The men, some half-shaved, some half-naked, looked at me as if I were crazy. Then 61-mm mortars started exploding. I huddled under the poncho tent against the creek bank. O.E. dived in beside me.

Mortar rounds exploded everywhere. Shrapnel screamed overhead. The earth shook as rounds exploded nearby. Shaking and terrified, I expected a round to hit on top of me any second. Mixed with the mortar were screams of the wounded and dying.

The barrage intensified. Something had to be done: the NVA were blowing the hell out of us. I got the radio and called for artillery. Since I had no idea where the mortars were located, I just called in the coordinates for the middle of the town and asked for a fire-for-effect.

Eighteen rounds of 105-mm artillery were on their way immediately. They hit in the middle of Mai Xai Ti west, and I called for a right fifty repeat. The enemy mortar stopped instantly. No doubt the NVA mortar gunners were heading for their own bunkers.

I halted the fire mission, and men hurried out of bunkers to help the wounded. The survivors moved as marines are supposed to move: they stayed under cover and moved quickly and stealthily from one place to another.

Screams, moaning, and cries for help came from all directions. O.E., members of the FAC team, and I made a beeline for the bunker on the front lines from which I had called in artillery fire the day before. Crying mixed with an unearthly animal keening came from that bunker. Someone was badly hurt.

I was prepared to see someone injured but I was not prepared to see what I saw. The bunker had received a direct hit. Three young infantrymen, replacements after Badger Tooth, stood outside the bunker in shock. Two were just staring with tears in their eyes, and the third was gagging and vomiting his guts out.

There in the bunker, back against the wall, was the tall, blond platoon sergeant who had returned to the front line just the day before. He didn't have his helmet on. He looked innocent and at peace. Funny, I had never noticed what a handsome man he had been. He didn't have a scratch on him as he sat motionless and very still. And very dead.

Across from him, lying on his back and still twitching, barely, was another friend and a veteran squad leader. Where his left arm had been was a bloody stump. Blood oozed from holes that punctured his body. He was dead.

But what did the most to unnerve us was a creature, curled in a fetal position, in the middle of the bunker. It was Sergeant Havelok, the bearlike platoon leader who had been such an asset and inspiration to us all. That picture of him still haunts me in nightmares. Since the other two were dead, we rushed directly to Sergeant Havelok, but he, for all practical purposes, was beyond help. A once powerful arm kept moving aimlessly and helplessly up and down his tortured body.

The men with me were all veterans. We had handled wounded before and knew what to do. One man slid a poncho, often used as emergency stretchers in the field, as far as possible under the sergeant. I took the sergeant by the shoulder and tried to roll him onto the poncho. Now I saw the real extent of his injuries.

One arm was a bloody mass, riddled and useless. The other, the one he kept moving over his body, was intact but had only two fingers and three bloody stubs on the hand. Most of the left side of his forehead was gone, leaving a bloody hole behind. His jaw was broken, and as he moaned and cried, blood poured steadily out of his mouth. How could he possibly be alive?

I yelled for a corpsman and cursed the other men into helping me get the man on the poncho. I wanted so badly to comfort him, but how was that possible? I looked into his one good eye and tried to see the spark that divides men from animals. The eye, though seemingly trying to focus, was dull and showed no spark of recognition.

Numb from horror, the six of us carrying the poncho were silent. The sun had disappeared and rain had started, making the poncho slick and that much harder to hold. This was hell. We were straining our guts, trying to carry the sergeant to the eastern side of the town where medevac helicopters would land. What was left of him kept thrashing, moving about, and kicking. Looking down, I saw that part of his boot on his right leg was gone, and a bloody stub protruded from what was left of the boot. All his toes and part of his foot were gone.

After going about fifty yards, we reached a small ditch. We had to go down one side and up the other. At the ditch, from sheer exhaustion, we had to let him down for a moment. Once the poncho touched the ground, the sergeant, with an animal scream, jerked upright. He started swinging his bloody stub of a hand and twisting his head from side to side. He was like a demon. The hole in his forehead spouted blood as he gibbered and cried. I dove on him, trying to hold him down, and buried my head in his shoulder. The other men helped, and we held on to him with all our strength. We were covered with blood, and all were crying.

Suddenly one of the men with us went berserk. He threw down his helmet and rifle and started cursing and swinging at bamboo trees and anything else in striking distance. This marine, a black from North Carolina, had been in Sergeant Havelok's platoon. The fatigue, the many deaths, the hopelessness of it all, had brought him to the breaking point. Trying to help his leader, who now was a pathetic mass of bleeding, blubbering flesh, had been more than his system could take.

Then the captain came. He grabbed the man and, holding him firmly, took him to the side. The captain talked to the marine like a father to a son he cared for very much. Captain Hempel was effective because we all knew his concern and feelings for us were real. There was nothing phony about him. Once the marine had calmed down, he retrieved his helmet and rifle and sat staring at nothing while the rest of us resumed half carrying, half dragging Sergeant Havelok toward the safe landing zone.

Upon reaching our goal, we found helicopters already

there. As we laid the sergeant on the floor of a chopper, I paused, not wanting to leave him. I thought of the faith he had had in me and the confidence and courage he had instilled in all those around him. It didn't seem fair that I should be alive and in one piece and he should be gone.

I grabbed his pitiful stub of a hand and held it for a moment. I looked at his good eye, and for a second I thought I saw a hint of recognition. Then I jumped off the helicopter to make room for more dead and wounded. The sergeant resumed crying and moving his hand over his body. The gunners and copilot of the aircraft gave me a look mixed with respect and sorrow as the craft lifted off.

As we five headed back to the front lines, things seemed gloomier and sadder than ever. No one said a word. The rain deepened our depression. We were all thinking the same thing: How much longer can we hold out? We had already done the impossible. How much more could we do?

But we were disciplined soldiers. We would stay until orders came to move out, or until we were all dead. There was no question about that.

There had been real danger of the front lines breaking, but while we were carrying the sergeant, officers and staff sergeants had moved among the men, talking to and reassuring them. And now everything was under control. The lines would hold.

As O.E. and I got back to the creek bed and the headquarters bunker we called home, I looked around. There was a trail of blood by the small creek where we had dragged the platoon sergeant. The smell of blood and death was on everything. The NVA soldiers we had killed days before were still lying where they had fallen, rotting, stinking.

The marines had disappeared underground. The place looked deserted, but in reality it was inhabited by the deadliest predators the world has ever known: desperate and bloodthirsty United States Marines who could and would kill anything that tried to dislodge them from this town.

I snapped out of my reverie when I heard, again, mortars on their way. "Incoming!" I shouted, and dove for the creek bed. Scattered mortar rounds exploded up and down the front lines, but the barrage was light and inspired no panic. Once again, the marines would hold the line.

27

Duel

I CALLED FOR ARTILLERY, AND THE 105-MM GUNS AGAIN blasted Mai Xai Ti west. The mortars ceased just before the artillery started. Finally I realized that the firings followed a definite pattern. Then it dawned on me: The enemy was monitoring our radio broadcasts! They knew exactly when our artillery was coming in and would get their mortars under cover and get into bunkers until the barrage was over. When they heard me halt the fire mission, they would set up their mortars and start all over again. Thus we never knew when their fire was on its way, but they always had advance warning of ours.*

I wondered why the officers and noncoms had not noticed this.

An ironic thing: We later learned the NVA used telephones to call in artillery. That explained why their artillery was so effective.

After telling the captain about what I had discovered, he, the FAC team, and I made a beeline for Battalion Headquarters to make a phone call. The captain got permission to use the phone and soon had the first sergeant of the artillery

---

*It was not till many years later when I was reading about World War II that I learned the marines never used radios in that war to call in artillery; they used either the telephone or a messenger. It is just as well that I did not know at the time. The officers had not done their groundwork about artillery. Many marines died because of the ignorance or laziness of some of these officers.

battery on the line. The captain handed me the phone. I talked to the First Sergeant and along with the command group of the artillery battery, the sergeant, and the captain, we worked out a code whereby we could call in artillery without talking.

The artillery battery had the grid coordinates exactly for the middle of Mai Xai Ti west, where the North Vietnamese forces were concentrated. The system we worked out was as follows: If I clicked my handset once it meant fire-for-effect right into the middle of Mai Xai Ti west immediately. If I clicked my handset twice it meant fire-for-effect 50 meters right of the target. If I clicked my handset three times it meant fire-for-effect 50 meters left of the middle of Mai Xai Ti west. The artillery radio frequency would stay silent except for my transmissions. It was a simple system, but with it we could cover Mai Xai Ti west with artillery without saying a word over the radio. Hopefully we could confuse the North Vietnamese and knock out the mortars.

This finished, we went back to the front lines and waited. Soon the familiar pop, pop, pop, of the mortars started. I clicked the handset once. Almost immediately the artillery whooshed overhead and blasted at the mortars. The enemy barrage ended abruptly.

After talking with the captain, I decided to click the handset at forty-minute intervals. Sometimes I would click twice and the artillery hit fifty yards right of the target, and sometimes I clicked three times and the rounds hit fifty yards left of the target. We were able to cover the village well. One particular volley got the mortars: suddenly there were a lot of screams and other noises coming from across the river. The NVA mortar attacks had ended. At least until they could get replacements.

The next day the NVA decided to punish us. We had been receiving heavy artillery all day when O.E. and I had a bright idea. We would climb to the top of our damaged brick building and keep our binoculars trained to the north. When the NVA fired, we would spot the muzzle flashes and get an exact direction from which the flashes came, and when the rounds hit, we would have a pretty good idea of the locations of the guns.

In artillery school I had learned that shrapnel always goes

to the side, never up. I reasoned we would be safe atop the building. Unfortunately, we found out our teachers had not told the shrapnel what direction it was to take.

Within ten minutes of climbing to the top of the building, we spotted muzzle flashes, far away but distinct against the low clouds. We took an accurate direction and started counting the seconds until the rounds hit. This would give us a pretty accurate location of their guns. Then we could call for naval gunfire and air strikes.

The first NVA rounds hit near the middle of the town a good distance from us. Suddenly O.E. got excited and yelled, "Look! Look! I see the muddafuckahs."

His binoculars were trained on two large French buildings we had seen on a patrol to the north a few days before. "They was lookin' at us with binoculars," he continued. "They was calling shit in on us!"

I trained my binoculars on the two buildings and thought I saw movement, but could not be sure. One thing was certain: The two buildings made perfect observation posts for the NVA. Although three miles away from Mai Xai Ti, from atop the buildings NVA FOs had a perfect view of our movements and could call in and adjust artillery right on top of us, just as they had been doing ever since we got there. Their position was perfect. They could see everything and yet they were out of range of small-arms fire. If we were going to stay in this town, we would have to take or destroy that village to the north.

Then we saw muzzle flashes again. This time the artillery was right on top of us. The NVA FOs had seen us on top of the building and had guessed what we were doing. As we crouched there, my logic told me that we were safe from shrapnel, but as I have said, nobody told the shrapnel. It was ricocheting off brick and through tree limbs around the building. It definitely was high enough to get us.

I looked at O.E. O.E. looked at me. If I looked half as scared as he did, I looked terrified. We bolted for the stairs and set a going-down-stairs speed record, both reaching the bunker door at the same time; for a second we found ourselves wedged in the doorway. Other marines were there as well.

"Well, girlies," one marine said, "I thought shrapnel went sideways, not up."

"So much for our brave FOs watching enemy artillery firings," joked another.

O.E. and I answered with sheepish smiles.

Men cautiously came out of their bunkers, and we quickly noticed that the artillery was still firing, not at us, but to the east of our rear positions. The NVA were shelling our artillery battery and supply depots.

I tried to call the artillery battery to report the positions of the NVA guns, but could not get through. What was going on? I wondered. I hurried to the captain's bunker and told him I couldn't get communications with the artillery battery.

"I'd better do some checking," he said, looking worried. He started toward the Battalion Command Post. He soon returned and told us the NVA had shelled the hell out of our rear positions. The fire-direction control center in our marine artillery battery had taken a direct hit and was destroyed. Several guns were knocked out. We would be without artillery for a while. There were casualties, but he did not know how many.

I was dumbfounded. Out of the numerous war stories I had heard from veterans of Vietnam, I had never heard of the Americans losing artillery support. Our not having such support for several days was terrible news.

And all the time I was thinking about casualties. All the men in the battery were good friends of mine, and I had always assumed they would be safe in a rear area. Later we learned that the artillery firing team was knocked out, with many men killed or wounded. I would never see those friends again.

The captain soon had good news for me. Colonel Mac had found a battery of 4.2 mortars somewhere and had gotten them set up to provide fire support until the artillery was back in operation. I was to call in 4.2 mortars for the time being.

I knew that 4.2 mortars, or four-deuce mortars as we called them, were excellent saturation fire weapons. The explosive power was greater than that of the 105-mm artillery, but they were not nearly as accurate. They had a high

155

trajectory and thus did not have the pinpoint accuracy of the artillery with its flat trajectory. It would be hairy trying to call 4.2 mortars in within fifty meters of our own lines. But we would have to try.

O.E. told the captain about seeing the NVA on the buildings to the north. The captain was very interested and immediately carried the information to battalion headquarters.

It was almost dark. Men prepared their evening meal of C rations and waited for the captain's return. It was gloomy, what with the rain, the death of friends, the constant fire from the enemy, and on and on.

An hour after dark the captain returned and told us what decisions had been made at the Battalion Command Post. Since it was obvious that the NVA observation posts in the village to the north had to be captured or destroyed, we would have to send some of our troops to do the job. The colonel was gambling that the move would take the enemy by surprise and that the forces across the river would not guess how much weaker we would become. Whatever the results, Colonel Mac knew we could not keep holding Mai Xai Ti east unless that village was taken. We had no choice.

The force moving north would consist of one platoon from L Company and one platoon from K Company, a total of sixty men. Captain Hempel would be in charge. Naturally, since I had been there before, he wanted me to come along to provide fire support in the form of 4.2 mortars.

I was thrilled.

28

The Attack

THAT NIGHT O.E. AND I STUDIED OUR MAPS, CLEANED OUR rifles, got our gear in order, and prepared to move out. As usual, I knew this would by my last trip, but this time at least we would be leaving this hellhole for a while.

It was pitch-dark when we started out the next morning. To my surprise, the trip seemed to last only a few minutes. That is how sleepy I was. As we neared the two grass huts we had shelled on our recent patrol, the captain and two platoon commanders had a quick conference. One of the lieutenants was the man who had blasted me about the way I had called in artillery the other day. I hoped he was as tough as he looked. He needed to be.

To reach the village we would have to cross an open rice paddy. There was a dirt road in the center of the paddy that had a good bit of brush on each side. The captain and his radioman and O.E. and I used the road. We were just behind the infantry assault lines, which were spread out on each side of us. Just before daybreak the assault started.

The first shots came from the grass huts. The North Vietnamese were trying to trap us, to get us to attack the huts and thus get us into the open so that they could massacre us from the two large permanent buildings. But we were wise to that old trick. Leaving five grunts behind to keep the enemy in the huts busy, the rest of the infantry moved forward to the village itself.

All hell broke loose. Heavy machine-gun and rifle fire erupted from both large buildings. Firing back, the marines tried a quick assault but were forced back. We were stopped. I knew only too well what those shapes scattered about the paddy field were.

After an hour of fighting, the situation was grim. Our M-16s were no match for their AK-47s and Chinese machine guns. We didn't have enough cover to use our M-60 machine guns. At times a solitary marine would attack, but every time he was either killed or wounded. It looked like a slaughter.

Then word came back to me. "Artillery up!" I thought, "Up where? We're on the front lines now." But O.E. and I crawled forward, past wounded marines who had either crawled out or been carried out of the water. One of the wounded was the lieutenant who had given me such a hard time. He had been shot in the pelvis, and he had the same look on his face that Lieutenant Callahan had had, a look apologizing for having been wounded and a look that showed guilt because he could no longer help. I wanted to go to him, take his hand and try to comfort him, but there was no time for that.

We found the captain crouched behind a paddy dike. The situation was desperate. I already had the map coordinates plotted when he said, "Get some mortars in here. They're cutting us to pieces."

"Get the men's heads down. You never know where the 4.2 mortars will land."

He just smiled and said, "Get some!"

I called in the first round and couldn't believe what happened. It hit directly on top of one of the big buildings, went through the roof, and exploded inside. What a booster to the morale of the grunts!

"How did you do that?" The captain looked at me in disbelief.

"Hell, I don't know," I answered.

"Do it again," he ordered.

No doubt the marines had gained fire superiority over the building hit, for now only one AK-47 was firing from it. I called for more mortars, and quickly grass huts were badly damaged, but the NVA still had superior fire from the undamaged French building. During each firing I was conscious of one mortar exploding somewhere in the distance; it was off target, and I hoped it would not decide to drop in on us.

With continued mortar fire we were slowly gaining superiority over the enemy. Then out of nowhere a rocket slammed into one of the French buildings. To my surprise, I saw three marine helicopter gunships hovering above us and firing into the village. They were beautiful!

The pilots knew their business. They stayed below the trajectory of the mortar and high enough to get good rocket and machine-gun fire into the village. The enemy, though having a hard time of it, were still fighting back, and turned their heavy Chinese machine guns toward the gunships.

I kept the mortar fire coming in, but the gunships ran out of rockets. Machine-gun fire was hitting the helicopters and disorienting them. One was damaged badly enough to withdraw. The other two were having a machine-gun duel with the communists.

Marines erupted from cover and stormed over the ruins of the French buildings and on into the village. By the time the North Vietnamese realized what was happening, it was too late to lower their machine guns and fire at the attackers. I stopped the mortar fire, and the gunships withdrew. The enemy lines were broken and the battle was over quickly.

I moved with the captain into the village behind the infantry. Most of the enemy had fled into North Vietnam, only a few miles north. We did not have the men nor the energy to pursue. We were just glad to have accomplished our mission. But we had paid a heavy price: fifteen killed and ten wounded.

We were losing men every day and still not getting replacements. How long could this go on? Soon, it seemed, we would have to give up the village and Mai Xai Ti east as well.

As we set up camp, the enemy dead, thirty of them, were piled unceremoniously in the middle of the village. As always, they had been well equipped, well fed, and looked in the peak of condition. Then something happened that bothers me until this day.

The men lost all traces of being civilized. Everyone knew that souvenirs from the front brought good prices from troops in the rear. Many a field marine had gotten on a good drunk or even financed an R and R by selling captured NVA equipment. An NVA helmet, cartridge belt, rifle, or just about any piece of communist gear would bring a good price. Especially valuable were souvenirs with blood on them or with bullet holes in them.

Once the village was secured, the marines ripped into the dead enemy soldiers, stripping them of everything that could be sold. More or less automatically, I took a cartridge belt, complete with bullet holes and blood. Then I stepped back to watch. It was gruesome.

After collecting all salable gear and equipment they could find, the marines started cutting off ears, a prized souvenir in the rear. I never once engaged in this practice, but at the time, I saw nothing wrong with it. I went along with what everyone else said: "Hell, they're dead. Cutting off their ears can't hurt them." The practice was common on front lines.

Hell, the North Vietnamese would and did do the same things to our dead. And I heard over and over reports of finding corpses of marines badly mutilated, some even of having testicles cut off and stuffed in the mouth. I never came across such corpses myself, but I had seen the NVA deliberately burn marines alive. When a person knows that an enemy is going all out to kill and then mutilate him, he does not have any compassion for that enemy. At least I didn't.

Let me say that I never saw nor heard of a marine torturing, striking, or otherwise mistreating a prisoner. It just wasn't done, at least to my knowledge.

Now, as the marines pulled and jerked at the corpses, I was reminded of a pack of wolves over their kill. Their eyes shone with an unearthly light that cannot be described in words. These predators were eighteen and nineteen years old, dirty, ragged, hungry for a good meal, thirsty for a drink. They had gone full circle and were now marines, the type of creatures Marine Corps boot camps taught them to be.

While I was watching the grunts collecting their trophies, I did not notice the captain and the company gunnery sergeant approach. The others didn't either. All of a sudden the captain and sergeant flew into the middle of the pile of dead men. They tossed two marines from the middle of the pile. The grunts landed like cats, and in a second had their rifles ready.

This was the most tense and electrifying moment of my entire stay in Vietnam. I stiffened and took the safety off my rifle. I did not have any idea what would happen. Would the men kill the captain and sergeant? They could have easily done so, for neither man was armed. I did not know what I would do if the men shot the captain. I knew I could not keep them from doing it if that was what they decided to do.

"Get away from these dead men," the captain ordered. "You're not vultures nor hyenas. You're U.S. Marines, and don't forget it. As long as I'm in command here, you'll act like marines and not like grave robbers."

All the men stood still, staring at the captain with that weird glow still in their eyes. Then slowly and reluctantly they withdrew.

All the men respected and liked the captain. Both he and the gunnery sergeant always fought beside them and helped them in any way they could. They knew that both men would die in an effort to save them. Perhaps this, along with Marine Corps discipline, caused the men to obey the captain now.

Had the captain been killed, all would have been chaos. What would the men here and at Mai Xai Ti east have done? Who knows?

After the captain had regained control, the gunnery sergeant got some of the grunts to bury the dead. We had not done this in a long time, but maybe the captain wanted to get temptation out of sight. Before leaving the site, the captain walked straight to me. I guess he just needed someone to talk to.

"Dammit," he said, "don't our men realize that those dead men were soldiers who died for what they believed in? We should show some respect for the dead."

"Aye, aye, sir," I said, but I didn't agree with him.

The captain's compassion and feeling for his fellow human beings was something I would never understand. To me the North Vietnamese were monsters, not human beings. They had killed my friends, and I felt sure they would kill me soon. Like the grunts, I had obeyed the captain because he was the captain, our leader. But as far as the North Vietnamese were concerned, I could have cut them up into little pieces and then fed them to dogs without batting an eye. I am sure that ninety-nine percent of the men felt the same way. A man does not feel compassion for people who are trying their damnedest to kill him.

We settled in for the night. Helicopters medevacked out our dead and wounded. I plotted fire missions for sites all around the village, and we kept flares coming in around the village all night, but once again the North Vietnamese did not counterattack. First and foremost they were guerrilla fighters.

29

K Company Fools the NVA

THE NEXT MORNING WE MOVED OUT, LEAVING K COMPANY to occupy the village, and Lieutenant Michaels as their forward observer. Back at Mai Xai Ti, days were much like the preceding ones except enemy artillery was not as accurate nor as effective as before.

Within two days after being knocked out, our artillery battery was restored. This was a blessing, especially since the NVA had just resumed their mortar attacks. With our new artillery we quickly stopped the mortar attacks.

Even though we were still taking casualties daily, we climbed on top of high points late every afternoon to watch the ships go up the river. That always gave us a lift. Cua Viet River still belonged to us. But for how long?

The village to the north, though relatively quiet, was a

sitting duck for an enemy attack. It was almost an hour's march from where we were and was defended by a company that was much undermanned. The NVA were known to attack isolated, weakly defended outposts and to massacre the occupants. Usually they attacked only at night and when they had heavy numerical superiority. We all knew an attack would come. When?

A week later I was awakened at 1:00 A.M. K Company was under attack. We were ordered to hold our positions just in case the North Vietnamese were playing a trick to attack us at Mai Xai Ti east when most of our men were gone. Lieutenant Michaels was calling in artillery, and since his radio was too far away from the artillery battery to get good contact, I had to relay his instructions.

Here is what happened:

The marines received reports from villagers that an attack on the northern village was to come soon. The North Vietnamese intended to retake their excellent observation post. For two nights K Company had been ready. They had set up a horseshoe-shaped ambush around their encampment so that the marines would have excellent fields of fire on the NVA when they entered the village, and they would be out of sight of the enemy. Lieutenant Michaels had artillery fire spotted on the encampment and on all avenues of approach and retreat.

Since the marines knew the attack was coming at night, they kept everything in the encampment looking normal during the day. They cooked meals, cleaned weapons, and built fortifications. At night they put ponchos over sandbags to look like sleeping marines, stacked sticks of bamboo to look like rifles, and put jungle utilities and helmets on dummies to make them look like marines sitting up. After doing this, the marines moved to their ambush positions. On the third night a battalion of 600-1,000 handpicked NVA soldiers hit the marine encampment.

They walked into hell!

They charged into the encampment, bayoneting what they thought were marines but were actually sandbags and dummies. The marines waited until the NVA were well within their ambush lines and then opened up with all their firepower. It was a perfect ambush.

In their surprise, the NVA at first milled around in confusion. Then an NVA officer got his men organized and led a charge to try to break the thin marine line. The line wavered but held, despite the enemy having a nearly five-to-one advantage. One of the heroes was the black marine who had fallen apart when Sergeant Havelok was blown apart by a mortar round. This marine, when the NVA had almost overrun his position, stood up with an M-60 machine gun and personally killed thirteen enemy soldiers. This had enabled his section of the line to hold.

A fierce battle raged all night. Lieutenant Michaels kept the artillery coming in and wreaked havoc on the NVA forces. By daylight the enemy forces were destroyed. Those not killed had fled either back north or west across the river.

This was one of the most complete victories for the United States forces in Vietnam. The official and true count was 148 NVA killed and an unknown number wounded since there were numerous blood trails leading toward the river. We suffered eight fatalities and twenty-five wounded. This is not an exaggerated body count. An enemy dead was not counted unless a marine could stand on his chest and say he was dead. There was absolutely no putting a rifle over a paddy dike, firing, and calling in ten dead. We didn't work it like that.

We had held our position and had the pride of victory, but the thirty-three men we lost for combat duty was a greater loss to us than I imagined the large number of deaths and wounded was to the NVA.

We had taken one casualty that we definitely could not replace. Close to daylight, when the battle was winding down, Lieutenant Michaels's radioman told me over the radio that the lieutenant had been hit. The radioman had enough knowledge of artillery to keep the fire coming in until the battle was over. I thought surely that the lieutenant had just been wounded, probably slightly, and that he wouldn't even be medevacked.

After the battle was over, I learned Lieutenant Michaels was dead. It hit me like a thunderbolt. I couldn't believe it. Lieutenant Michaels was like Captain Hempel: he was indestructible, he couldn't die. But he was dead. He had been shot in the chest and had died about daybreak. He had skillfully directed the artillery fire on enemy positions, repeatedly exposing himself to enemy fire and contributing significantly to his unit's victory. But Lieutenant Michaels was dead. It was unbelievable. And now I was the only forward observer left in the battalion.

I was exhausted the next morning, after the battle, but I couldn't sleep. I staggered to the ditch that I called home and stared at the mud bank. I should have cried, but the tears wouldn't come. I thought of the lieutenant. He had been tall, thin, proud, every inch a marine. I remembered his soft smile and how he laughed at the way I talked and acted. He was an excellent forward observer and an excellent soldier. I knew that I could never understand him. We came from different worlds. He was an officer, well educated, and had had a brilliant future ahead of him.

We were very different, but we had a common bond in that we both were forward observers even though he was much better than I. There was nothing I could do for him now, but I would miss him. So now I just sat for a while and thought of everything I could about him, and I knew the human race and the Marine Corps had lost a good man.

The NVA must have been in shock at having lost the battle for the northern village. In Mai Xai Ti east we received very little incoming fire, only a few heavy artillery rounds that did little damage, and even the small-arms fire slacked off to nearly nothing. No doubt after such a disastrous defeat, the North Vietnamese had to regroup.

With our forces in Mai Xai Ti east dwindling, Colonel McCown took a risk by not sending any replacements for K Company. The risk paid off.

30

Another NVA Strategy

THE NEXT FIVE DAYS WERE PRETTY MUCH THE SAME AS usual: From across the small river came the same old artillery rounds, the same old occasional mortars; above were the same old low clouds which brought us the same old rain. Of course, there was the same old routine of our artillery blasting the NVA. There was little rest and no comfort. It seemed that this was the only life we had ever had.

But the NVA had been planning, and we had no advance warning about those plans. About 3:00 A.M. on the fifth day after the battle in which Lieutenant Michaels was killed, I was awakened and told to saddle up. Half-asleep, I got binoculars, maps, rifle, and all the ammunition I could carry and staggered after the marine sent to fetch me. Of course, O.E. was accompanying me with his radio on his back.

After forced marching in the dark for about ten minutes, we got aboard amtracs. Once the amtracs got rolling, one of the men gave me the poop. The NVA forces had circled around to the north and had reached, and were attacking, the marine supply base at the mouth of the Cua Viet River. If their attack was successful, they could hit us at Mai Xai Ti from both sides. We would be doomed, and the NVA would have the Cua Viet River back.

As we moved eastward through the dark on the bumpy dirt road, we heard the continuous roar of rifle fire and the occasional boom of a cannon being fired at close range. If the North Vietnamese were taking our supply base, they were paying a heavy price!

As always, terror crept into us as we neared the fighting.

We didn't know what we would find. I wondered what we would do if we found the supply base wiped out. But sounds of the fighting indicated that the marines were at least holding their own. As the minutes went by, it became obvious that the M-16 fire was growing heavier, whereas the AK-47 fire was growing weaker. The marines were winning! The enemy would eventually learn that attacking a fortified position manned by United States Marines exacted a heavy price.

Traveling in the amtracs instead of walking was faster but still was pretty slow on the bumpy road. It had just become full daylight when we reached the gate of the supply depot.

The depot and rear area at the mouth of the Cua Viet River was typical of a marine emplacement in hostile territory. The outside lines were barricaded with a wall of sandbags, ammo boxes, and logs. There were observation towers at the corners and at regular intervals around the site. The land for about one hundred yards around the walls was clear of all vegetation and was laced with four rows of barbed wire. Cans were tied on the wire so that any movement of the wire would make a noise. Most of the observation towers had M-60 machine guns, and all had sentries armed with LAWs, grenade launchers, and rifles. This was a formidable emplacement. The wall stretched around the rear echelon and supply depot at the mouth of the Cua Viet River and thus controlled the supply route to Dong Ha and Khe Sanh. This was where our artillery battery was located, where our supplies were landed, and where any replacements, if we ever got any, would first land.

Marine guards manned the fortress walls, and sailors usually handled the supplies. If the NVA ever overran this position, our ass, needless to say, would be in a sling.

A grisly sight met our eyes on arriving. The haze of rifle smoke hung over the compound like a fog. Marine and navy supply personnel peered over the fortifications, their faces black from smoke and their eyes like tired, glowing embers. I had seen those eyes before.

I couldn't keep from comparing what I saw with movies I had seen of the old West. It looked like a frontier fort after the cavalry had been attacked by Indians. I swear I expected to see arrows sticking out of some parts of the fortifications.

The attack had started about 2:30 A.M., and after two hours of hard fighting, the NVA had been beaten off. The enemy had never made it through the wire. We saw enemy dead all around the compound, many of them hanging in the wire in various postures of death.

When we arrived, the defenders were just beginning to come out from behind their fortifications. One of the first things we saw was a dead North Vietnamese officer propped up at attention, his right hand tied in a salute to the American flag. The men in our convoy broke into loud cheering when they saw this. We gave thumbs-up to the defenders, and they greeted us with cheers and applause. I saw tears in many eyes. It had been a tough night for them.

Once inside the compound, I headed for the artillery battery. The men there were exhausted and pale. I found the first sergeant. He was busily trying to get some tired and shaken gunners to get one of the 105-mm howitzers back in position. Once he had time, the sergeant gave me details about what had happened.

Between two and two-thirty the North Vietnamese had made their first probe at the marine lines. A marine had spotted a sapper trying to get through the wire. After verifying that no friendly troops were in the area, the sentry opened fire. Reports of movement in the barbed wire started coming in from all around the compound. Then all hell broke loose.

The sergeant said that the men remained calm. After the attack recently on K Company, they had been expecting a night attack. Everyone slept with weapons and ammo ready, and all rushed to the wall to help in its defense. Since everyone knew a North Vietnamese would kill a man trying to surrender as quickly as he would one attacking him, everyone was more than willing to fight.

As marines and sailors, some armed with old Springfield rifles, rushed to the wall, the M-60 machine guns in the towers laced the barbed wire with death. Flares went up all around. The North Vietnamese were all around the compound, thick as ants. The barbed wire, the terrible M-60 machine-gun fire, and the flares seemed to make them hesitate and slow down for a moment. They had not expected to be discovered until they were through the wire. They paid a terrible price for their moment of confusion. For a moment it was a turkey shoot as marine gunners exacted a heavy toll on the NVA.

The NVA withdrew from the wire into the surrounding darkness, into typical South Vietnamese terrain: plenty of places for concealment in sand dunes, bamboo and scrub pine thickets, and rice paddies. For a short time the NVA kept their distance while pouring rifle fire, mortar rounds, and occasionally an RPG round into the compound.

As I listened, I thought that the NVA had to have had at least a thousand men to surround the entire compound except for the side that bordered the South China Sea. This says a lot about their ability to move large numbers of troops swiftly and quietly.

After about twenty minutes, the NVA troops launched a full-scale human-wave assault. The fighting was furious. Even with light from the flares, the enemy was hard to see, but they were taking heavy casualties. Still the enemy pressed on, many taking cover behind bodies of dead comrades. I could identify with how they felt. I am sure that all we marines knew how the North Vietnamese felt terror as they charged into machine-gun fire. We had all done it.

After some of the enemy got through the barbed wire and hand-to-hand fighting was taking place, the first sergeant had ordered two 105-mm howitzers loaded with antipersonnel shot brought to the lines. These shells shot something like a load of buckshot from a shotgun and were very effective against ground personnel. A dark look came over his face as the first sergeant described the firing into charging NVA with the cannons. Although he was as tough as nails, he had not enjoyed the slaughter. The howitzers, though unwieldy and clumsy against a ground attack, had helped stop the NVA attack. The sergeant said it had been like firing a shotgun into a bunch of baby chicks.

On a battlefield like those in Vietnam, a coward dies as quickly as a brave man. If a person is a pilot or a high-ranking officer, he can probably surrender by throwing his arms up. As a prisoner, he might be mistreated, but eventually he will be exchanged and end up a war hero. But if an enlisted man tries to surrender, he will be shot on the spot. And so enlisted ground troops learn that they might as well keep fighting until they die. The niceties of war are reserved for fly-boys and higher ranking officers. For the enlisted ground pounders, it is kill or be killed, and let God sort out the good from the bad.

Eventually the NVA leaders realized that their attempt to gain control of the compound was futile, and just as daylight was about to break, they had begun a slow and painful withdrawal, taking with them as many of their dead and wounded as they could. They had been gone for only about twenty-five minutes when we arrived. Except for the crazy sailor who had run out and propped the NVA officer into a permanent salute to the American flag, the troops had remained wary and invisible.

Members of L Company manned the lines of the supply compound while the defenders got some much-needed rest. As we manned the lines, I thought about our having ridden in amtrac from Mai Xai Ti east. Evidently marines and Seabees had opened the dirt road that ran along the northern bank of the Cua Viet River while we were securing our hold on the river. It was much safer to deliver our supplies to Mai Xai Ti by amtrac than by helicopter.

Well, we didn't even get a regular meal! I found out that even in rear areas, men were surviving on C rations, and no one got a cooked meal. Anyway, we didn't stay around long enough for one. Before dark we were back on amtrac heading out to the boonies. The picnic was over. Later I heard that the NVA had left behind over two hundred dead. We still controlled the river, but we were having to work to do so.

31

More Endurance

WE ARRIVED BACK AT MAI XAI TI EXHAUSTED, TO FIND THE men left behind nervous and worried. We were getting shorter and shorter on manpower, and evidently we would get no more men from the rear. They needed all they could get. To this day I can't figure out why we couldn't get any fresh troops. The real estate we held was vital, and if we lost it, the whole effort of the United States in northern Quangtri Province was doomed.

I know it takes time to train new troops, but look at all the reserve units that had taken government money for years. Why wouldn't the president activate them? And how about the National Guard? At the time I knew nothing about politics, I only knew we needed help! But fresh troops never came.

By this time I had discarded the battle dressing the corpsman had put on the boil on my neck and was applying fresh battle dressings when I could get one every day or two. I also was using a tube of antiseptic salve that a different corpsman had given me. My neck was still stiff and the boil was still an open sore the size of a silver dollar, but the killing infection did not return.

The monsoon rains were constant. Everything was soaked, and everybody was miserable. We lived like rats. We stayed in holes and never exposed ourselves to enemy fire from across the river. Artillery came in every day; the NVA knew our location, so all they had to do was to set the coordinates on their guns and fire away. They couldn't pinpoint the artillery right on our lines, but they could keep it in the town, and that was enough. The 61-mm mortar fire

171

was picking up. The NVA must have gotten some new mortars and ammunition from the north, and they began blowing the hell out of us.

I was constantly on the go. Being the only forward observer left, I was constantly calling in artillery fire to silence the mortars or try to kill a sniper as he scurried back to his bunker. It was either constant artillery missions, or trying to pinpoint NVA artillery to the north. There was no rest.

The men, gaunt and hollow-eyed, were becoming more like zombies every day. The constant pounding and lack of rest took its toll on them. Arguments broke out over nothing. Things were said by men who were friends that never should have been said and never would have been said under any other circumstances. They were at one another's throats. Things looked hopeless. The captain, other officers, and staff sergeants, were doing all they could to keep our hopes up and to keep us together. Morale sank to its lowest point since I had been in Vietnam.

Still, in the late afternoon we could see supplies go up the river. We knew we had to hold the river, but we also knew that soon, if we kept taking casualties, none of us would be left to do anything.

One day I remember well. The rain was falling, and we had just dragged a crying, wounded young man to be medevacked. As usual, we were wet and miserable. And as usual, the captain was helping us. We had taken heavy artillery fire that morning, the heaviest since we had returned from relieving the supply depot. Our air power was still next to useless.

As we were getting back to our bunkers, we looked around as if seeing things for the first time. The desolation and death hit us like a ton of bricks. We seemed to be standing in our own graveyard.

"Captain, we can't stay here any longer. They're blowin' us apart," one of the men said.

"We got to have some relief, Captain," another said.

"If they attack us now, we're gone."

"We couldn't stop a platoon of Cub Scouts."

"Can't anybody do anything about those guns to the north?"

"Do something, Captain!"

This was the first time that Captain Hempel had heard the men complain. They weren't really complaints, just statements of fact. Somebody had to do something. We were sitting here getting blown apart, and there was nothing we could do.

As the captain looked at us, his face darkened. He had made a decision. He didn't say a word, he just headed for the Battalion Command Post. Then 61-mm mortars started coming in, and we rushed to our bunkers. I had no more time to think of the captain as I called in artillery to silence the mortars. None of us were making future plans.

32

Back to the Rear

THE NEXT DAY, FIRING FROM BOTH SIDES WAS MUCH THE same, but something new was in the air. While keeping hidden from the NVA, marines were moving about, excited. Word was out that we were moving. Where? Nobody had any idea, that is, nobody except the officers and noncoms. Enlisted men asking, at any time, where they were going were always given the same old answer: You'll know when you get there.

K Company arrived from the north. Now I knew for sure we were leaving. A marine company in Vietnam could always be ready to move in minutes. It was just a matter of getting a poncho rolled up, being sure you had all your gear, and putting a few mementos, such as a skull, a couple of ears, or a bloody cartridge belt into a sack. When you have no personal possessions, even the most trivial or bizarre object can be very important to you.

Headquarters Platoon was ready to go when the captain came around, looking pretty sad but determined.

"Where are we going, Captain?" I asked.

"For a rest" was his answer.

We men looked at one another blankly, feeling neither elation nor sorrow. By now we certainly did not expect a break. We just automatically went where we were told to.

Just then the NVA greatly increased their fire. The captain grinned. This was his element. Our M-16s answered their AK-47s, and I had our 105-mm howitzers answering their heavy artillery.

Noticing the captain staring toward the Cua Viet River, I followed his gaze and could not believe what I saw: a flotilla of the light amphibious tanks used by the Marine Corps to transport troops. It was beginning to penetrate my brain that we actually were leaving. We were evacuating!

When the vehicles came ashore and marines started getting aboard, I had mixed feelings. We had to get out. There was no doubt that we had to have a rest, but somehow I hated to leave. It just did not seem right. We had paid such a high price for this town, and the thought of just letting the enemy reoccupy it was hard to take.

And I had gotten used to living here. It is odd how a person can become adapted to any type of existence, and when change threatens, he is afraid. He has become a part of that existence, and so the hell that we had been living in was normal. The town was our home.

As it turned out, both the colonel and the captain knew the men were at the breaking point, a point where they could no longer be effective fighting machines. There was no choice: they had to have a rest. They came up with the idea of taking us to the rear for a couple of days to rest before we went back to combat.

The flotilla of vehicles had landed at the southeastern edge of the town, out of sight of the NVA forces. We hoped that we would be gone before the enemy knew what was happening and be back before they could set up effective defenses against an attack.

I was awed at seeing the amphibious vessels start down the river, full of marines on the inside and covered with marines on the top. The men, as always, were fully armed, looked haggard and exhausted, and had dark faces and cold eyes. The only thing clean about them were their rifles, which were spotless. The eighteen- and nineteen-year-olds had lost all their youth on the battlefields. As I looked at the men, I felt very proud and fortunate to be a part of a group that had helped so much to keep a supply route open. I knew our part in the overall effort was important. We had been, and we were, contributing.

By now I didn't want to leave. I was enveloped by the destruction. I was part of this. The artillery was mine, and I wouldn't leave it. I suppose I was mad. Anyway, I was numb. Things were again in slow motion. The artillery was beautiful.

I was thinking like this and keeping the artillery coming in when I noticed that O.E. and I were the only ones left. Just then the captain ran up and grabbed me by the arm.

"Come on, Mac," he said. "Let's go."

I heard him from a distance. Most of the vehicles were already far from shore, but one was waiting for us.

I held back. The captain tugged on my arm.

"Dammit, Mac. Let's go!" He spoke as if he meant it.

O.E. was looking at me with his "You're crazier than hell" look.

I still couldn't snap out of it. The captain pulled me all the way to the waiting vehicle. Like a drunkard I got on and, half-dazed, watched the town recede from sight.

The NVA were still pounding the town. We got a kick out of that. It was a beautiful sight. Then I started laughing. O.E. started laughing. The captain started laughing. As the town rapidly disappeared from sight, we hurled curses upon Ho Chi Minh's heritage and laughed all the way to the rear.

As the grunts entered the rear compound, they sought shelter where they could find it, Some shared bunkers with rear-echelon personnel, and some just found a hole big enough to lie down in. Rest was in the offing, and rest was what was welcome. No one bothered to undress, take a shower, or do anything else: we just dropped, exhausted, where we could.

The next day we were up early. We from Mai Xai Ti, as impossible as it may seem, felt refreshed and ready to go. A hot breakfast would start us off right. Well, we had a hot breakfast—C rations! The compound had no regular food and no beer. But we had plenty of C rations, and we really enjoyed them.

Discipline was lax. We wandered pretty much where we pleased, and neither the officers nor noncoms harassed us in any way. They needed a rest, too. We renewed acquaintances and swapped stories with old friends. It was the best of times, but it was short-lived.

In late afternoon we were lounging around, eating extra C rations, cleaning rifles, and getting ready for another good night's sleep when hell broke loose. The first artillery round did not hit close to me, but I suppose I looked as shocked as the man next to me did. Some yelled, "Incoming!" Those who had available covers scrambled for them. We who had none just flattened out where we were and hoped no round would hit on top of us.

It had not taken the NVA long to figure out where we had gone, and even less time to figure out where we were. And they no doubt knew that this rear compound was crowded.

They hit us with everything they had: heavy artillery mixed with mortar and recoilless rifle fire. It was the worst bombardment that any of us could remember. Screams and moans came from the dying and the wounded. There was nothing we could do: to stand, much less to move around, would be suicide.

The bombardment seemed to last forever, and it was getting dark before the shelling stopped. By then the compound was in a shambles. I looked around. Everyone able to was helping the wounded, fighting fires, or gathering up the dead. A heavy black cloud of smoke came from near the South China Sea; the main fuel dump had caught fire and was lost. Many were trying to keep the fire from spreading. The total casualties—thirty-four killed or wounded. A terrible loss. But we were lucky there were not more.

Those of us who had been outside bunkers were dazed and were useless until we got our heads back together, but finally we were able to help also.

The physical damage was great, but the most terrible effect of the bombardment was the effect it had on the men. It was a terrible shock just to have our manpower further depleted, but the loss of buddies and seeing the suffering of the wounded made all other losses seem small. Among those killed was that corpsman who had bandaged my hand recently. One of the artillery shells had landed almost on top of him. His body was not torn in any way, but the shock of the explosion had killed him. I just could not believe it. He had been one of those who could not be killed. But he was dead. Familiar faces were becoming scarce indeed.

Although the bombardment had been a psychological success in one way, in another it hurt the enemy more than it did us. They had spurred the marines to leave the compound. The marines, of course, would attack. Colonel Mac was not about to sit back and let himself be killed while he was trying to rest. If he and his men were going to die, they would die attacking, not like rats in a hole. In addition, we had a better chance outside the compound because we could attack and destroy the artillery's forward observers. We really had no choice. Despite not having enough men to mount an effective offensive, the colonel was getting ready to run another bluff. We would see whether it would be successful, or if we would die trying to carry it out.

33

Back to the West

THAT NIGHT CAPTAIN HEMPEL HELD A MEETING AND TOLD us about what had happened that day and what we were going to do next. When the supply boats had tried to go up the Cua Viet River that afternoon, they had been met with highly accurate recoilless rifle fire. One boat had been damaged, and the others had followed it back to the base. The river was closed to our traffic.

Military intelligence and recon reports told that the NVA had sent a forward observer team, which had called in the heavy artillery on the compound that we were now in. The mortars and recoilless rifles that had hit us had to be close by, but there was no sign that the NVA were refortifying the villages we had taken earlier. We knew the enemy had moved back into the villages, but did not know with what force nor how determined they were to hold them. Colonel McCown had decided to move before daylight next day before the NVA had time to refortify them.

L Company would be the point company. I was, as usual, scared shitless. Our ranks were so decimated that the odds were terribly against us. I could picture the horrible battles ahead, and I could not see how we could keep from being slaughtered.

The colonel was both a good field commander and a gambler. He felt sure the NVA did not know how weak we were. If they had known, they would have overrun us long ago at Mai Xai Ti east. Also, the colonel remembered, and he gambled the enemy remembered, that every time they had stood up and fought, the marines had destroyed them. He was gambling that the NVA would think it suicide to stand and fight, and would run before having a solid contact with us. Our lives and the lifeline of the power of the United States in Quangtri Province depended on the colonel's bluff paying off.

Before daylight the next day, we moved out of the compound. I was half-asleep and expected to be fired upon as soon as we left. Happily, I was wrong. As the morning wore on, the day seemed brighter than usual even though the rain was still falling. It was as quiet as a graveyard except for the sound of falling rain. The marines moved like jungle animals, silently and almost invisible, among the bamboo thickets and scrub brush.

It was eerie, like being on the moon or on another planet. The men were so played out that they wasted no breath on conversation. Nothing seemed real in the silence.

About midmorning we came across the ruins of the first village. Not an animal or person moved, but we knew the

NVA were there. Grunts spread out into assault lines as we moved across the rice paddies into the village. The rain had eased off, and for a minute the clouds cleared up. Visibility was good.

This was no surprise attack: we wanted the NVA to see us coming. Their commanders must have been having some anxious moments. Were they seeing just an advance patrol that had a large force ready to launch a full-scale attack? They had to decide whether to open fire with their machine guns and try to hold the village or retreat to their main force.

Colonel McCown was counting on their retreating. We men just hoped they would. When we crossed the rice paddies and entered the village unopposed, it was unbelievable. The adrenaline started to flow, and all our senses heightened.

Then we heard the sharp crack of an AK-47. The captain and his radioman, and O.E. and I, rushed to the front line of grunts. We froze behind a large bunker, slightly ahead of the grunts. The marines had disappeared into whatever cover was available, prepared for a firefight.

We soon realized the main body of NVA troops had fled, leaving behind a few men to slow our progress. After a brief fight, the rest of the enemy disappeared, though we tried our best to trap them. One thing the Vietnamese were good at: disappearing. The colonel's bluff had worked.

We camped for the night in the village, keeping the artillery on the alert and the countryside lit up with flares. But no counterattack came.

The next village was more or less a repeat. After a brief firefight, the North Vietnamese fled. The colonel's bluff had worked again.

As we prepared to spend the night in this village, the rain became a downpour which lasted all night and into the next day. We kept guards posted at all times, but there was no enemy movement. Maybe the NVA were just as content as we were to stay put for the moment.

Everything was soaked. Since all grass huts had been destroyed, we just crawled under our ponchos, cleaned our rifles, ate cold C rations, and rested.

Because I was the last forward observer around and because I might be killed at any time, I gave most of the platoon sergeants and any grunt who would listen crash courses on calling in artillery fire.

The men were becoming ever more exhausted and morale was low, but the night of rest helped. About noon the rain let up. We got our weapons ready, and some men even managed to dry a pair of socks. We knew the colonel would not stay put long. That was not his style.

34

The Second Assault on Mai Xai Ti East

I HAD A PAIR OF SOCKS HANGING UP TO DRY AND WAS EATING cold C rations when the captain came up.

"Mac," he said, "we're sending a platoon-sized patrol probe to Mai Xai Ti. I want you to go with it."

"Yes, sir," I replied, and got my gear ready. In fifteen minutes O.E. and I had joined First Platoon and were heading west. The colonel must have gotten some intelligence about to Mai Xai Ti and was sending us to check it out.

The platoon sergeant was the same one who had led the patrol north from Mai Xai Ti east earlier. He was thin, tough as a briar, and was "old Marine Corps" all the way. He did not like headquarters personnel, especially one who seemed to be the captain's favorite.

He eased up to me while we were moving out and said in a drill instructor's voice, "Okay, hotshot, we may see what you've got now." I didn't say anything. I just looked straight ahead and kept walking.

After humping for several miles over slick and muddy

ground, we drew near Mai Xai Ti. We concealed ourselves behind bamboo, scrub brush, and paddy dikes. The sergeant had his three squads of ten men each spread out into an assault line. O.E. and I were left to our own resources to keep just behind the grunts. When the time came to call in the artillery, we would be ready.

While we were waiting, I half imagined the sergeant would have liked to see me fall behind or get lost and killed. I was convinced that he just plain hated me and that perhaps he was a little jealous. I had no particular feelings toward him, but thought he must be an excellent platoon sergeant. Anyway, I was not about to try to be a hero just to prove myself to him. I knew that when I called artillery in, it would hit exactly where I wanted it to.

We got through the rice paddies and to the edge of the town without being fired upon. We were beginning to wonder whether the town was occupied when the enemy sprang a trap. AK-47s opened fire on our front lines, and a heavy artillery adjustment round fell about two hundred yards north of us. Luckily we had kept ourselves pretty well invisible, and the attack was no more than we had expected.

The NVA game had been to let us get across the rice paddy, and then when we tried to retreat, to mow us down in the open rice paddy, our only means of escape. Already we had two men wounded, one too seriously to walk.

Another artillery round hit, this time close to us. We were about to get panicky. The next round would be on top of us, and when we tried to cross the rice paddies, machine-gun fire would mow us down.

I immediately called for a fire-for-effect, and eighteen rounds of high explosives hit right on target. I kept the artillery coming in, and then another enemy round hit so close to us that we were nearly deafened. Their next round would get us for sure. The sergeant and I looked at each other.

"The shit is going to hit the fan soon!" I shouted. "Get your men the hell out of here!" He nodded.

Our artillery had thrown the NVA into momentary confusion, and before they could reorient themselves, the sergeant started his retreat, but not before another man was wounded. With help, two of the wounded could walk, but the third had to be carried. It was slow going.

O.E. and I stayed with the last marines until they moved away. As usual, the men showed a great deal of gallantry and courage and finally were out of the rice paddies and into the bamboo and pine thickets. But O.E. and I were crouched behind a paddy dike keeping the artillery on target, adjusting it as necessary. On looking across the paddies, I realized we were alone.

The NVA supplemented their small-arms fire with 61-mm mortars and kept firing in the direction of the retreating men.

We kept the artillery coming in, and I was thinking that O.E. and I were goners. We were alone, and once we became visible, all the enemy fire would be directed at us. Then I heard someone shouting. It was the sergeant standing at the edge of the underbrush and waving for us to come on. O.E. and I looked at each other.

"You ready?" I asked.

He nodded, and we took off like halfbacks bursting through a hole in the line in a football game, zigzagging across the paddy field while small-arms fire hit all around us. Then, like magic, we were in the bamboo thicket, and once again both O.E. and I had not gotten an expected bullet in the back.

After giving us a second to get our breath, the sergeant said, "Come on."

The sergeant, O.E., and I were the last to leave the area, and I kept the artillery coming in as we retreated. We laughed as the NVA mortars destroyed a grass hut they had built in an attempt to lure us into it so that they would have easy prey for their mortars. We knew that North Vietnamese trick and so had avoided the hut.

As we struggled back to our command post, no one said a word. O.E. and I brought up the rear, ready to call the artillery in at the slightest hint that we were being followed.

We made it back in drizzling rain, and the sergeant went immediately to report to the captain and to call in medevac choppers for the wounded. As he passed me, he said, "You did a helluva job, Mac!"

I couldn't believe what I was hearing. The sergeant who

hated all headquarters personnel, especially me, had paid me a sincere compliment. Did I appreciate it? I walked on air the rest of the afternoon and slept well that night. A compliment from a staff sergeant in the Marine Corps is a rare and important event.

The next day the captain told us we were going to attack Mai Xai Ti east. No! I couldn't believe it. The men could barely walk and yet they were expected to attack a fortified village. The captain himself was excited at the prospect and tried to encourage us. In addition to artillery fire, we would have two tanks for backup. Too, the attack would be a surprise to the NVA. They surely would not expect us to attack again so soon after they had reoccupied the town. I saw a glint of doubt in the captain's eyes, just a glint. I had served with the captain for a long time now and knew him well. He was a marine through and through, and regardless of any doubt he might have, he would march through hell if orders came for him to do so. Now, we who knew him realized he thought we could not regain Mai Xai Ti east. But he would die, if need be, trying.

The awful truth was that tomorrow we would all be lying dead in a rice paddy. It had been all we could do to take the town the first time, and then we had a much greater force and were much fresher. But we would go and we would die, if necessary. That is why they call us marines.

Long before dawn we were moving out, not marching but just shuffling and staggering. Nobody said much, everyone being absorbed in his own thoughts. Just before daylight we could make out the outline of Mai Xai Ti east. There was a mist; even so, the day looked brighter than usual.

As I glanced at the gaunt, drawn faces around me, I thought of a picture I had once seen in a history book of the remnants of Lee's Army of Northern Virginia just before their surrender in 1865. The artist had captured the look perfectly. The men were worn-out and defeated. There was a dullness in their eyes just like that in the eyes of these marines, and their faces were drawn and hollow-eyed just like ours were. But we hadn't complained, and like Lee's army, we would die for our country with no questions asked.

My admiration for my comrades cannot be expressed in words. They all knew what they were facing, and all were willing to die. As for me, I was filled with dread. O.E. and I would be going in just behind the grunts, directing artillery support, and our radio would be like a red flag drawing enemy fire. Somehow I controlled my shaking and got in place as we lined up for the assault.

This was not a village we were about to attack, it was a small city with permanent buildings, and it covered a much wider area than the villages we had captured. As we lined up for the assault, we felt like sitting ducks in a shooting gallery. Even the staff sergeants were grim and subdued.

Daylight came, and the NVA could see us coming. If they chose to fight, we simply did not have the strength to win. But the colonel was still pushing his bluff.

I called in the first artillery barrage. Soon the thin line of ragged scarecrows moved forward across the rice paddies toward the exploding artillery, their faces grim and pale. They walked upright, stiff and tired, too tired to run and try to find cover. They were zombies.

When we got within one hundred yards of the town, I stopped the artillery to avoid the chance of the shrapnel hitting our own men. O.E. and I now joined the grunts in the infantry line. Then the machine guns started.

The marines dropped to the ground by reflex action and started firing back. The enemy fire had spurred them to action. They kept low, firing their M-16s as they moved forward. They moved forward, but not with the zip they usually displayed. They had the skills and the knowledge, but the energy was gone. Their movements were just a little slow and jerky.

The machine-gun fire was intense. Once again I saw rice paddies dotted with fallen marines. But there was little screaming and moaning from the wounded. I guess they were so tired that they just died or suffered their wounds in silence.

Somehow, through countless individual charges and acts of heroism, the marines made it into the village. The machine-gun and AK-47 fire was like a swarm of hornets around us. Eventually they fought their way to a trench halfway through the town, and there they were stopped.

This was a long, shallow trench that ran almost the length of the town. It had been built by the North Vietnamese as a line of defense against the marines and was about two feet deep and wide enough for a man to crouch in.

O.E. and I dropped into that ditch with the grunts. The machine-gun and AK-47 fire whizzed overhead and thudded into the ground in front of us. I looked at the grunts, at their dead, listless eyes. There was no fight left. I tried to encourage some of the men to go over the top of the ditch and attack.

"Come on. Let's go. If we stay here, we're dead! I'll go first if you'll follow. We've got to attack!" I yelled.

The captain crawled along the trench trying to encourage the men to assault, but they just looked at him with lifeless eyes. Finally, maybe to shut me up, a veteran squad leader turned to me.

"Dammit," he said, "if we attack now, we're dead. The men are worn-out. The gooks have got the range for their machine guns, and you know they've got more men than we have. It's suicide to attack them. Go on if you want to, but you won't last ten seconds."

"Well, what the hell are we gonna do?"

The squad leader looked around, a fatalistic look in his eyes. "Hell," he answered, "call in artillery on us. Blow the hell out of them and us, too. We're gonna die anyhow."

I slowly made my way over to O.E. The squad leader was right. Our only chance was to call the artillery in on ourselves and hope more of the enemy would be killed than we were. Then we possibly could retreat during the confusion. What I didn't know was that retreat was not in Colonel Mac's plans, and he was calling the shots.

I hesitated, knowing I would be court-martialed if I called the artillery in, but I decided, "What the hell? I'll never live to worry about it."

Just as I was about to call, I heard shouting to our south. I turned and saw an awesome sight. One of the tanks that the captain had promised for support had made it to the village. It was moving forward like a juggernaut, its cannon firing point-blank into the North Vietnamese positions, and the M-60 machine guns firing a steady stream of fire at the enemy.

Standing on top of the tank was a grizzled staff sergeant with a handlebar mustache. He was known by most of the men. He was a blood-and-guts career marine who had seldom left a bar without at least one good fistfight in progress. He was waving a .45-caliber pistol in one hand and yelling encouragement to the grunts.

"Come on, jarheads," he screamed. "Out of the ditches! Move forward. You're dead if you stay here. By God, move!"

The marines hesitated.

Enemy small-arms fire converged on the tank, and at least one RPG rocket round exploded close to it. But the M-60 gunner on the tank kept the NVA from taking careful aim.

The tank pulled up to the ditch and hesitated, for to plow into the enemy positions without infantry support was suicide. The infantry kept the NVA from climbing all over the tank and dropping grenades in the turret. Without the infantry, the tank would be doomed.

The staff sergeant kept screaming for us to charge, but the men seemed not to have another charge left in them. They had fought all up and down this river, lived on C rations, had had no rest, and no relief. They were beaten. They had given all they could give.

The tank sat there a split second. The M-60 machine gunner was hit, and he slumped forward and was pulled back into the tank. Then a bullet hit the staff sergeant. He paled and slumped behind the turret. He kept screaming, weakly: "Come on, boys, attack! Don't die like dogs. Move out!"

Then something happened. About twenty feet to the north of me, a single marine, one of the newer men whom I didn't recognize, stood up with a look of terror on his face, fixed his bayonet, and shuffled forward. Then another marine followed. Then with one impulse, all the marines on the line charged. I was carried away in the momentum, fixed my bayonet, and charged too.

It was incredible. The men had no strength, they were worn-out and beaten, but they came out of the ditch like zombies, each certain he would die, fixed their bayonets, and stumbled forward. The tank slowly moved forward.

The staff sergeant was still shouting weakly. "That's it, boys, kill 'em. We got the little bastards now."

The battle was brief. The bluff had worked. When the marines came out of the ditch, the NVA panicked and fled. It seemed that no matter how many marines they killed, the marines kept coming. Had they known how tired we were, how few men we had, the North Vietnamese could have learned that under certain conditions, the marines were not invincible. The colonel's bluff was beautiful.

Not many North Vietnamese were killed, but we suffered several casualties. When I came out of the ditch, I stayed with the assault line. I kept firing from the hip and moving forward, still expecting to be shot any second. It was incredible! Small-arms fire was everywhere, we kept firing, and I didn't see a thing to shoot at.

My rifle barrel got so hot, I could barely touch it, and I was running low on ammunition. Exhausted, I dropped behind an NVA bunker for protection, numb with fear. I didn't even realize the enemy was gone, but was expecting one of them to kill me instantly. The captain came toward me, smiling. He walked hunched over and low to the ground, the normal way of walking in Mai Xai Ti east.

"Well, Mac," he laughed, "looks like we did it again."

I looked at him dumbly. It was as if I were looking through a television screen. I nodded numbly and tried to sit up, but I was shaking too badly. He grasped my shoulder with his right hand and shook me.

"You'll be okay, Mac," he reassured me.

I finally got enough nerve to sit up. I watched in a stupor as dead and wounded marines were carried toward the eastern part of the town, probably to be loaded on trucks since the road was now open to our rear supply base and because helicopters always drew so much fire.

Still trembling, I got to my feet and started helping with the dead and wounded. One of the tanks had hit a mine, killing all aboard. Luckily for us, one tank had made it through. After we had helped with the dead and wounded, O.E. and I found our old home in the ditch and immediately fell asleep.

It had been another victory for the marines, but at a high price. The river again belonged to us.

35

Replacements

THE NEXT DAY WE HAD THE SAME LOW CLOUDS, THE SAME steady rain, and both the NVA and the marines seemed content to fire just enough to keep each other honest. But as the day wore on, excitement grew in our encampment. Keeping out of sight of the enemy, our troops started moving about. Then the news was out: A six-man team of marine recons was on the site.

What the hell do we need with recons? was my first thought. Why didn't they send us six grunts instead? The grunts were desperately needed.

That night I was called over to the Battalion Command Post to go over maps with the leader of the recons, to give him the target numbers and locations of the fire missions already plotted in case his team was discovered and they needed help to escape. He was an unusually nice person and was courteous to all. He seemed to think I was an authority about the terrain on the other side of the small river, and I guess I did know as much as anyone else in our battalion did about it.

I wished him luck, but at the same time was resentful. Why waste money and effort for a dangerous mission that would reveal nothing we didn't already know? I had a hell of a time staying awake to be alert in case artillery was needed. I lit a cigarette, but since I don't smoke, I couldn't inhale, and then I used the cigarette to burn my wrists and hands to try to stay awake. I got coffee but spilled it all over myself. I was just too tired to get the cup to my lips. At different times the captain came by and shook me awake.

Anyway, the mission was successfully completed, and guess what was found out that we did not already know? Nothing!

The next morning the recon team moved out. Where they went and what their next mission was, nobody knew except the officers. Enlisted men were not given such information.

The rain tapered off and visibility improved. The NVA engaged in their usual small-arms fire, and at any time we expected the artillery and mortars to come in.

But something was up. Again there was a feeling of excitement. Officers and noncoms continued having meetings. Then we heard many trucks and helicopters coming in from the east. Supplies, we all thought, and remained in our holes. Working parties would be assigned to handle the supplies, and we saw no use in exposing ourselves.

Soon we heard a lot of commotion and noise as if a herd of cattle were coming down Main Street. The grunts peeped out of bunkers, and I did also. I couldn't believe it! It couldn't be true! Replacements had arrived! Beautiful!

They wore new jungle fatigues, new jungle boots, fresh haircuts, were clean and freshly shaved. Some even had Stateside fat on their bodies. God, they were huge! Any one of them would have weighed more than any two of us. They had the full necks and broad shoulders developed in boot camp. They looked as fresh as daisies.

To me they looked both clumsy and slow, for they had not yet developed the catlike speed and the stealth necessary to survive in combat. Those who lived long enough would quickly get those qualities, and that Stateside fat would melt off like magic.

They kept coming, several hundred of them, until our depleted ranks were filled up to a formidable fighting force again.

We all stared out of our fighting holes as if we had never seen a fresh marine before. I can only imagine the horror these men felt as they came through the camp. Many or most had never seen a dead person except in a funeral home, and here they were passing NVA dead lying everywhere in various stages of rot. The worms and rats and insects had not completed their work yet. The stench that we no longer smelled must have been overpowering to them. Everywhere they saw destruction and desolation, destroyed buildings, splintered trees, mortar holes.

And what did they think and how did they feel when they saw us old-timers gawking wild-eyed at them from out of fighting holes and bunkers? That we were subhuman? If so, they were right. They certainly had to know that they were in a world of shit.

I admired their nerve to be able to walk into a hellhole like this without cracking up, and I wondered whether some of them were now regretting their choice to become marines. We were overjoyed to see them, of course. Our confidence rose, and our spirits breathed new life. Maybe we would get out of this place alive after all. Maybe with the new men, we would defeat the North Vietnamese, and the war would be over.

The new men were immediately assigned to infantry squads, and I overheard veteran squad leaders telling them what to do and what not to do if they wanted to stay alive. They would have to learn quickly. Mistakes were almost always fatal.

Before long everyone had disappeared into either a bunker or fighting hole, for enemy artillery started coming in. The NVA had sighted the choppers and had called the guns in. The new men would get a taste of real fear immediately.

In about an hour our planes were in the air and the artillery stopped.

That night I slept soundly even though I knew we would attack tomorrow. I had that old familiar feeling that tonight would be my last night on earth.

36

Attack on Mai Xai Ti West

LONG BEFORE DAYLIGHT WE WERE UP AND GETTING READY for the assault. Since it was supposed to be a surprise, there was no artillery preparation. M Company, K Company, and I Company were to do the assault. L Company, the one I was with, was to be held in reserve. Captain Hempel, of course, was disappointed, but I was relieved. I might survive.

The attack started before daylight. As the assault companies crossed the river in LVTs, there was sporadic firing from our M-16s and M-60s. I hadn't yet heard an AK-47 or Chi-Com machine gun. I felt uneasy. Was something wrong? This was too easy. They were not about to go away and leave a town they had held so long.

As the assault continued, our company became nervous. The waiting was tough. At the first hazy light of dawn, I sat down and tried to relax. "Hell," I thought, "they've left."

Just then small-arms fire, mixed with grenades, satchel charges, and RPGs, exploded and became a steady roar. Most of the small-arms fire came from AK-47s and Chi-Com machine guns.

The news came back to us by that invisible grapevine which exists in a combat zone that the NVA had waited until the marines had gotten inside the village and had caught them in a cross fire. The enemy knew about our replacements and had prepared for our attack. They had built camouflaged bunkers along their side of the riverbank with firing parapets pointing into the town and had surrounded the town with machine-gun bunkers and snipers. The trap was set.

By now the North Vietnamese knew that even in pre-dawn darkness, veteran marines would spot and destroy the camouflaged bunkers, but they were counting on our new men falling for their tactics. And they were right. Our replacements walked right by the camouflaged bunkers without even noticing them. Too late they realized that when assaulting a place occupied by the NVA, you throw a grenade into every hole and anything that faintly resembles a bunker. A few of the camouflaged bunkers were destroyed by veterans, but most were overlooked by the inexperienced newcomers.

When the marines had bypassed the bunkers and reached the center of town, the communists sprang their trap. Our men were caught in a brutal cross fire from which there seemed no escape. Radio messages said that K Company was hardest hit, and that M and I companies had found some cover and were trying to fight their way out.

Word came for L Company to get ready to move out. We would have to attack and try to break the NVA trap: that was the purpose of a reserve company.

As soon as word came for us to get ready, the captain, other officers, and staff noncoms started making last-minute checks on ammunition and weapons and giving last-minute instructions to the new men. They gave the squad leaders and platoon sergeants a general idea of the attack plan, and then we all waited for the word to move out.

As the assault troops boarded the tanks (amtracs), I tried to disguise myself as a rock or a palm tree. I tried to become invisible. I was terrified, and the thought of charging up a riverbank in broad daylight into NVA machine-gun fire didn't seem exactly appealing.

Before getting on the amtrac, the captain started looking around. "I'm forgetting something," he kept saying. "Something's not right."

I turned pale. I knew damn well what was coming.

The captain spotted me and broke into a big smile. "You better go with us, arty. I almost forgot you. It just wouldn't be right without you along."

O.E. and I were already ready. With a sinking feeling I

got on the amtrac with the captain. As the crew closed the huge door, I thought of a coffin closing. No wonder they called these vehicles floating coffins. As we crossed the river, no one said a word. The silence was like a roar. We all knew that when the doors opened, the only thing to do was to charge forward. God would choose who made it and who didn't.

We heard the small-arms fire getting louder and even heard enemy rounds striking the outer armor of the amtrac. We also heard the M-60 on top of the tank firing steadily and felt the tank leave the water. Everyone was so intense that he felt like being on coiled springs. I was wondering what it would be like to feel a bullet tear through me. I was certain I would find out within minutes.

When the front doors to the amtrac dropped, light burst into the tank like an exploding bomb. There was no time to think. We all rushed out into bullets hitting everywhere. A man beside me, a short, stocky marine who belonged to battalion headquarters and had been brought up to help the infantry in this assault, turned pale and dropped. There was no time to help him. We had to get away from the door of the amtrac before we all were killed.

The infantry quickly formed a skirmish line and charged up the riverbank so fast that they were on the enemy before the enemy knew what hit them. The vitality of the new replacements was what we had needed. I stayed with the captain as we worked our way up the bank, destroying every bunker and throwing a grenade into anything that faintly resembled a hole where a North Vietnamese could be hiding. The amtrac rolled right behind the men, keeping up a steady fire with its M-60 machine gun.

As we broke the NVA lines, the captain laughed. He was in his element. It was a rout. The North Vietnamese fled in panic. Whatever plans their commanders had had were gone now. The marines were in their element. They were on the attack and overrunning the enemy. At this they were supreme.

As we swept around the edge of town, the other three grunt companies launched an attack on the main enemy lines. The communist lines crumbled and the trap was broken. Now it was a turkey shoot. The grunts were like a pack of wolves after rabbits in the brush. The North Vietnamese dropped their weapons and fled in panic.

As the marines broke out of the trap and formed an assault line that ran the whole length of the town, the day brightened, giving the grunts a better field of vision with which to kill. It was as if God had finally come over to our side. Our troops swept swiftly to the northwest.

Looking through my binoculars, I saw scattered groups of terror-stricken North Vietnamese running and trying to hide. It was bedlam. I didn't join in the rabbit hunt. Although I could at that time kill a North Vietnamese and never bat an eye, I was not as bloodthirsty as many of the others. I looked around and noticed the slope littered with dead marines. Many other dead marines lay in the middle of town where the trap had been sprung. I couldn't blame the grunts for their rampage. The enemy had planned to kill every one of them; why should the marines show mercy?

I kept up with the assault lines, not to seek revenge, but just to see how everything turned out. I was walking up the main road, lined with palm trees and destroyed thatch houses. It seemed as if every bush had an enemy rifle or pack behind it. The area was becoming littered with North Vietnamese dead. There were shouts and small-arms fire ahead as the grunts kept moving forward, killing any enemy soldier who tried to fight or who lagged behind the full-scale flight of their fellows.

I slowed down, checking the extent to which the North Vietnamese had fortified the town. I checked out one large bunker that had been used as a field hospital. There were bunk beds on the walls. I saw the very latest in medical equipment: syringes, new battle dressings, IVs, bottles of antibiotics, and on and on. All made in the U.S.A.! There was even a magazine rack complete with the ever-present *Playboy*.

The medical supplies furnished by American sympathizers to the North Vietnamese were not used for civilians. They went straight to the North Vietnamese armed forces to be used against American troops.

There was a dead North Vietnamese in one of the bunk beds. Obviously the field hospital staff had left too fast to worry about their wounded. The dead man had a neat hole right between the eyes. The grunts knew now to take care of NVA wounded.

I left the bunker and caught up with our assault lines. As I moved up the wide main road, I heard something hit a tree near the road. I whirled and brought my M-16 to bear at the movement. Then I saw a familiar face. It was Private Binge from Kentucky! He had been Lieutenant Michaels's radioman. The last time I had talked with Binge, he had been bright and cheerful, more like a kid from back home than a soldier. I had not seen him since Lieutenant Michaels had been killed. I lowered my rifle and walked swiftly to him, a smile on my face. I was really happy to see him.

I was ready to laugh and talk over old times. Binge had been standing in the road throwing a K-bar into a large banana tree. From the way the tree bark was torn up, he must have been throwing the knife for half an hour or more. He had blood on his hands and in his hair, but he didn't seem wounded. His eyes were dull, listless, and his face cold and dark.

He ignored my greeting and continued to throw the K-bar. He would throw the knife about thirty feet, go pull it out of the tree, return to his spot, and throw again. He seemed in a trance.

I slowly eased up to him, calling his name. He just looked dully at me and kept throwing the knife. I was afraid he was wounded, so I got close enough to put my arm on his shoulder.

"What's the matter? You okay?" I asked.

I could smell the blood and death on him.

He jerked away. He wasn't physically wounded, but his eyes had a wild, faraway look in them.

"Fuck it! Just leave me alone," he answered.

Clearly he wasn't right. His rifle was leaned against a tree, and a marine never lays his rifle down in a combat area. He turned away from me and kept on throwing his K-bar. I didn't know what he had done that day, but whatever it was, it must have been wild, because the demons were working on him hard.

When I left, he was still throwing the knife into the tree and muttering curses. After that he was never the friendly, good-natured man he had been before that battle. He remained cold and distant and acted as if he was nursing a grudge. We were never friends again.

After leaving Binge, I caught up with the advancing infantry and got with the captain and staff sergeant and traveled with them. The grunts were moving so fast in trying to catch the NVA that I had a hard time keeping up. As we swept north, I entered several more bunkers, which were interesting in that they reflected the quality of life of the enemy. Rice, fish, and American canned goods were in abundance. There was plenty of ammunition and medical supplies also. I expected at any time to find an American color television set.

I did not see another live NVA soldier in that town. The grunts ahead of us were on a killing binge, and nothing ahead would survive except United States Marines. The grunts set fire to grass huts, and the scenery was changing quickly to one of death and desolation. As we swept north, I had the exhilarating feeling of total victory.

I realized that we must be a part of a huge marine offensive clearing the NVA units from around Dong Ha and Khe Sanh. It made me feel good to know we were doing our part.

As we moved northward, we broke into a near run. The thrill of victory and the adrenaline gave us energy. Nothing could stop us. The captain had a look of sheer joy on his face. He was tireless as he humped along behind the grunts. The staff sergeant, grim as usual, urged the men forward, but he never smiled. Like all marine staff sergeants, he was all business.

Through my binoculars I saw scattered groups of North Vietnamese running or trying to hide and heard scattered firing as grunts found or overtook them. I couldn't come close to guessing how many rifles or how much rice we found in bushes along the way, but there were more than enough rifles to outfit an army and more than enough rice to feed them.

We kept moving north for hours, and then a thought hit me. "Hell, we must be in North Vietnam!"

At one time we swept for an hour along a wide, sandy stretch of ground laced with bamboo thickets and stunted evergreens. Everything had gotten quiet. We were in another world. We were in North Vietnam! But the momentum of our pursuit didn't slow down, and we didn't intend to slow down.

For two more hours we swept northward. There was absolutely no one around. It was eerie. Then we came upon a slight rise in the land. It was a group of sand dunes ahead, with bamboo and pine thickets surrounding it. Warily the captain, staff sergeant, and I approached the dunes. The sight was awesome.

Surrounded by the dunes was the biggest single mass of NVA weapons I ever saw in Vietnam. There were hundreds of AK-47s in perfect condition. There were mortars, recoilless rifles, machine guns, and thousands of rounds of ammunition. There were even some vintage French carbines. This must have been a major supply depot for the NVA.

Fortified bunkers surrounded the dunes, but evidently the NVA forces occupying this fortress fled north with the remnants of the communist force that had been occupying Mai Xai Ti. I was happy they were gone, for this would have been a tough fortress to take.

L company occupied the sand dunes fortress. I was with the staff sergeant as we looked over the fortifications. Then he, several veteran squad leaders, and I walked to the top of one of the largest sand dunes. We found an NVA observation post complete with binoculars, maps, compasses and a field telephone. The sergeant got a gleam in his eye as he picked up the phone. It was still in service and had the underground lines running north, probably all the way to Hanoi. When he picked up the receiver, we heard a North Vietnamese voice jabbering excitedly on the line. I'll be damned! The staff sergeant smiled! The first time I had ever seen that. He put the handset to his ear and keyed the transmit button to talk. He laughed and said, in his North Carolina drawl, "You little sloe-eyed bastard, you tell your Uncle Ho Chi Minh that we just kicked his ass!"

We all burst out laughing. The good feeling I had at that moment has never been surpassed in my life. We cheered and kept laughing as the sergeant smashed the phone against an ammo box. I have wondered what the North Vietnamese on the other end of the line thought when he heard that North Carolina accent. I would say that he and other big shots in North Vietnam had to change their pants.

This was a complete victory. We thought we had won the war. We knew that after a long, hard struggle, we had secured the Cua Viet River indefinitely. We weren't very good with politics.

After setting up a defensive perimeter around the sand dunes, we started disposing of the weapons. There was a rumor that if a soldier put a tag on a weapon, he could take it home with him. But captured weapons were shipped to the rear, and normally they were destroyed, given to South Vietnamese units, sold on the black market back to the communists, or confiscated by rear-echelon personnel for war trophies. Since the staff sergeant had some tags, we all tagged about six rifles each with our names just in case we could keep one for a souvenir. We never saw the rifles again.

The captured weapons were loaded aboard helicopters and sent to the rear. Weapons and ammunitions not loaded were destroyed with plastic expolsives. It made a beautiful fireworks display that, I'm sure, cost Russia and China a pretty penny.

The helicopters brought orders to Captain Hempel and the other officers to withdraw south of the DMZ. Neither the captain nor the staff sergeants looked pleased.

At this moment the United States of America lost the Vietnam War. Had the marines been allowed to continue north, they could have captured Hanoi within a week and hanged Ho Chi Minh and General Giap on the main street of the city. We had already beaten the armies of North Vietnam and had already taken about all the casualties that we were going to take to insure our victory. (You always have to take a percentage of casualties against a fortified enemy to gain the advantage.) The rest of the conquest of North Vietnam would have been gravy. All we had to do was just move in against token resistance and take over. Once the civilian population saw their armies running in terror, they would have offered little resistance.

American generals have known for generations that you *cannot* defeat an enemy nation without invading that nation. That is why General Sherman marched through Georgia, that is why we occupied Germany and Japan at the end of World War II, that is why we invaded North Korea, and why we invaded Mexico in the Mexican War. Defeating a nation's army in the field is just not enough, especially if that field is not even on that nation's soil.

But the weakling politicians in Washington vacillated and worried, and became more and more confused. For years they couldn't make up their minds what they wanted. They did not want to lose, but neither did they want to win. So the golden opportunity was never taken advantage of.

The attitude of the men was very different from that of a couple of days before, when they had had no replacements, had had no rest, and were totally exhausted. Now we had fresh troops and had the enemy on the run. I felt safe inside the line of marines. My terror, which had lasted so long, was gone. We all felt invincible.

But here were orders to withdraw south. Well, we were marines and we obeyed orders. The only logical conclusion I could come to was that North Vietnam had surrendered. We were a tired but happy lot who force-marched south to a secure area for a much-needed rest. As I looked at the line of weary and tired marines, I felt pride that I will never feel again. I saw few familiar faces, but all the men were veterans now.

I envisioned history books telling about the American forces defeating the communists in 1968 and winning the Vietnam War. But one thing did seem odd to me. The captain and staff sergeant, though they seemed relieved, did not seem happy about returning south. They were older and more experienced than we enlisted men, and they probably knew that we had not gone far enough in our defeat of the NVA forces.

But we enlisted men were happy and never dreamed that media reporters back home were hailing the Tet Offensive as a great communist victory. Little did we realize that back home, thousands of college students were rioting in the streets and on college campuses, burning draft cards, and spitting on the American flag.

I guess we were a little naive.

37

Resting in Mai Xai Ti

IT WAS LATE WHEN WE REACHED MAI XAI TI WEST, WHERE we would set in for the night. Setting up a defensive perimeter was just a formality. The communists were beaten and we knew it, but we would take no chances on sapper or hidden enemy units out for revenge.

Although laughter and good feelings abounded, the marines were still armed to the teeth and were deadly. They weren't ready to mix with ordinary people yet. We still smelled like blood and death, and most of the marines had killed several men that day—some for the first time, but for many veterans, killing had become commonplace. We would be kept at Mai Xai Ti until we calmed down and had become somewhat adjusted to regular civilization.

The first attempt at readjustment was a disaster. But before you read what happened, remember that most of these men had been under enemy fire for two and three months. They had had no food except C rations. They had become accustomed to living with rotting corpses all around, had not had an opportunity to bathe, had seen their best friends slaughtered, and had become totally unused to most things that people take for granted, such as sleeping on a bed or sitting in a chair. Most of us sat on our haunches the way primitive people had. We looked, and we were, as savage as the Huns who ravaged Eastern Europe during the time of Attila the Hun.

Just as soon as we got our perimeter set up, we heard choppers coming in. In the light of flares I saw they were the huge U.S. Army supply choppers used to transport large numbers of men and great quantities of supplies and equipment.

Marines flocked to the area to see what was going on. When the doors opened, we were dumbfounded. It was like seeing people and equipment from another world. Aboard were army cooks and field kitchens! The cooks were immaculate. They had fresh haircuts, new uniforms, and new boots. The stainless-steel stoves and cookware glistened in the light of flares as they were unloaded.

As the cooks started setting up equipment, some marines approached them wide-eyed. A few even ventured to touch the glistening cookware. No one wanted to harm them, but the cooks got nervous. They must have thought they had landed on another planet or had gone back in time twenty thousand years. The wild-eyed marines staring at them did not resemble any civilized being they had ever seen. Our bodies stank, we were extremely thin (except for those who had arrived the day before), hollow-eyed, ragged, and radiated blood and death.

The dead North Vietnamese killed that morning and lying all around had had their ears and noses sampled by rats. We were used to dead bodies laying around, but to the cooks, the sight and stench must have been overpowering. At the same time, the cooks were about as out of place here as a freshly groomed poodle among a pack of timber wolves. We had just returned from a killing spree, but we meant the cooks no harm, we were just fascinated by the bright cooking gear and the clean, neat army helicopters and equipment.

After getting their stoves hot, the cooks got steaks from ice chests they had brought along and started cooking thick, fresh steaks. Now, these hungry marines had not eaten fresh food, much less steak, for a long time, and they were starved! And here, from out of nowhere, army cooks were preparing thick, red, juicy steaks. I didn't know such food existed in Vietnam. Maybe some marine staff sergeant in the rear area had pulled some strings. I wondered whether First Sergeant Michelle had had a hand in getting the steaks. He probably did.

When the first steaks hit the hot stoves, marines edged closer and closer. Then the odor of broiling steaks hit our nostrils. It was indescribable! My stomach growled, and I had the most irresistible urge for fresh meat that I have ever had in my life. Unless you have been raised on beef and then suddenly do without it for a long period, you will never experience this craving for fresh meat.

The eyes of the men were wild and dancing. It was like some savage ritual. It was like when prehistoric tribes of Europe returned home from a successful hunt or a successful war. They had indulged in orgiastic feasting and telling of war stories or feats of bravery during the hunt. They just pigged out and let off steam.

As the smell of the cooking steaks spread, the excitement of the crowd increased and the men started milling around, too nervous to be patient. I don't know how, but some marine grabbed a steak off a stove and savagely bit into it. Immediately a second marine grabbed one, and then the whole group started grabbing steaks. The cooks fled. Awestruck, I stood back and watched.

Marines were laughing and shouting. They started passing out raw steaks to everybody. A huge marine with a grimed and blood-blackened face handed me a large raw one. He was laughing, and his eyes were wide and wild. I took the steak and laughed. It smelled great. I hesitated an instant and then thought, "What the hell? Meat is meat."

I bit into the steak. It was delicious. I joined the laughing, pushing crowd and helped myself to another one. By now the field kitchen was destroyed. The shining stoves were in various positions of disarray and destruction. The iceboxes had been quickly emptied of steaks and then turned over. Marines grabbed handfuls of ice to sample. They laughed, fired rifles into the air, and some even danced for joy. To us, the war was over and this was our first celebration.

I saw a lone figure sitting on the edge of a bunker eating a raw steak. It was Captain Hempel. He smiled when he saw me. His face was black with blood and grease, but his eyes were calm and peaceful.

"Sit down, Mac," he invited, "and watch the fun. It's been a long time since we've had meat."

We sat and watched the marines blow off steam. Oddly,

there was not one fistfight all night. All were so glad to be alive that they danced, wrestled, hugged one another, and fired rifles into the air all night long. No one got mad. It was one helluva good time.

38

Getting Ready for the Rear

LATE THE NEXT MORNING WHEN I AWOKE, I COULD STILL taste raw, red steak, and it still tasted good! I had slept in the bunker on the ground with all my combat gear on.

The field kitchens and all the army gear were gone. I bet the cooks had some wild stories to tell their buddies and folks back home about the primitive savages they had fed in the jungles of South Vietnam. I had to snigger at that.

I found O.E., and we looked up the rest of headquarters platoon. I was relieved to find that no one else had been killed or wounded. We stuck together pretty close now, and as we set up camp, nothing much was said.

It was quiet in Mai Xai Ti. A deadly fog had lifted, leaving the air clean and clear of danger. We could actually feel the absence of the NVA. It was not just that we were receiving no incoming fire, we could feel the difference. We felt safe going anywhere.

Around noon on the second day back from the north, the captain said, "Mac, there's supposed to be a doctor in the field a few miles east of here. Why don't you let him check your neck?"

By now the boil on my neck had healed, leaving a scarred-over hole about a quarter inch deep beyond my ear. O.E. and I were bored sick, and any diversion would be welcome, even though my neck, for all practical purposes, was well.

"Okay, Captain," I said, and O.E. and I got our rifles and ammunition and started east.

Our being able to make the trip alone showed just how badly the NVA had been beaten. Just a week earlier it would have been dangerous, if not foolhardy, for a fully armed platoon to travel the same route. Admittedly, we were fully armed, experienced, and watchful, but just the same, we were relatively safe. It was strange to just walk outside of the defensive line of the perimeter and start walking east.

As soon as we left the perimeter, our combat instincts took over. At first we didn't realize what was happening to us. Our systems reacted the same as in a combat situation: the adrenaline flowed and created a superawareness that we ordinarily do not have. As had happened in combat situations, colors got incredibly bright and our vision became so acute, we saw tiny things that under ordinary conditions we would not even see.

We walked eastward along the road close to the Cua Viet River, which connected the villages along the northern bank of the river. We didn't say a word. The destruction and desolation was heartbreaking. All isolated grass huts had been destroyed. Shell craters from both American and NVA weapons dotted the area. Rice paddies were still there, but they were barren. Nothing seemed alive or growing.

Villages we passed were in total ruin. The North Vietnamese had accomplished one of their goals: they had turned a happy, prosperous part of South Vietnam into a wasteland. At times we saw the bloated bodies of NVA soldiers killed in the recent battle. There were too many dead bodies for the rats and vultures to take care of adequately.

As we marched on, I got an increasing feeling of freedom. When we were mounting our assaults and digging in to hold a position, it was as if we were trapped in a box and couldn't get out. Back then, if we wandered away from the main group, it could easily have been fatal. So we had to stay pretty close to a confined area.

Now we were actually moving around, just O.E. and me, between military posts. For a moment I wanted to run and scream and shout and wave my rifle in the air. But the desolation and death around us dampened our spirits to the point that we simply marched along without saying anything.

After a while I thought, "One thing for sure. This doctor is far enough in the rear that he would have a good running start if the fighting ever starts up again." About three miles later we came across a large, sturdy hut that had been partly rebuilt. This had to be the doctor's office, I thought.

O.E. and I walked inside without knocking, since there was no door. The office was dimly lit by a propane lantern. Sure enough, there sat a real, live doctor, complete with a black bag and stethoscope. Things must really be secure to get him off that ship!

He was a big man and was wearing new jungle fatigues and new jungle boots. He was sitting in a bamboo chair looking out a window. Within easy reach was a fully loaded M-16, a combat helmet, and a flak jacket. Here, everyone had to be ready to play grunt at a moment's notice.

Apparently the doctor had seen us coming and was not surprised when we walked into the room. No doubt he had become used to seeing emaciated, wild-eyed scarecrows hobble in and out of the hut. He turned to face us, and at the same time a navy corpsman came out of a side room. He was armed with a loaded .45. Around these parts, no one went anywhere without being fully armed.

"What can I do for you boys?" the doctor asked without smiling but in a friendly enough voice.

I told him about the boil and the shrapnel wound and said they were healed but the captain had asked me to come see him.

He seemed amused, as did everybody, by my Kentucky accent. He almost smiled.

"Well, let's look at them," he said.

He first looked at the boil and then checked the hand, which he examined for only a minute or so. He went back to the hole behind my ear.

"Damn, son," he said seriously. "You should have seen a doctor for this infection. It could have killed you, especially in this climate. Why didn't you see a doctor?"

"They couldn't spare me long enough."

"You mean that they couldn't spare you for a few days to get an infection like that cleared up? Bullshit!" I didn't say anything. The doctor was an officer, and in the Marine Corps you learn that privates don't argue with officers. But I was thinking: "Mister, you don't know anything. You weren't there. You don't know what it's like to be short of men and fighting for your life. I wouldn't have left Captain Hempel then even if he had let me. You sat back on your air-conditioned ship and tended to men flown to you by helicopters. If you want to judge what was going on, you should have come out and helped. We could for sure have used the help."

But I didn't voice my opinion. Despite my thoughts, I appreciated this doctor being in the field at all. Regardless of what is seen in movies and on television, doctors in Vietnam were much too valuable to send anywhere near a combat area. I was surprised that this one was here at all.

Well, the doctor gave me a shot of antibiotics and a tetanus shot. He then put salve on a battle dressing and wrapped my neck again.

As we left, I said, "Thanks, Doc. We really appreciate your being here."

He looked surprised. I think I made his day.

Nothing more was said, and O.E. and I headed out the door and started a mile-eating march back to our company area. It was back to the Marine Corps.

EPILOGUE

Back at camp, O.E. and I found the men still in a festive mood. Although there were many inspections, especially of rifles and combat gear, discipline was rather loose and so the men had plenty of time to horse around, retell war stories, and talk about what they were going to do when they got home. But actually, everything that happened after our eating-raw-steak orgy was anticlimactic.

The marines were shaved, clean, and were wearing new jungle fatigues and new boots. All our old clothes and shoes had been heaped into a big pile and burned. It felt good to be clean, and those new boots felt wonderful!

About the fourth day back from the north, the officers decided that our adrenaline had slowed down greatly and that regular Marine Corps discipline had been reestablished sufficiently for it to be safe to start the trip back to civilization. We marched to the supply depot at the mouth of the Cua Viet River, where we were greeted with cheers, handshakes, and a happy atmosphere.

The day after we arrived, Second Battalion, Fourth Marines, came ashore to relieve us of the security of the Cua Viet River. On the second day after they got there, 2/4 swept west and set up defensive positions in Mai Xai Ti. As soon as they had secured the area, we boarded the ship.

Colonel Mac gave a short eulogy honoring those killed and those wounded, and his eyes filled with pride as he praised the rest of us. As soon as he finished talking, every marine dashed to the showers. A hot bath! Oh, man!

Our getting off the ship at Da Nang was like a big bunch of kids getting into Disneyland. We quickly found out that

Da Nang was very different from the city we had been in so recently. Then, a grunt was a novelty. Now, grunts were everywhere. The NVA had attacked Da Nang three times during the past two months, and now everyone there knew what war was like.

It seemed that everybody in town was partying. Bars were wide open, and drunk marines leaned on prostitutes or staggered into bars. The party was going on all the way to our encampment, though the bars in that area were simple grass huts.

As soon as we got set in our area, the whole battalion was given overnight leave but with strict orders to be back by daylight. Da Nang that night would be an easy place to get killed.

A sergeant from Texas and I headed down a muddy road with loaded rifles, knives, and intentions to get drunk. We visited bars, drank, and visited more bars. My companion, however, was somewhat subdued, and I, instead of getting rowdy, was content to forgo the party and just sit and watch.

As I drank more and more beer, I began to see the faces of dead heroes. Like a line from Hades, corpses marched up to me, looked me in the eye, and gave me an accusing look that said, "You're here and we're dead. Why?" All night it was like that. At times the sergeant caught me talking to no one and would shake me back to reality. I had fewer than sixty days to go in country, and then I would be home, but these men appearing before me would never go home again. They would forever be in that stinking hell along the Cua Viet River. Forever they would be starving, worn-out, and sick.

I don't remember getting back to our encampment, but I awoke there wishing I were dead. It turned out that during the night, three of our men were stabbed, two shot, and about half the battalion ended up with black eyes. By some miracle, no one was seriously injured.

After leaving Da Nang, what was left of Third Battalion, First Marines, was scattered along Highway 9 to guard bridges. This duty was a pain in the ass. Marines don't make good occupation troops: they are geared for action. Soon the boredom told on us. Friends exchanged bitter words, and heated arguments started over the most trifling things. Snakes and scorpions were everywhere, and though relatively safe, we all were completely miserable.

After this stretch of duty, I really did nothing for the next few weeks. Because of my war record and the forbearance of First Sergeant Michelle, I stayed out of trouble and was finally shipped home.

Today I often think of those glory days when we won the Vietnam War. I think of my old companions: of those who didn't make it back—what would they be doing if they had lived? And of those who survived—what are they doing now? I wonder whether any of them ever thinks of me.

I still have the scar from the boil on the back of my neck and it still gets infected now and then. I still also have the scars on my hand from the shrapnel. But I consider myself extremely lucky. As far as the United States government official records are concerned I was never injured while in the Marine Corps. I consider myself lucky to have had the privilege of serving in the United States Marine Corps.

Every battle, every incident, in this book is based on fact. Although memories change over the years and I realize that my perceptions of what happened could vary greatly from military records or anyone else's interpretation of events, this is the story the way I remember it and the way I thought it happened.

It is a fact that we could have won the war in 1968. But the war is over now and we lost. I absolutely couldn't believe what I saw on television in 1975: the fall of Saigon. The marines and members of the other services did their part: did our presidents and our other leaders do theirs?

By virtue of the authority vested in me as President of the United States and as Commander-in-Chief of the Armed Forces of the United States, I have today awarded

THE PRESIDENTIAL UNIT CITATION (NAVY)

FOR EXTRAORDINARY HEROISM TO

FIRST MARINE DIVISION (REINFORCED), FLEET MARINE FORCE

For extraordinary heroism and outstanding performance of duty in action against enemy forces in the Republic of Vietnam from 16 September 1967 to 31 October 1968. Operating primarily in Quang Nam Province, the First Marine Division (Reinforced) superbly executed its threefold mission of searching for and destroying the enemy, defending key airfield and lines of communication, and conducting a pacification and revolutionary development program unparalleled in the annals of warfare. With the Division responsible for over 1,000 square miles of territory, it extended protection and pacification to more than one million Vietnamese. The countless examples of courage, resourcefulness, and dedication demonstrated by the officers and men of the First Marine Division attest to their professionalism and esprit de corps. Their combat activities were skillfully carried out in the face of adverse weather and difficult terrain such as canopied jungles, rugged mountains, swampy lowlands, and hot, sandy beaches. During the enemy Tet-offensive in late January of 1968, the First Marine Division dealt a devastating blow to enemy forces attempting to attack Danang. Again, in May 1968, the Division totally crushed an enemy drive directed against the Danang area through the Go Noi Island region southwest of Danang. The Division achieved this resounding victory through the skillful coordination of ground forces, supporting arms, and aircraft support. Most action in the I Corps Tactical Zone during August of 1968 was centered in the First Marine Division's tactical area of responsibility. The enemy, now looking for a victory which would achieve some measure of psychological or propaganda value, again mounted an attack of major proportions against Danang but were thoroughly repulsed, sustaining heavy casualties. The valiant fighting spirit, perseverance, and teamwork displayed by First Marine Division personnel throughout this period reflected great credit upon themselves and the Marine Corps, and were in keeping with the highest traditions of the United States Naval Service.

Richard Nixon

The Secretary of the Navy takes pleasure in presenting the NAVY UNIT COMMENDATION to the

BATTALION LANDING TEAM
THIRD BATTALION, FIRST MARINES

for service as set forth in the following

CITATION:

For exceptionally meritorious service in the northern I Corps Area, Republic of Vietnam from 23 January to 16 April 1968. Acting on the knowledge that elements of the 803d North Vietnamese Army Regiment had been successfully interdicting traffic along the Cua Viet River, thereby threatening the vital supply link between the sea and Dong Ha combat base, the Battalion Landing Team was assigned the mission of engaging and destroying this enemy force and of keeping the river open to friendly traffic. On the evening of 23 January 1968, operations against the enemy commenced with a combined heliborne and amphibious landing. For the next eleven days the Battalion Landing Team was heavily engaged with the formidable enemy on the north bank of the river. Five major attacks were conducted against the North Vietnamese Army forces which were firmly entrenched in intricate, mutually supporting, heavily fortified positions. Maintaining continuous contact with the enemy day and night, the Battalion Landing Team systematically reduced the fortified positions to rubble, seized the villages, and inflicted grievous losses upon him when he was forced to retreat. The enemy forces on the northern bank of the Cua Viet routed, the Marines crossed to the southern side, and on 16 February commenced a search and clear operation which yielded stores of enemy supplies and equipment in a series of engagements which also netted a high toll of enemy dead. Crossing back to the north bank on 1 March, the Battalion Landing Team assaulted the village of Mai Xa Thi (West) and was met with extremely heavy resistance. Forced to attack across a creek in the most difficult of terrain, the Marines fought, faced with blistering enemy fire, to secure a beachhead on the opposite side. The vital life-line of communication, the Cua Viet River, was once again secured enabling supplies to reach the beleaguered forces on the Demilitarized Zone as far west as Khe Sanh. On 5 March the Battalion Landing Team was diverted from the Cua Viet area and moved by helicopter to Camp Carroll with the mission of providing security for the Camp and the two key bridges along Route 9. Through aggressive patrolling and detailed sweeps, the enemy was denied freedom of movement in the area and Route 9 was kept open for the vital supply convoys moving from Dong Ha to the "Rockpile", Ca Lu, and Khe Sanh. Continuously in contact with enemy forces during the entire period, the Battalion Landing Team participated in Operations BADGER CATCH, SALINE, NAPOLEAN SALINE and CHARLTON. By their effective teamwork, agressive fighting spirit and individual acts of heroism and daring, the men of the Battalion Landing Team and supporting Marine aviation units achieved significant results. Their courage, professional skill and devotion to duty were in keeping with the highest traditions of the Marine Corps and the United States Naval Service.

All personnel attached to and serving with the following units of Battalion Landing Team, Third Battalion, First Marines during the period 23 January to 16 April 1968 or any part thereof are hereby authorized to wear the NAVY UNIT COMMENDATION Ribbon.

Headquarters and Service Company
Companies I, K, L and M
Battery C (-) (Rein), 1st Battalion, 11th Marines
Mortar Battery, 2d Battalion, 11th Marines
3d Platoon (Rein), Company C, 1st Tank Battalion
4th Platoon, Company B, 1st Amphibious Tractor Battalion
(27Jan-5Mar68) (Operation SALINE/NAPOLEON–SALINE)
Detachment, 1st Platoon, Company A, 1st Amphibious Tractor
Battalion (14-18Feb68) (Operation SALINE)
Detachment, 1st Armored Amphibious Company, 1st Amphibious
Tractor Battalion (31Jan68) (Operation SALINE), (29Feb-1Mar68)
(Operation NAPOLEON/SALINE)
Detachment, 1st Platoon, Headquarters and Service Company,
1st Amphibious Tractor Battalion (29Feb-1Mar68) (Operation
NAPOLEON/SALINE)
Detachment, 4th Platoon, Company B, 1st Amphibious Tractor
Battalion (14-18Feb68) (25-26Feb68) (Operation SALINE)
4th Platoon (Rein), Company B, 3d Amphibious Tractor Battalion
3d Platoon, Company C, 5th Anti Tank Battalion
1st Platoon, Company A, 5th Tank Battalion (27Jan-5Mar68)
(Operation SALINE/NAPOLEON–SALINE)
1st Platoon (Rein), Company D, 1st Reconnaissance Battalion
1st Platoon (Rein), Company A, 1st Motor Transport Battalion
2d Platoon (Rein), Company C, 1st Medical Battalion
3d Platoon (-) (Rein), Company A, 1st Engineer Battalion
Detachment, Postal, Disbursing, Radio Relay, Headquarters
Battalion, 1st Marine Division
Detachment, Company A, 1st Shore Party Battalion
Detachment, Dental Company, 9th Marine Amphibious Brigade
Detachment, Logistics Support Unit, Force Logistics Command
Detachment, (Naval Gunfire Liaison Team) Headquarters Battery,
11th Marines
SLF Bravo (Attached Command Group 79.5)
Marine Medium Helicopter Squadron-165

U. S. NAVY SUPPORTING UNIT

Detachment, NSAD, Cua Viet

John H. Chafee
Secretary of the Navy

THE FOLLOWING LIST CONTAINS THE NAMES OF THE OFFICERS, ENLISTED MARINES, AND HOSPITAL CORPSMEN WHO DIED IN ACTION OR OF OTHER CAUSES WHILE SERVING IN VIETNAM WITH BATTALION LANDING TEAM 3/1, DECEMBER 1967–JUNE 1968

In Memoriam

NAME	RANK	COMPANY	DATE OF DEATH	WALL LOCATION
ABNER, CARL E.	LCPL	LIMA	27 DEC 1967	32E-66
ADAMS, RICKY F.	LCPL	MIKE	1 MAR 1968	42E-12
ALFRED, BRUCE C.	PFC	LIMA	27 DEC 1967	32E-67
ALLEN, EDWARD J.	PFC	MIKE	16 MAY 1968	61E-06
ALLEN, RONALD P.	LCPL	LIMA	27 DEC 1967	32E-67
ANDERSON, ROBERT C.	LCPL	MIKE	3 FEB 1968	37E-03
ANTONIO, JOHNNIE, JR.	LCPL	MIKE	27 DEC 1967	32E-67
APPLEGATE, DONALD L.	PFC	KILO	27 DEC 1967	32E-68
ARMSTRONG, BILLY C.	SGT	LIMA	21 APR 1968	51E-16
ARNOLD, MOSES A.	CPL	KILO	2 FEB 1968	36E-65
BACA, JOHNNY L., JR.	PFC	LIMA	4 FEB 1968	37E-17
BANNISTER, RICHARD W.	PFC	MIKE	27 DEC 1967	32E-68
BARANOSKI, JOHN F.	PFC	INDIA	20 FEB 1968	40E-36
BARNES, LAWRENCE M.	LCPL	LIMA	27 DEC 1967	32E-68
BARREIROS, SILVINO F.	PFC	INDIA	27 JAN 1968	35E-44

Name	Rank	Unit	Date	Panel
BARRETT, STEPHEN O.	HM3	H&S	25 JAN 1968	35E-29
BEERS, EDWARD N.	CPL	KILO	23 MAY 1968	66E-06
BERNARD, GUY N.	LCPL	MIKE	2 MAR 1968	42E-27
BILES, CALVIN W.	LCPL	KILO	27 DEC 1967	32E-69
BOBKOVICH, STEPHEN J.	SSGT	MIKE	1 MAR 1968	42E-13
BOYCE, JOHN M.	LCPL	KILO	2 MAR 1968	42E-27
BRENNAN, JAMES A.	CPL	LIMA	31 JAN 1968	35E-88
BRISCOE, JOHN A.	LCPL	INDIA	26 JAN 1968	35E-36
BROCKMAN, PHILIP L.	PFC	MIKE	31 MAY 1968	62W-06
BROWN, WILLIAM J.	PVT	LIMA	27 DEC 1967	32E-69
BROZ, GEORGE M.	2NDLT	LIMA	27 DEC 1967	32E-69
BRUNT, ARTHUR L.	PFC	MIKE	1 MAR 1968	42E-14
BURNETT, RICHARD J.	PFC	INDIA	1 MAR 1968	42E-14
BURRIS, ROY N.	LCPL	MIKE	27 FEB 1968	41E-48
CARABEO, LEONARD	LCPL	INDIA	28 APR 1968	52E-35
CARDENAS, RAMIRO	LCPL	MIKE	27 FEB 1968	41E-48
CARPENTER, WILLIAM H., JR.	PVT	H&S	27 DEC 1967	32E-70
CARRANZA, HORACIO	PFC	MIKE	2 MAR 1968	42E-29
CAULTON, WILLIAM R.	LCPL	INDIA	26 JAN 1968	35E-41
CHAPPELL, KENNETH L.	LCPL	LIMA	27 DEC 1967	32E-70
CLEARWATER, NORMAN W.	SGT	LIMA	27 DEC 1967	32E-75
CLEMONS, LARRY R.	LCPL	MIKE	31 JAN 1968	36E-02
COURTEMANCHE, CALLEN J.	CPL	MIKE	31 JAN 1968	36E-10
CRUDEN, DONALD J.	SSGT	LIMA	27 DEC 1967	32E-71

NAME	RANK	COMPANY	DATE OF DEATH	WALL LOCATION
CUNNANE, DENNIS T.	PFC	MIKE	31 JAN 1968	36E-04
CURRY, JAMES L.	PFC	INDIA	28 APR 1968	52E-35
CUSSINS, LOUIS W.	LCPL	KILO	18 FEB 1968	40E-03
DAY, DENNIS P.	HN	H&S	2 FEB 1968	36E-69
DENHOFF, THOMAS E.	PVT	KILO	25 JAN 1968	35E-29
DESO, BERTRAM A.	CPL	MIKE	1 MAR 1968	42E-14
D'EUSIACHIO, THOMAS G.	PFC	LIMA	1 FEB 1968	36E-45
DODSON, DAVID P.	PFC	H&S	25 JAN 1968	35E-31
DULEN, RENDLE	PFC	MIKE	9 MAY 1968	57E-19
DUNCAN, MITCHELL J.	PFC	INDIA	21 DEC 1967	32E-35
EDWARDS, EDWIN R.	SSGT	MIKE	3 MAR 1968	42E-50
EDWARDS, TED W.	1STLT	BTRY C	2 FEB 1968	36E-69
EMMONS, JUDSON W.	PFC	MIKE	27 DEC 1967	32E-71
EKART, PAUL D.	HM3	H&S	26 JAN 1968	35E-38
FALK, FREDERICK J., JR.	LCPL	INDIA	26 JAN 1968	35E-39
FISCHIO, JOHN A.	PFC	INDIA	6 MAR 1968	43E-18
FLETCHER, BRUCE J.	PFC	KILO	25 JAN 1968	35E-31
FOLEY, ROBERT P.	PFC	MIKE	2 FEB 1968	36E-71
FOSTER, GARY N.	PFC	INDIA	26 JAN 1968	35E-38
FRITZE, TIM L.	PVT	INDIA	19 JUN 1968	56W-33
GABRIEL, GARRY L.	PFC	LIMA	27 DEC 1967	32E-72
GALLAGHER, RICHARD	LCPL	H&S	8 MAR 1968	43E-53

GARCIA, ANGEL A.	PFC	LIMA	28 JAN 1968	35E-54
GARLICK, RICHARD L.	PFC	MIKE	1 MAR 1968	42E-16
GONZALES, CARLOS L.	PFC	MIKE	1 MAR 1968	42E-16
GOODSON, THOMAS H.	SGT	MIKE	31 MAY 1968	62W-09
GORDON, GERALD E.	PFC	LIMA	16 FEB 1968	39E-57
GREGORY, CHARLES L.	LCPL	MIKE	31 JAN 1968	36E-11
HADDOCK, EDWARD	PFC	LIMA	28 JAN 1968	35E-54
HAMILTON, MICHAEL E.	CPL	INDIA	16 MAY 1968	61E-10
HAMPTON, CHARLES V., JR.	PFC	MIKE	31 JAN 1968	36E-12
HASTINGS, MICHAEL K.	HN	H&S	1 MAR 1968	42E-18
HAWES, ROBERT C.	CPL	MIKE	20 APR 1968	51E-07
HENRICKSON, COMBLY H.	SSGT	LIMA	31 JAN 1968	36E-14
HENTSCHEL, ROBERT E.	LCPL	LIMA	27 DEC 1967	32E-73
HICKS, EARLIE H., JR.	PFC	H&S	18 APR 1968	50E-39
HOLMES, NATHAN	PFC	INDIA	1 MAR 1968	42E-17
HOPEWELL, DONALD C.	LCPL	LIMA	27 DEC 1967	32E-73
HORNER, ALBERT L.	CPL	LIMA	27 DEC 1967	32E-73
HUBBELL, THOMAS S.	CAPT	LIMA	27 DEC 1967	32E-74
HUGHES, MITCHELL, Jr.	LCPL	LIMA	27 DEC 1967	32E-74
HUMPHREY, CECIL H., JR.	CPL	MIKE	31 MAY 1968	62W-11
HUNT, WILLIAM S.	PFC	MIKE	11 MAR 1968	44E-17
JAKO, JAMES L.	LCPL	H&S	27 DEC 1967	32E-74
JENKINS, ROBERT W.	PFC	INDIA	31 JAN 1968	36E-17
JONES, BOYD E.	SGT	H&S	27 DEC 1967	32E-70

NAME	RANK	COMPANY	DATE OF DEATH	WALL LOCATION
JONES, DUBOIS R.	PFC	MIKE	31 JAN 1968	36E-18
KAPP, RICHARD W., JR.	2NDLT	H&S	1 MAR 1968	42E-18
KASSATKIN, PAUL	LCPL	H&S	24 APR 1968	51E-47
KAZEKEVICIOUS, JOSEPH H.	PFC	KILO	5 MAY 1968	55E-17
KEEHNER, CARROL G.	LCPL	INDIA	21 DEC 1967	32E-36
KENNEDY, WILLIAM H.	PFC	INDIA	21 DEC 1967	32E-36
KESLING, RONALD L.	CPL	KILO	27 DEC 1967	32E-75
KIRBY, DONALD R. III	LCPL	MIKE	27 DEC 1967	32E-75
KLORAN, THOMAS W.	PFC	KILO	17 FEB 1968	39E-73
KREC, FRANK	LCPL	MIKE	2 MAR 1968	42E-35
LAFFERTY, DAVID N.	PFC	MIKE	27 DEC 1967	32E-76
LAUER, JOSEPH E.	PFC	MIKE	31 MAY 1968	62W-12
LEDFORD, DANNY	PFC	MIKE	1 MAR 1968	42E-19
LENTZ, DOUGLAS A.	PFC	MIKE	29 FEB 1968	42E-07
LEWIS, EARL LEROY	PFC	LIMA	27 DEC 1967	32E-77
LEWIS, RICHARD E.	PFC	KILO	27 DEC 1967	32E-77
LINDSAY, MICHAEL C.	PVT	MIKE	1 FEB 1968	36E-54
LIPINSKI, VERNON R.	PFC	LIMA	27 DEC 1967	32E-77
LLOYD, RODNEY D.	LCPL	INDIA	1 MAR 1968	42E-20
LONSDALE, GEORGE E.	PFC	LIMA	27 DEC 1967	32E-77
LOZANO, CARLOS FELIPE M.	PFC	LIMA	27 DEC 1967	32E-78
MALDONADO, ANTHONY G.	PFC	MIKE	31 JAN 1968	36E-23

MANSON, JAMES E., JR.	LCPL	KILO	25 JUL 1968	50W-08
MARKWITH, GERALD W.	PFC	MIKE	1 MAR 1968	42E-20
MARTELL, GARY W.	PFC	LIMA	27 DEC 1967	32E-78
MARTIN, CHARLES J.	LCPL	INDIA	19 FEB 1968	40E-25
MARTIN, DONALD E.	LCPL	BTRY C	2 FEB 1968	36E-78
MCMASTER, GLENN L.	PFC	INDIA	21 DEC 1967	32E-39
MEEHAN, ROBERT E.	PFC	LIMA	23 APR 1968	51E-40
MELTON, DAVID L.	PFC	MIKE	2 MAR 1968	42E-36
MEYER, JAMES F., JR.	PVT	LIMA	17 FEB 1968	39E-75
MILLER, RICHARD D.	PFC	MIKE	1 MAR 1968	42E-20
MILLER, ROBERT T.	LCPL	MIKE	27 DEC 1967	32E-78
MISIUTA, EDWARD M.	PFC	KILO	1 MAR 1968	42E-21
MONSKA, BRUCE W.	PFC	INDIA	5 FEB 1968	37E-40
MOORE, DAVID C.	PFC	LIMA	2 MAR 1968	42E-37
MOORE, JIMMY L.	LCPL	H&S	26 MAY 1968	66W-10
NEFF, LARRY L.	PFC	LIMA	20 APR 1968	51E-10
O'DAFFER, RICHARD D.	HN	H&S	19 FEB 1968	40E-26
OLSEN, CHARLES E.	HM3	H&S	19 FEB 1968	40E-27
PALMA, RAYMOND B.	PFC	LIMA	27 DEC 1967	32E-79
PARKER, MICHAEL L.	LCPL	MIKE	27 DEC 1967	32E-79
PARKINSON, GRAY C.	HN	H&S	4 MAR 1968	42E-69
PETERS, EDWARD K.	CPL	LIMA	28 JAN 1968	35E-53
PIERSON, LARRY J.	LCPL	H&S	26 MAY 1968	66W-11
PLUNKETT, ROBERT S.	CPL	LIMA	28 JAN 1968	35E-56

NAME	RANK	COMPANY	DATE OF DEATH	WALL LOCATION
POPE, CHARLES D.	CPL	H&S	27 DEC 1967	32E-80
PRESLEY, DONNIE D.	LCPL	INDIA	21 DEC 1967	32E-39
RADONSKI, KENNETH W.	PFC	H&S	17 FEB 1968	39E-76
RACHON, CHARLES J.	PFC	MIKE	22 APR 1968	51E-33
RALLS, RAYMOND B.	PFC	KILO	22 MAY 1968	66E-01
REED, SHELLIE J.	LCPL	KILO	27 DEC 1967	32E-80
REID, JOHN L.	HN	H&S	26 JAN 1968	35E-37
REMBERT, HARVEY L.	LCPL	LIMA	27 DEC 1967	32E-80
RICHARDSON, ARPHALIA L.	PFC	LIMA	27 DEC 1967	32E-78
RIDDLE, ROBERT T.	CPL	MIKE	27 DEC 1967	32E-81
RITCHIE, DOUGLAS R.	PFC	MIKE	2 MAR 1968	42E-39
ROBERTS, ARTHUR J., JR.	PFC	H&S	31 JAN 1968	36E-33
SAUNDERS, EARNEST ROLLIN	PFC	MIKE	1 JUN 1968	61W-07
SANCHEZ, PAUL F.	CPL	MIKE	31 MAY 1968	62W-17
SCHATZMAN, ROBERT J.	PFC	MIKE	31 MAY 1968	62W-19
SCOTT, DENNIS L.	LCPL	MIKE	27 DEC 1967	32E-82
SCOTT, ROBERT L.	PFC	INDIA	26 JAN 1968	35E-41
SELIG, RONALD J.	LCPL	KILO	2 FEB 1968	36E-86
SHEKELL, STEVEN E.	LCPL	KILO	27 DEC 1967	32E-82
SHEPPARD, JOHNNIE A.	CPL	KILO	31 MAY 1968	62W-17
SHUBERT, DARNAY	PFC	LIMA	27 DEC 1967	32E-82
SILLER, PETER L.	2NDLT	INDIA	26 JAN 1968	35E-41

SILVERS, MITCHELL F.	PFC	KILO	25 JAN 1968	35E-35
SINEGAL, LARRY J.	PFC	H&S	26 MAY 1968	66W-12
SMITH, CHARLES A.	CPL	KILO	28 FEB 1968	41E-73
SMITH, HURLEY A.	LCPL	H&S	2 FEB 1968	36E-86
SMITH, KENNETH W.	1STLT	LIMA	28 JAN 1968	35E-57
SOROKA, DOUGLAS M.	LCPL	LIMA	28 JAN 1968	35E-57
SPADARO, THOMAS	PFC	MIKE	1 MAR 1968	42E-24
STILES, THOMAS N.	LCPL	MIKE	27 DEC 1967	32E-82
STRINGER, ANTHONY O.	HM3	H&S	1 MAR 1968	42E-25
SULLIVAN, MICHAEL X.	CPL	LIMA	8 FEB 1968	38E-40
TILLMAN, JOHN III	PFC	INDIA	1 MAR 1968	42E-25
TINAJERO, JOSE A.	PFC	INDIA	21 DEC 1967	32E-36
VARNER, THOMAS A., JR.	CPL	MIKE	27 DEC 1967	32E-83
VAUGHAN, ROBERT L.	LCPL	MIKE	27 DEC 1967	32E-83
VINCENT, JOHN L.	PFC	LIMA	23 APR 1968	51E-43
WHITE, RICHARD E.	LCPL	INDIA	19 JUN 1968	55W-03
WHITLEY, ROBERT L.	LCPL	MIKE	31 JAN 1968	36E-42
WILLIAMS, JAMES E., JR.	LCPL	LIMA	27 DEC 1967	32E-83
WILLIAMS, STEPHEN	PFC	LIMA	27 DEC 1967	32E-84
WYATT, JOHN W., JR.	PFC	LIMA	4 FEB 1968	37E-30
ZELASKI, LEONARD J., JR.	LCPL	KILO	2 MAR 1968	42E-45
ZENKEWICH, GEORGE W.	PFC	LIMA	28 JAN 1968	35E-58

The Explosive
Autobiography
of the Controversial,
Death-Defying Founder
of the U.S. Navy's
Top Secret
Counterterrorist Unit
SEAL TEAM SIX

The
#1
<u>New York Times</u>
Bestseller!

"Fascinating....
Marcinko...
makes Arnold
Schwarzenegger
look like
Little Lord
Fauntleroy."
*—The New York
Times Book Review*

ROGUE WARRIOR

RICHARD MARCINKO
with JOHN WEISMAN

995